Querying Graphs

Synthesis Lectures on Data Management

Editor
H.V. Jagadish, *University of Michigan*

Founding Editor
M. Tamer Özsu, *University of Waterloo*

Synthesis Lectures on Data Management is edited by H.V. Jagadish of the University of Michigan. The series publishes 80–150 page publications on topics pertaining to data management. Topics include query languages, database system architectures, transaction management, data warehousing, XML and databases, data stream systems, wide scale data distribution, multimedia data management, data mining, and related subjects.

Querying Graphs

Angela Bonifati, George Fletcher, Hannes Voigt, and Nikolay Yakovets

ISBN: 978-3-031-00736-1   paperback
ISBN: 978-3-031-01864-0   ebook
ISBN: 978-3-031-00091-1   hardcover

DOI 10.1007/978-3-031-01864-0

A Publication in the Springer series
SYNTHESIS LECTURES ON DATA MANAGEMENT

Lecture #51
Series Editor: H.V. Jagadish, *University of Michigan*
Founding Editor: M. Tamer Özsu, *University of Waterloo*
Series ISSN
Print 2153-5418   Electronic 2153-5426

Querying Graphs

Angela Bonifati
Université Claude Bernard Lyon 1

George Fletcher
Technische Universiteit Eindhoven

Hannes Voigt
Neo4j/Technische Universität Dresden[1]

Nikolay Yakovets
Technische Universiteit Eindhoven

SYNTHESIS LECTURES ON DATA MANAGEMENT #51

ABSTRACT

Graph data modeling and querying arises in many practical application domains such as social and biological networks where the primary focus is on concepts and their relationships and the rich patterns in these complex webs of interconnectivity. In this book, we present a concise unified view on the basic challenges which arise over the complete life cycle of formulating and processing queries on graph databases. To that purpose, we present all major concepts relevant to this life cycle, formulated in terms of a common and unifying ground: the property graph data model—the pre-dominant data model adopted by modern graph database systems.

We aim especially to give a coherent and in-depth perspective on current graph querying and an outlook for future developments. Our presentation is self-contained, covering the relevant topics from: graph data models, graph query languages and graph query specification, graph constraints, and graph query processing. We conclude by indicating major open research challenges towards the next generation of graph data management systems.

KEYWORDS

graph databases, property graphs, graph query languages, graph constraints, graph query specification, graph data representation, graph query processing

Contents

Foreword

The current surge of interest in Graph Data Bases (GDBs) reflects the popularity of their data models based on nodes and edges, which, in many applications, provide a more intuitive conceptualization for entities and relationships than the one offered by Relational Data Bases (RDBs). This has inspired the design and development of many GDB systems and their use in a wide range of applications. Indeed to date, we counted more than 20 GDB systems developed and used in application areas such as Semantic Web, Social Networking, Fraud Detection, Recommendation Systems, Life Science, and Knowledge Bases.

For all their remarkable achievements, GDBs still lack the conceptual coherence that RDBs have been blessed with from the beginning as a result of E.F. Codd's seminal contributions which, combined with the major research advances in theory and systems that followed, provide the subject of numerous textbooks. However, the fast-expanding technology of GDBs is still quite far from achieving similar levels of conceptual unification and this create hurdles for researchers, instructors, and students alike.

This book tackles this problem head on by presenting a comprehensive unified treatment of GDBs, as needed to serve as a reference book for experts and a textbook for graduate students. The book's coverage begins with a formal treatment of the Property Graph Data Model that is common to most GDBs. Then, the book discusses GDB query languages and, moving past their many differences, it proposes a core property graph query language and elucidates its properties both in terms of graph logic and graph algebra. After that, the book covers techniques for efficient GDB implementation, including data structures, indexes, query operators, and processing, for which the presentation underscores how solutions different from those of traditional DBs are often required. Furthermore, the departures from traditional technology are even more dramatic for (i) integrity constraints, which lose their key role in normal-form RDB schema design, but find new important uses in GDBs, and (ii) interactive query specification via examples and counter-examples that have proven to be surprisingly effective with GDBs. The book's comprehensive treatment is further enhanced by extensive references and suggestions on open research problems for further investigation.

Carlo Zaniolo
Computer Science Department
University of California at Los Angeles (UCLA)

Acknowledgments

The authors would like to warmly thank the many people who helped us to make this book a reality. First and foremost, we thank our families and partners for their patience and support throughout the many months dedicated to the writing of this book.

We also give many thanks to the Editor H.V. Jagadish and the Founding Editor M. Tamer Özsu for the opportunity and encouragement to publish this book. During the writing, the staff at Morgan & Claypool were just awesome, especially Diane Cerra. Thank you all for keeping the writing moving forward. We also thank the three reviewers for their critical and insightful feedback.

Our sincere thanks further go to Carlo Zaniolo for kindly writing the Foreword. We are greatly honored by your contribution!

Finally, we give our heartfelt thanks to colleagues for reading early drafts. We especially thank Sourav Bhowmick, Stefania Dumbrava, Jan Hidders, Wilco van Leeuwen, Davide Mottin, Oskar van Rest, and Kaijie Zhu for their detailed proofreading and helpful comments.

The work presented here was supported in part by a donation from Oracle Labs and by the CNRS Mastodons grant MedClean (2016–2018).

Angela Bonifati, George Fletcher, Hannes Voigt, and Nikolay Yakovets
September 2018

CHAPTER 1

Introduction

Things are interesting only in so far as they relate themselves to other things; only then can you put two and two together and tell stories about them. Such is science itself and such is all the knowledge that interests [hu]mankind.

D'arcy Wentworth Thompson (1860–1948)

Graph data management systems have experienced a renaissance in recent years. The reason for this is clear: with a confluence of trends in society, science, and technology, graph-structured data sets are increasingly being constructed, collected, and made available for analysis. Common everyday examples of massive and ever-growing graph data collections include social, biochemical, ecological, citation, communication, mobility, and transportation networks [Newman, 2018]. Graph data modeling and querying arises in such applications where the primary focus is on *things* and their *relationships* and the rich patterns in these complex webs of connectivity. In a social network such as LinkedIn[1] or Viadeo,[2] for example, we primarily have people and institutions as the things (i.e., nodes, vertices) and social connections such as "follows" and "works for" as the relationships (i.e., edges). In this domain, a job-seeker may be interested in answers to queries such as "Who are the people in my social network with a shared professional society membership who live in my city?" As another example, in biological network data sources such as BioGRID[3] or UniProtKB,[4] we typically have entities such as proteins as the things and the interactions between proteins as the relationships. Here, a scientist might be interested in querying for interaction pathways which have not been explored before in the literature, toward insight for new medical treatments. Teasing out such hidden patterns in graph databases are often a basis for knowledge and value creation in many contemporary application domains across the sciences and society.

The study of query languages is central in the design and engineering of data intensive systems. Reflecting the interest and tremendous growth in graph database systems, much progress has been made recently in our understanding of graph query languages, ranging from their theoretical foundations to their practical use and efficient realization. Several recent surveys have

---

[1] https://www.linkedin.com
[2] http://www.viadeo.com
[3] The Biological General Repository for Interaction Datasets, https://thebiogrid.org.
[4] The Universal Protein Resource, http://www.uniprot.org.

covered different aspects of graph analytics, ranging from graph data models and query languages [Angles and Gutiérrez, 2008, Angles et al., 2017] to graph mining [Koutra and Faloutsos, 2017], distributed graph processing [Heidari et al., 2018, Kalavri et al., 2018, McCune et al., 2015], and big graph analytics platforms [Yan et al., 2017].

To the best of our knowledge, a comprehensive overview of the "life of a graph query" is currently missing in the literature. The present book complements existing surveys and monographs on graph data management, addressing this important gap in the literature. Given the fundamental role of query languages, there is a clear need for such a treatment. Furthermore, as the study of graph query processing solutions is reaching a first stage of maturity, both in academia and in industry, we believe that now is an especially crucial moment for such an overview.

Our overarching goal is to present a unified coherent view on the current understanding of the basic challenges arising over the complete life cycle of a graph query. To that purpose, we present all major concepts relevant to this life cycle, formulated in terms of a common and unifying ground: *the property graph data model*, the predominant data model adopted by practical graph database systems [Francis et al., 2018, van Rest et al., 2016]. As part of the life cycle of graph queries, we present in-depth the various components of this cycle, encompassing graph data models, graph query languages and query specification, graph constraints, graph data structures and indexes, graph query processing, and graph physical operators.

In particular, in Chapters 2 and 3 we introduce the property graph data model and a core property graph query language. This is followed in Chapters 4 and 5 with a presentation of the state of the art in graph constraints and query specification. We then turn to core concepts in efficient graph representation, query processing, and query operators in Chapters 6, 7, and 8. We conclude in Chapter 9 by indicating major open research challenges in each of the topics surveyed. Each chapter includes a bibliographical and historical discussion, giving pointers into the rich history and literature on graph data management.

The primary audience of the book is developers or researchers of graph database and graph analytics systems and tools. Another important audience of the book is students and teachers interested in graph data management. We have written the book to be self-contained. The reader is only assumed to have a background in the basics of computer science and information systems. Hence, the book is accessible to senior undergraduate students and graduate students, and can be used as a textbook for an advanced seminar.

Our hope is that this unified presentation of the state of the art in querying graphs will contribute toward further coherence and consolidation in the graph query processing community, setting foundations and directions for the next generation of graph database systems.

CHAPTER 2

Data Models

In this chapter, we introduce the property graph model. The property graph model is important for graph-based data management as it is implemented in many systems and used as a reference model for various research work. Our aim in this chapter is two-fold. First, we introduce the basic concepts of the property graph model, following the LDBC's Graph Query Language Task Force [Angles et al., 2018a].[1] Second, we discuss a number of variations of the property graph model in terms of specializations and structural extensions. This illustrates how the property graph model fits into the family of existing graph models.

2.1 PROPERTY GRAPH MODEL

The Property Graph Model (PGM) represents data as a directed, attributed multi-graph. Vertices and edges are rich objects with a set of labels and a set of key—value pairs, so-called properties. Figure 2.1 shows a simple example of a property graph. The graph has the three vertices (10, 11, and 12) and three directed edges (20, 21, and 22) connecting them. Labels are descriptive class information tagged to the objects and indicate which kind of real-world entity an object represents. As can be seen in the figure, we denote labels prefixed with a colon. In the example, vertex 11 has two labels: :Expert and :Father. Properties provide the actual data an object represents. The property key specifies the meaning of the property value. For instance, edge 22 has one property with key since and value 2006. Since labels are purely descriptive, they do not imply any properties. Objects can instantiate an arbitrary set of properties independent of their labels.

For a formal definition, let $\mathcal{O}$ be a set of *objects*, $\mathcal{L}$ be a finite set of *labels*, $\mathcal{K}$ be a set of *property keys*, and $\mathcal{N}$ be a set of *values*. We assume these sets to be pairwise disjoint. A *property graph* is a structure $(V, E, \eta, \lambda, \nu)$ where

- $V \subseteq \mathcal{O}$ is a finite set of objects, called vertices;

- $E \subseteq \mathcal{O}$ is a finite set of objects, called edges;

- $\eta : E \to V \times V$ is a function assigning to each edge an ordered pair of vertices;

- $\lambda : V \cup E \to \mathcal{P}(\mathcal{L})$ is a function assigning to each object a finite set of labels (i.e., $\mathcal{P}(S)$ denotes the set of finite subsets of set S); and

- $\nu : (V \cup E) \times \mathcal{K} \to \mathcal{N}$ is a partial function assigning values for properties to objects,

[1]The Linked Data Benchmark Council, http://ldbcouncil.org/.

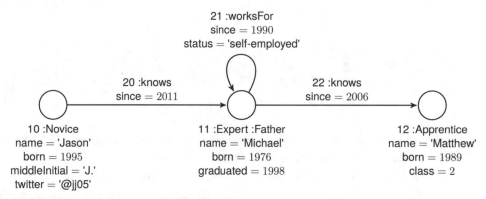

Figure 2.1: An example of a property graph.

such that the object sets V and E are disjoint (i.e., $V \cap E = \emptyset$) and the set of domain values where v is defined is finite.

Figure 2.2 shows a larger property graph example G_{ex} used later on in the book. The displayed graph is defined as $G_{ex} = (V, E, \eta, \lambda, v)$, where $V = \{10, 11, \ldots, 16\}$, $E = \{20, 21, \ldots, 29\}$, λ is defined as visualized (e.g., $\lambda(11) = $:Expert and $\lambda(21) = $:worksFor), η is defined as visualized (e.g., $\eta(20) = (10, 11)$), and v is defined as follows: $v(10, salary) = 1000, v(11, salary) = 3000, v(12, salary) = 2000, v(12, level) = $ 'A', $v(20, year) = 2016, v(23, year) = 2017$, and $v(29, since) = 1997$.

For convenience, we assume the following notation. $\mathtt{in}(v)$ denotes the set of incoming edges of vertex v, with $\mathtt{in}(v) = \{e \in E \mid \pi_2(\eta(e)) = v)\}$.[2] Likewise, $\mathtt{out}(v)$ denotes the set of outgoing edges of vertex v, with $\mathtt{out}(v) = \{e \in E \mid \pi_1(\eta(e)) = v)\}$. Further, $\mathtt{adj}(v) = \mathtt{in}(v) \cup \mathtt{out}(v)$ is the set of all edges adjacent to v. $\mathtt{src}(e)$ denotes the source vertex of edge e, with $\mathtt{src}(e) = \pi_1(\eta(e))$. Analogously, $\mathtt{trg}(e)$ denotes the target vertex of edge e, with $\mathtt{trg}(e) = \pi_2(\eta(e))$.

---

[2] π_i projects an n-tuple to its i-th element, i.e., $\pi_i((x_1, \ldots, x_i, \ldots, x_n)) = x_i$.

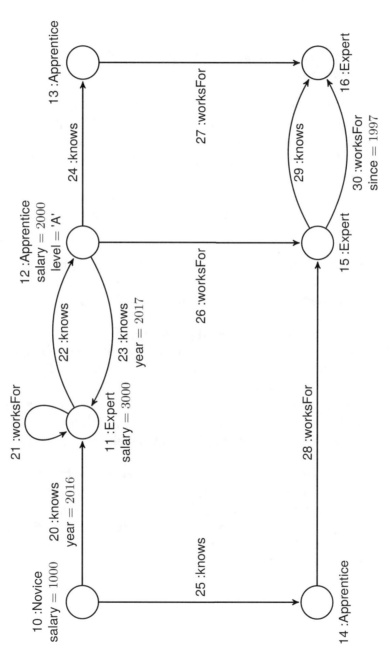

Figure 2.2: A larger example of a property graph.

2.2   VARIATIONS OF THE PGM

2.2.1   SPECIALIZATIONS

The PGM incorporates four basic traits of contemporary graph data models, namely *direction*, *multi-graph*, *labels*, and *properties*, in one unifying model.

Direction.   A property graph is a directed graph; the PGM defines edges as ordered pairs of vertices. Hence, edges have a direction. Graphs with undirected edges consider edges as 2-element subsets of the set of vertices, i.e., the codomain of η is $\text{codom}(\eta) = \{\{x, y\} \mid x, y \in V, x \neq y\}$. Several practical systems support a "mixed" model where graphs can have both undirected and directed edges.

An undirected edge $\{x, y\}$ can be represented in a directed graph by two oppositely directed edges (x, y) and (y, x). In this sense, directed graphs are a generalization of undirected graphs.

Multi-graph.   A property graph is a multi-graph; the PGM allows multiple edges between a given pair of vertices. Simple graphs (in contrast to multi-graphs) additionally require η to be injective (one-to-one). Multi-graphs are a generalization of simple graphs.

Labels.   A property graph is a multi-labeled graph; the PGM allows vertices and edges to be tagged with zero or more labels. This trait exists in other variations of graph data. A graph model may require exactly one label per vertex and edge, i.e., $\text{codom}(\lambda) = \mathcal{L}$. Some graph models allow labels for either vertices or edges only, i.e., $\text{dom}(\lambda) = V$ or $\text{dom}(\lambda) = E$, respectively. Unlabeled graphs can be represented in a labeled graph model by simply not assigning any labels, so that $\forall x \in V \cup E : \lambda(x) = \emptyset$, or assigning a dummy label 0, so that $\forall x \in V \cup E : \lambda(x) = \{0\}$. Multi-labeled graphs are a generalization of all of these variations.

Properties.   A property graph is a key—value-attributed graph; the PGM allows vertices and edges to be enriched with data in the form of key—value pairs. This trait also exists in other graph data model variations. Instead of key—value pairs "data-attributed" graph models only support vertices and edges being attributed with a chunk of binary data, i.e., $\upsilon : V \cup E \to \{0, 1\}^*$. Binary data can be represented in a key—value pair with a dummy key 0. Other graph models allow to attribute either vertices or edges only, i.e., $\text{dom}(\upsilon) = V$ or $\text{dom}(\upsilon) = E$, respectively. Key—value-attributed graphs are a generalization of data-attributed graphs as well as non-attributed graphs.

2.2.2   STRUCTURAL EXTENSIONS

Various extensions to the PGM have been proposed in recent years. We will briefly discuss the most important of these, with a focus on extensions that add or enrich object types of the model, i.e., those that concern the graph structure.

Objectified paths.   We can extend the PGM with objectified paths, i.e., having paths as first-class citizens along side vertices and edges. We refer to this extended model as Objectified Paths PGM (OPPGM). Vertices are the first-order objects in a graph. In multi-graphs, such as property graphs, edges are second-order objects. Edges attach data, in the form of labels and properties, to (ordered) pairs of vertices, i.e., they are statements about specific subsets of lower-order objects. In that sense, objectified paths are third-order objects that attach labels and properties to sequences of edges. Figure 2.3 shows an example of an objectified path. Path 30 presents the edge sequence [20, 22] and has the label :knowsIndirectly and two properties. Obviously, a graph can have multiple objectified paths which can represent identical or overlapping edge sequences.

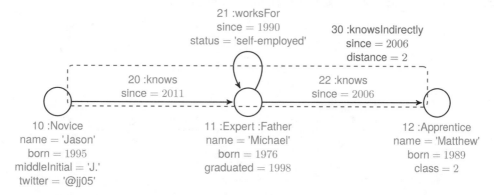

Figure 2.3: A property graph with an objectified path.

Formally, an OPPGM graph extends a PGM graph as defined in Section 2.1 to a structure $(V, E, P, \eta, \delta, \lambda, \nu)$ where

- $P \subset \mathcal{O}$ is a finite set of objects, called paths;

- $\delta : P \to \bigcup_{n \geq 0} E^n$ is a total function assigning to every path a sequence of edges;[3]

- $\lambda : V \cup E \cup P \to \mathcal{P}(\mathcal{L})$ is a function assigning to each object a finite set of labels; and

- $\nu : (V \cup E \cup P) \times \mathcal{K} \to \mathcal{N}$ is a partial function assigning values for properties to objects,

such that

- the object sets V, E, and P are pairwise disjoint;[4]

- for each $p \in P$, it holds for $\delta(p) = [e_1, \ldots, e_\ell]$ that $\mathtt{trg}(e_i) = \mathtt{src}(e_{i+1})$ for each $0 < i < \ell$; and

- the set of domain values where ν is defined is finite.

[3] $E^n = \underbrace{E \times \cdots \times E}_{n \text{ times}}$.

[4] For example, $V \cap E = V \cap P = E \cap P = \emptyset$.

Objectified subgraphs. We can also consider extending the PGM with objectified subgraphs—in short, OSPGM—which has subgraphs as first-class citizens next to vertices and edges. As with objectified paths, objectified subgraphs are higher-order objects and allow us to make statements about specific subsets of vertices and edges that constitute a graph themselves. Figure 2.4 shows a property graph with two objectified subgraphs. Subgraph 31 labeled :TrainingTandem consists of vertices 10 and 11 and edge 20, while subgraph 32 labeled :Interview encompasses vertices 11 and 12 and edges 21 and 22. The objectified subgraphs of a base graph may overlap and their union may also be a subset of the base graph. Each individual objectified subgraph must have at least one vertex. Since a OSPGM graph can have an empty set of subgraphs, clearly OSPGM is a strict generalization of PGM.

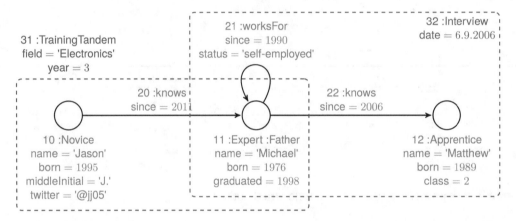

Figure 2.4: A property graph with two objectified subgraphs.

Formally, an OSPGM graph extends a PGM graph as defined in Section 2.1 to a structure $(V, E, G, \eta, \gamma, \lambda, \nu)$ where

- $G \subset \mathcal{O}$ is a finite set of objects, called subgraphs;

- $\gamma : G \to \mathcal{P}(V) \times \mathcal{P}(E)$ is a total function assigning every subgraph a pair of vertex set and edge set;

- $\lambda : V \cup E \cup G \to \mathcal{P}(\mathcal{L})$ is a function assigning a label to objects; and

- $\nu : (V \cup E \cup G) \times \mathcal{K} \to \mathcal{N}$ is a partial function assigning values for properties to objects,

such that

- the object sets V, E, and G are pairwise disjoint;

- the subgraphs $g \in G$ are well-formed graphs, in the sense that all edges of subgraph g are adjacent to vertices of g, i.e., for every $e \in \pi_2(\gamma(g))$ it holds that $\eta(e) \in \pi_1(\gamma(g)) \times \pi_1(\gamma(g))$; and

- the set of domain values where ν is defined is finite.

Hypervertices.   In another direction, we can extend PGM with hypervertices—in short HVPGM—where a (hyper)vertex denotes a (possibly empty) subgraph, i.e., it considers objectified subgraphs as vertices. Hypervertices denoting empty subgraphs represent vertices in the traditional sense while hypervertices denoting non-empty subgraph represent higher-order objects. Since hypervertices can be linked with edges, HVPGM allows linking a subgraph to other subgraphs and even to the hypervertices they contain. Figure 2.5 shows a property graph with hypervertices. Hypervertex 10 labeled :Novice denotes an empty subgraph. In contrast, hypervertex 32 labeled :Interview denotes a non-empty subgraph consisting of hypervertices 11 and 12 and edges 21 and 22. Hypervertex 32 has two outgoing edges 23 and 24 linking it to hypervertex 31—another subgraph—and to hypervertex 12—a vertex contained in 32—respectively. The hypervertices may overlap and their union may also be a subset of the whole graph. Since hypervertices may have no adjacent edges, HVPGM is a strict generalization of OSPGM.

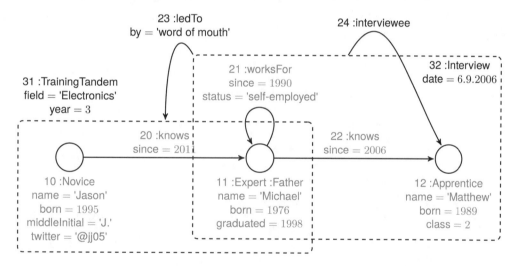

Figure 2.5: A property graph with hypervertices.

A HVPGM graph extends a PGM graph as defined in Section 2.1 to a structure $(V, E, \eta, \gamma, \lambda, \nu)$ where

- $V \subseteq \mathcal{O}$ is a finite set of objects, called hypervertices; and

- $\gamma : V \to \mathcal{P}(V) \times \mathcal{P}(E)$ is a total function assigning every hypervertex a hypervertex set and an edge set,

such that

- the object sets V and E are disjoint, i.e., $V \cap E = \emptyset$;

- the hypervertices are well-formed graphs in the sense that all edges of hypervertex v are adjacent to hypervertices of v, i.e., for every $e \in \pi_2(\gamma(v))$ it is the case that $\eta(e) \in \pi_1(\gamma(v)) \times \pi_1(\gamma(v))$; and

- the set of domain values where v is defined is finite.

Hyperedges. Finally, we can consider extending PGM with hyperedges—in short HEPGM—where a (hyper)edge links a non-empty sequence of vertices without repetitions. Figure 2.6 shows a property graph with hyperedges. Hyperedge 20 labeled :knows links the two vertices 10 and 11 like a standard directed edge, while hyperedge 21 labeled :worksFor links only vertex 11 with itself like a standard directed loop edge. Hyperedge 23, however, links the three vertices 10, 11, and 12. The hyperedges may have overlapping vertex sets and the union of their vertex sets may also be a subset of all vertices in the graph. Since all hyperedges may have exactly two vertices, HEPGM is a strict generalization of PGM. It is worth pointing out that hyperedges do not generalize objectified paths. Hyperedges represent sequences of vertices without repetitions, while objectified paths represent sequences of edges, which may involve repetition of edges and adjacent vertices.

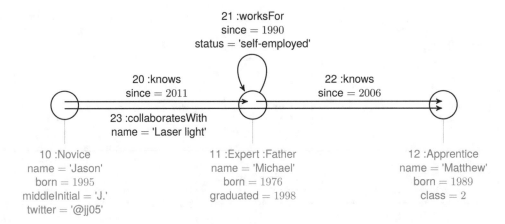

Figure 2.6: A property graph with hyperedges.

Formally, a HEPGM graph extends a PGM graph as defined in Section 2.1 to a structure $(V, E, \eta, \gamma, \lambda, v)$ where

- $E \subseteq \mathcal{O}$ is a finite set of objects, called hyperedges; and

- $\eta : E \to \bigcup_{X \in \mathcal{P}(V) \setminus \emptyset} \{[\pi(1), \ldots, \pi(|X|)] \mid \pi$ is a bijection from $\{1, \ldots, |X|\}$ to $X\}$ is a function assigning to each edge a non-empty sequence of vertices without repetition,

such that the object sets V and E are disjoint and the set of domain values where v is defined is finite.

Note that hyperedges as defined in the HEPGM are directed. For undirected hyperedges as common in the literature on hypergraphs the codomain of η is simply $\mathcal{P}(V) \setminus \emptyset$. However, undirected hyperedges do not generalize the directed edges of the PGM.

2.2.3 DATA REPRESENTATION EXTENSIONS

Data representation extensions to the PGM are less fundamental than structural extensions. They do not concern the graph structure but rather the data properties, i.e., value representations at the level of objects of a graph. These extensions are of practical relevance and are common in implemented systems. They increase practical convenience, for example, when specifying query predicates. Conceptual and theoretical work on graph querying typically neglects these extensions. We briefly discuss the most important of such extensions.

Value types.   Most implemented PGMs have typed values (e.g., integers and strings). Value types specify the default interpretation of a value in the context of query predicates. If $\mathcal{T}$ is the finite set of value types supported by a system, then the system maintains a function $\tau : \mathcal{N} \to \mathcal{T}$, which specifies the value type of every value.

Multiple values.   Some systems allow a property to have more than one value. For instance, a vertex representing a person may have a property hobbies with values $\{\text{'Hiking', 'Climbing', 'Reading'}\}$. With multiple values, the codomain of ν is $\mathcal{P}(\mathcal{N})$. Multiple values may also be seen as the support of just another type of values, namely sets.

Explicit identity.   Many systems expose an explicit identity of the objects. Let $\mathcal{I}$ be a set of identities used by a system, then the system exposes an injective function $\iota : \mathcal{O} \to \mathcal{I}$, which assigns an explicit identity to each object. Typically, the domain of a standard data type such as Integer or Long is used as $\mathcal{I}$.

2.2.4 SUMMARY

Figure 2.7 shows PGM in a hierarchy of model expressiveness with specializations (Section 2.2.1) and structural extensions (Section 2.2.2) of the PGM. Read bottom-up, the figure shows which trait has to be added to a graph data model to obtain a graph data model of richer expressiveness. Incorporating all the traits discussed in Section 2.2.1, the PGM subsumes many other more specialized graph data models. While the discussed structural extensions certainly have an appeal, they also complicate the data model, multiply modeling alternatives, and are not necessarily intuitive for the common user. By omitting these extensions, the PGM strikes a good balance between expressiveness and complexity. This is a characteristic that renders the PGM particularly well-suited for data management, since it offers high modeling expressiveness while still being simple and intuitive.

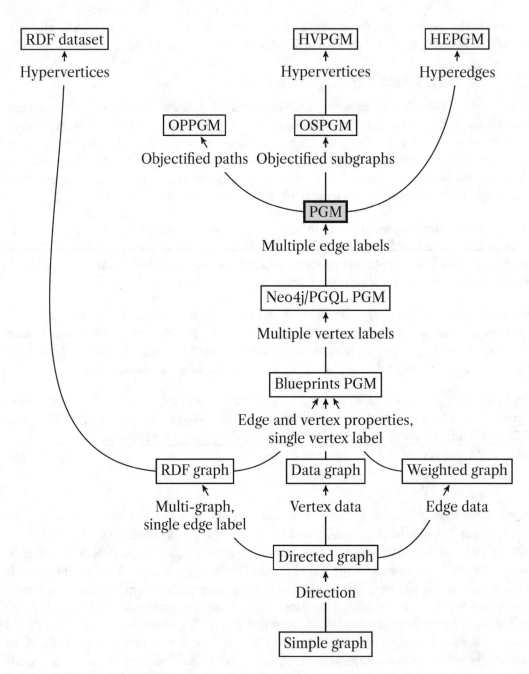

Figure 2.7: Hierarchy of PGM variants and extensions.

2.3   BIBLIOGRAPHIC AND HISTORICAL NOTES

Graph data models have a long history of study in the database community. Predating relational database systems, the CODASYL network data model resembles essentially graph data. Graph data models first gained broad academic attention in the late 1980s and the first half of the 1990s with the rise of object-oriented programming and advent of object-oriented database systems. Angles and Gutiérrez [2008] provide an excellent survey of the graph data models proposed and discussed at the time, where the reader can find a presentation and discussion of the precursors to the data models discussed in Section 2.2.2; as another recent overview of graph data models we also recommend [Gutierrez et al., 2018]. With the continued dominance of relational DBMSs at the time, none of these efforts gained sustainable traction in industry and attention declined.

With the emergence of XML in the 1990's, focus shifted to semistructured and tree-structured data. Today, tree-structured data models are still relevant particularly in the context of document stores. Popular document data models are XML [W3C, 2008] and JSON [Crockford, 2006]. JSON-based document stores, such as MongoDB [Chodorow and Dirolf, 2010] and Marklogic, are commonly used for web applications, where JSON is the dominant data model for data exchange between application servers and browsers. Using the same data model for persistence greatly simplifies application development.

In the 2000's, the graph concept, and with it graph data models, had a considerable revival in the wake of three major trends. The first trend is the Semantic Web movement [Berners-Lee et al., 2001]. The idea of the semantic web gave rise to the RDF data model. W3C published the first RDF recommendation already in 1999 focusing on meta data description [W3C, 1999] and reworked the standard twice in 2004 [W3C, 2004] and 2014 [W3C, 2014]. An RDF graph structures data as a directed edge-labeled multi-graph, cf. Figure 2.7. An RDF dataset consists of an unnamed default RDF graph and zero or more named RDF graphs. Since named RDF graphs can appear as vertices in RDF graphs, they resemble hypervertices. Today, RDF is widely adopted in the semantic web and linked open data [Heath and Bizer, 2011] communities. Thousands of open RDF datasets are published and maintained on the internet, most famously DBpedia [Auer et al., 2007] and Wikidata [Vrandecic and Krötzsch, 2014]. RDF also sparked research in every corner of the database community—ranging from works investigating the fundamental properties of query languages for labeled graphs to the design of storage structures and query engines for RDF data. Hartig [2017] extends RDF with statement annotation to RDF★, which lays the ground for edge properties. Effectively RDF★ lifts RDF to the expressiveness of a restricted form of HVPGM, where a hypervertex can denote only an empty subgraph or a subgraph containing a single edge and its two adjacent (hyper)vertices. RDF★ allows for instance the RDF store Blazegraph[5] to support also PGM data [Blazegraph, 2013].

The second trend is agility with respect to the management of data. New application domains (e.g., [Franklin et al., 2005, Werner et al., 2011]) as well as novel development methods [Beck et al., 2001] increased the demand for data models that are less rigid and schema-

---

[5]https://www.blazegraph.com

oriented but more ad-hoc and data-oriented. Graph data models typically excel in this regard as new nodes and edges can be added anytime, regardless of their properties. This propelled the proliferation of the PGM and corresponding graph DBMSs. Neo4j[6] and Apache TinkerPop Blueprints[7] implementations were among the first advocates of the PGM. By now the PGM is widely used and implemented by many others, such as IBM Graph,[8] Oracle [van Rest et al., 2016], SAP HANA [Bornhövd et al., 2012, Rudolf et al., 2013], and Sparksee[9] [Martínez-Bazan et al., 2007, 2011]. The Linked Data Benchmark Council (LDBC) proposes OPPGM as the foundation for a core property graph query language [Angles et al., 2018a, Gutierrez et al., 2018].

The third trend is big data analytics [Hey et al., 2009]. One major method in this discipline is network analysis, which puts the focal point of interest on the connectivity of entities. The toolbox of network analysis offers a rich set of algorithms and measures and targets a wide range of use cases, including network impact analysis, route finding, collaborative filtering, supply chain management and logistics, fraud detection, digital asset management, biomolecular engineering, scientific computing, and many more. Algorithms and systems as discussed in the research literature are typically based on a weighted graph or a data graph, cf. Figure 2.7. In practical systems for graph analytics, however, PGM gains ground. Frameworks such as GraphX [Gonzalez et al., 2014] on Apache Spark[10] and Gelly [Flink, 2015] on Apache Flink[11] also allow processing PGM data. Junghanns et al. [2016] argue that OSPGM forms the best ground for analytical questions in domains such as social networks, business intelligence, and life science.

---

[6]http://neo4j.com/
[7]http://tinkerpop.apache.org/
[8]https://ibm-graph-docs.ng.bluemix.net/
[9]http://www.sparsity-technologies.com/
[10]http://spark.apache.org/
[11]http://flink.apache.org/

CHAPTER 3

Query Languages

In this chapter we give a presentation of property graph query languages. We begin with the core language functionalities of graph navigation queries and (unions of) conjunctions of navigational queries. Our approach is then to give a presentation of major graph query language functionalities as restrictions or extensions of the recently proposed Regular Queries, a computationally well-behaved yet expressive fragment of Datalog for querying graphs [Reutter et al., 2017]. Our main contributions in this chapter are (1) giving a novel extension of the Regular Queries to the property graph model, (2) introducing a new algebra for this extended language, and (3) highlighting the realization of these features in practical languages. These contributions are important not only for the study of capabilities and limitations of practical graph query languages but also for the study of graph query processing methods and engineering of practical graph database engines.

3.1 BASIC FUNCTIONALITY

We begin by introducing in this section the basic capabilities which form the core of contemporary graph query languages.

3.1.1 REGULAR PATH QUERIES

A basic feature of graph querying was highlighted in the queries posed in the opening paragraph of Chapter 1: finding direct and indirect connections in social and biological networks. Such path navigation is a core ingredient of graph querying.

The *regular path queries* (*RPQ*) allow us to express such reachability queries. More precisely, an *RPQ* asks for all pairs of vertices that are connected by at least one path where the sequence of edge labels along the path forms a word in the language of a given regular expression over the graph's edge labels.

Syntax
The regular path queries are all and only those expressions recursively generated as follows.

- If $a \in \mathcal{L}$, then $a \in RPQ$.

- If $e \in RPQ$, then $(e)^- \in RPQ$.

- If $e, f \in RPQ$, then $(e)/(f) \in RPQ$.

- If $e, f \in RPQ$, then $e + f \in RPQ$.

- If $e \in RPQ$, then $(e)^+ \in RPQ$.

Note: In the sequel we will freely drop parentheses when doing so does not introduce ambiguity.

Semantics

As a query algebra, RPQ allows us to: select all edges (i.e., paths of length 1) sharing an edge label, take the inverse of a set of paths, concatenate paths from two sets of paths, take the union of two sets of paths, and to take the transitive closure of a set of paths. Alternatively, a pair of vertices is a valid answer to an RPQ if and only if the respective vertices are connected in the data graph by a path conforming to the RPQ. We formalize this as follows.

Let $G = (V, E, \eta, \lambda, \nu)$ be a property graph. The semantics of evaluating an expression $g \in RPQ$ over G is the set of vertex pairs $[\![g]\!]_G \subseteq V \times V$, recursively defined as follows.

- If $\quad g = a \in \mathcal{L}, \quad$ then $\quad [\![g]\!]_G = \{(s, t) \mid \exists edge \in E$ such that $\eta(edge) = (s, t)$ and $a \in \lambda(edge)\}$.

- If $g = (e)^- \in RPQ$, then $[\![g]\!]_G = \{(t, s) \mid (s, t) \in [\![e]\!]_G\}$.

- If $\quad g = e/f \in RPQ, \quad$ then $\quad [\![g]\!]_G = \{(s, t) \mid \exists u \in V$ such that $(s, u) \in [\![e]\!]_G$ and $(u, t) \in [\![f]\!]_G\}$.

- If $g = e + f \in RPQ$, then $[\![g]\!]_G = [\![e]\!]_G \cup [\![f]\!]_G$.

- If $g = (e)^+ \in RPQ$, then $[\![g]\!]_G = \{(s, t) \mid (s, t) \in TC([\![e]\!]_G)\}$, where $TC(R)$ denotes the transitive closure of binary relation R.[1]

Example 3.1 The query $q = $:knows/:worksFor/:knows$^+$ evaluated on G_{ex} of Figure 2.2 results in $[\![q]\!]_{G_{ex}} = \{(10, 11), (10, 12), (10, 13), (10, 16), (11, 16), (12, 12)\}$.

Note that in the sequel, given a graph G, we will let $\mathcal{L}_G$ denote the set of all and only those elements of $\mathcal{L}$ appearing in an edge or node label of G. To distinguish elements of $\mathcal{L}_G$, we will prefix them with ":" as we have in the preceding example.

3.1.2 CONJUNCTIVE GRAPH QUERIES

A second basic feature of graph querying highlighted by the example queries of Chapter 1 is the ability to identify substructures in a graph, e.g., pairs of people in a social network who have shared connections to both a professional society and the city where they live. The *conjunctive graph queries* (*CQ*) allow querying such subgraph patterns. Informally, a *CQ* asks for all subgraphs that match a given graph pattern. Hence, they are also known as "subgraph pattern matching queries."

---

[1]That is, $TC(R)$ is the smallest binary relation on $\pi_1(R) \cup \pi_2(R)$ that contains R and is transitive.

Syntax

A query pattern is given as a set of edge predicates. Each edge predicate consists of a pair of vertex variables and an edge label. The set of edge predicates forms a subgraph pattern.

Formally, let $\mathcal{V}$ be a set of *vertex variables*. The conjunctive graph queries are all and only those expressions of the form

$$(z_1, \ldots, z_m) \quad \leftarrow \quad a_1(x_1, y_1), \ldots, a_n(x_n, y_n)$$

where

- $m \geq 0, n > 0$,

- $x_1, y_1, \ldots, x_n, y_n \in \mathcal{V}$,

- $a_1, \ldots, a_n \in \mathcal{L}$, and

- for each $0 < i \leq m$, it holds that $z_i \in \{x_1, y_1, \ldots, x_n, y_n\}$.

We call m the arity of the expression.

Semantics

The semantics of *CQ* queries is given by bindings of variables to nodes in a graph. A set of variable bindings is a valid answer iff all predicates hold on the data graph.

Let $G = (V, E, \eta, \lambda, \nu)$ be a property graph and let $r = (z_1, \ldots, z_m) \leftarrow a_1(x_1, y_1), \ldots, a_n(x_n, y_n)$ be a *CQ*.

A *mapping* for r on G is a function μ with domain $\mathcal{V}$ and range V such that, for each $1 \leq i \leq n$, there exists an $edge_i \in E$ where $\eta(edge_i) = (\mu(x_i), \mu(y_i))$ and $a_i \in \lambda(edge_i)$. The semantics of evaluating r over G is the m-ary relation $[\![r]\!]_G \subseteq \underbrace{V \times \cdots \times V}_{m \text{ times}}$ defined as follows:

$$[\![r]\!]_G \quad = \quad \{(\mu(z_1), \ldots, \mu(z_m)) \mid \mu \text{ is a mapping for } r \text{ on } G\}.$$

Example 3.2 The query $q_1 = (a, b) \leftarrow \text{:knows}(a, b)$ evaluated on G_{ex} of Figure 2.2 results in $[\![q_1]\!]_{G_{ex}} = \{(10, 11), (10, 14), (11, 12), (12, 11), (12, 13), (15, 16)\}$. While the query $q_2 = (a_1, e_2) \leftarrow \text{:knows}(a_1, a_2), \text{:worksFor}(a_1, e_1), \text{:knows}(e_1, e_2), \text{:worksFor}(a_2, e_2)$ evaluated on G_{ex} results in $[\![q_2]\!]_{G_{ex}} = \{(12, 16)\}$.

A note on mapping semantics. A mapping is a function, i.e., every query variable is bound to exactly one graph vertex. However, different variables can be bound to the same vertex, as *CQ*'s find subgraphs to which the subgraph pattern is *homomorphic*. However, the definition of mappings can easily be adapted to other matching semantics such as *isomorphism*, i.e., where mappings must be injective. Hence, query classes—although typically defined in terms of subgraph homomorphism—can be considered as orthogonal to matching semantics.

3.1.3   CONJUNCTIVE REGULAR PATH QUERIES

Conjunctive regular path queries (CRPQ) combine subgraph pattern querying with path querying.

Syntax

A query pattern is given as a set of path predicates. Each path predicate consists of an *RPQ* and a pair of vertex variables.

Formally, let $\mathcal{V}$ be a set of *vertex variables*. The conjunctive regular path queries are all and only those expressions of the form

$$(z_1, \ldots, z_m) \quad \leftarrow \quad \alpha_1(x_1, y_1), \ldots, \alpha_n(x_n, y_n)$$

where

- $m \geq 0, n > 0$,

- $x_1, y_1, \ldots, x_n, y_n \in \mathcal{V}$,

- $\alpha_1, \ldots, \alpha_n \in RPQ$, and

- for each $0 < i \leq m$, it holds that $z_i \in \{x_1, y_1, \ldots, x_n, y_n\}$.

Again, we call m the arity of the expression.

Semantics

As we did for *CQ* queries, the semantics of *CRPQ* queries is given by bindings of variables to nodes in a graph. A set of variable bindings is a valid answer iff all predicates hold on the data graph.

Let $G = (V, E, \eta, \lambda, \nu)$ be a property graph and let $r = (z_1, \ldots, z_m) \leftarrow \alpha_1(x_1, y_1), \ldots, \alpha_n(x_n, y_n)$ be a *CRPQ*.

A *mapping* for r on G is a function μ with domain $\mathcal{V}$ and range V such that, for each $1 \leq i \leq n$, it holds that $(\mu(x_i), \mu(y_i)) \in [\![\alpha_i]\!]_G$. The semantics of evaluating r over G is the m-ary relation $[\![r]\!]_G \subseteq \underbrace{V \times \cdots \times V}_{m \text{ times}}$ defined as follows:

$$[\![r]\!]_G \quad = \quad \{(\mu(z_1), \ldots, \mu(z_m)) \mid \mu \text{ is a mapping for } r \text{ on } G\}.$$

Example 3.3   The query $q = (a, b) \leftarrow \text{:knows}/\text{:worksFor}/\text{:knows}^+(a, b)$ evaluated on G_{ex} of Figure 2.2 results in $[\![q]\!]_{G_{ex}} = \{(10, 11), (10, 12), (10, 13), (10, 16), (11, 16), (12, 12)\}$. This is the same query as the example given for *RPQs*, illustrating that *RPQs* are a subset of *CRPQs*. *CQs* are a subset of *CRPQs* as well, so that all examples given for *CQs* are also examples for *CRPQs*. The query $q' = (n, e) \leftarrow \text{:knows}^+(n, a_1), \text{:worksFor}(a_1, e), \text{:knows}(n, a_2), \text{:worksFor}(a_2, e)$ evaluated on G_{ex} results in $[\![q']\!]_{G_{ex}} = \{(10, 15)\}$. This *CRPQ* is neither a *RPQ* nor a *CQ*.

Alternative Visual Formalization

It is often handy to have an alternative visual formalization of *CRPQ*, which in the sequel we will call *graph patterns* (*GP*).

Given a *CRPQ* $r = (z_1, \ldots, z_m) \leftarrow \alpha_1(x_1, y_1), \ldots, \alpha_n(x_n, y_n)$, the *graph pattern* for r is the directed edge-labeled graph $r[z_1, \ldots, z_m]$ having node set $\{x_1, y_1, \ldots, x_n, y_n\}$ and, for each $1 \leq i \leq n$, an edge from x_i to y_i with edge label α_i.[2]

Given a property graph G, the semantics $[\![r[z_1, \ldots, z_m]]\!]_G$ of evaluating $r[z_1, \ldots, z_m]$ on G is based on mappings from the nodes of $r[z_1, \ldots, z_m]$ to the nodes of G and is exactly the same as the semantics of the underlying query r, i.e., $[\![r[z_1, \ldots, z_m]]\!]_G = [\![r]\!]_G$.

Example 3.4 An example of a graph pattern for the graph of Figure 2.2 is provided in Figure 3.1. This graph pattern corresponds to the query $(n, e) \leftarrow$:knows$^+(n, a_1)$, :worksFor(a_1, e), :knows(n, a_2), :worksFor(a_2, e), :worksFor(e, e).

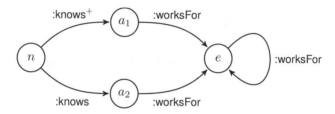

Figure 3.1: A graph pattern $r[n, e]$ defined on the graph of Figure 2.2.

3.1.4 UNIONS OF CONJUNCTIVE REGULAR PATH QUERIES

We next extend the expressive power of *CRPQ* by adding disjunction.

Syntax

A union of conjunctive regular path queries (*UCRPQ*) is a finite non-empty set $R \subseteq CRPQ$, each element of which is of the same arity m. We also say that R is of arity m.

---

[2]Going in the other direction, consider a pair $(G, [z_1, \ldots, z_m])$, where G is a directed graph with edges labeled with *RPQ*'s and nodes labeled with distinct variables from $\mathcal{V}$, and $[z_1, \ldots, z_m]$ is a list of node variables occurring in G, possibly with repetition, of length $m \geq 0$. Then it is easy to establish that $(G, [z_1, \ldots, z_m])$ corresponds to the unique *CRPQ* $(z_1, \ldots, z_m) \leftarrow \bigwedge_{\alpha(x,y) \in G} \alpha(x, y)$.

Semantics

For a given property graph $G = (V, E, \eta, \lambda, \nu)$ and $R \in UCRPQ$ of arity m, the semantics of evaluating R over G is the m-ary relation $[\![R]\!]_G \subseteq \underbrace{V \times \cdots \times V}_{m \text{ times}}$ defined as follows:

$$[\![R]\!]_G \quad = \quad \bigcup_{r \in R} [\![r]\!]_G .$$

Example 3.5   The following *UCRPQ* evaluates on the graph of Figure 2.2 to all people x who know or work for someone in-between (not necessarily distinct from x) who works for a person y (not necessarily distinct from x or the person in between):

$$(x) \quad \leftarrow \quad \text{:knows/:worksFor}(x, y)$$
$$(x) \quad \leftarrow \quad \text{:worksFor/:worksFor}(x, y) .$$

In the graph of Figure 2.2 such people x are $\{10, 11, 12, 14\}$.

To summarize our discussion so far, we make the following observations, which are straightforward to establish:[3]

- *RPQ* $\subset$ *CRPQ* $\subset$ *UCRPQ*,

- *CQ* $\subset$ *CRPQ*,

- *CQ* $\not\subset$ *RPQ*,[4] and

- *RPQ* $\not\subset$ *CQ*,

where $\mathcal{L}_1 \subset \mathcal{L}_2$ denotes that every query of $\mathcal{L}_1$ can be expressed by a query in $\mathcal{L}_2$ but not vice versa.

3.1.5   RELATION ALGEBRA

We conclude our survey of basic graph query functionality with a generalization of *RPQ* with negation.

Syntax and Semantics

The *relation algebra* expressions are defined by the grammar of the *RPQ*'s extended with two additional production rules:

- *id* $\in$ *RA*.

---

[3] For example, $\alpha \in RPQ$ can be equivalently expressed in *CRPQ* as $(x, y) \leftarrow \alpha(x, y)$.
[4] This holds even if we restrict *CQ* to binary queries, i.e., all and only those *CQ* queries of arity 2.

- If $e, f \in RA$, then $e - f \in RA$.

The semantics of RA expressions on graph G is as expected.

- If $g = id$, then $[\![g]\!]_G = \{(s, s) \mid s \in V\}$.

- If $g = e - f$, then $[\![g]\!]_G = \{(s, t) \mid (s, t) \in [\![e]\!]_G \text{ and } (s, t) \notin [\![f]\!]_G\}$.

Note that we can also now express intersection $e \cap f$ (i.e., a limited form of conjunction), defined as $e - (e - f)$.

Example 3.6   The query $q_1 = (\text{:worksFor}^+ \cap \text{:knows}^+) - \text{:worksFor}$ evaluated on our running example retrieves all pairs of people (x, y) such that x knows y (either directly or indirectly) and x indirectly works for y. As another example, the query $q_2 = (\text{:worksFor} \cap id)/\text{:knows}$ finds all pairs (x, y) where x is a person who works for themselves and y is someone x knows.

    RA properly generalizes RPQ in the direction of $UCRPQ$'s with the ability to express conjunctive patterns as in both queries q_1 and q_2 of Example 3.6. Furthermore, RA can express queries which are inexpressible in all of the languages above, e.g., nonmonotonic queries[5] such as our example q_1 above cannot be expressed in RPQ, $CRPQ$, CQ, or $UCRPQ$. However, it is easy to exhibit conjunctive queries expressible in $CRPQ$, CQ, and $UCRPQ$ which are in turn inexpressible in RA.

3.2   REGULAR PROPERTY GRAPH QUERIES

We next present the *regular property graph queries* (*RPGQ*s), an extension of the *regular queries* [Bourhis et al., 2014a,b, Reutter et al., 2017] to the property graph data model. The regular queries were introduced as a well-behaved generalization of all the languages presented in the previous section,[6] well-behaved in the sense that query containment is decidable [Reutter et al., 2017]. However, these queries do not support reasoning over the features of the property graph data model not found in earlier models, such as the property values associated with nodes and edges in the property graph data model.

    We present two formalisms for this new language: *regular property graph logic* and the *regular property graph algebra*. We establish that these two formalisms are equivalent in expressive power and demonstrate in the following sections of this chapter how the regular property graph queries are well suited as a vehicle for the study of foundations and practical engineering of property graph query languages.

---

[5]A query Q is monotonic if and only if, for every pair of database instances I and I', it holds that if $I \subseteq I'$, then $[\![Q]\!]_I \subseteq [\![Q]\!]_{I'}$.

[6]With the caveat that we restrict RA to its positive fragment, i.e., where we replace "$-$" with "$\cap$".

3.2.1   REGULAR PROPERTY GRAPH LOGIC

Regular property graph logic (*RPGLog*) is a fragment of standard non-recursive Datalog [Green et al., 2013] adapted to property graphs. Informally, *RPGLog* corresponds to unions of conjunctive queries on graphs (i.e., all predicates are binary or unary, corresponding to edge labels and node labels, respectively), augmented with edge variables and a transitive closure operation "*". In addition to being tailored to the features of the PGM, *RPGLog* queries can have nesting of subqueries.

Syntax

Let $\mathcal{E}$ be a set of *edge variables* and $\mathcal{V}$ be a set of *vertex variables*, where $\mathcal{E} \cap \mathcal{V} = \emptyset$. Edge and vertex variables allow refer to edges and vertices in the head predicate or in other body predicates of a rule, e.g., to filter on their properties. Furthermore, let $\mathcal{C}$ denote a set of *context identifiers*. The role of context identifiers is to distinguish or identify (i.e., unite) edges created by different rules. An *RPGLog rule* has the form

$$head \quad \leftarrow \quad body_1, \ldots, body_n, constraint_1, \ldots, constraint_m$$

for some $n > 0$ and $m \geq 0$, where

- each body predicate $body_i$ is of one of the following forms:

    - $p(x, y)$ AS e
    - $p^*(x, y)$
    - $p(x)$,

    where $p \in \mathcal{L}$ is a label, $x, y \in \mathcal{V}$ are vertex variables, and $e \in \mathcal{E}$ is an edge variable;

- each body predicate $constraint_i$ is either of the form

$$x.p \; \theta \; y.q \quad \text{or} \quad x.p \; \theta \; val,$$

    where $x, y \in \mathcal{V} \cup \mathcal{E}$, both x and y appear in a non-constraint body predicate (not necessarily the same predicate), $p, q \in \mathcal{K}$, $val \in \mathcal{N}$, and $\theta \in \{=, \neq, <, >, \leq, \geq\}$, or, of the form

$$x = y,$$

    where $x, y \in \mathcal{V}$ and both x and y appear in a non-constraint body predicate (not necessarily the same predicate);

- the head predicate *head* is either of the form

$$p(x, y) \text{ IN } c,$$

where $p \in \mathcal{L}$ is a label, $c \in \mathcal{C}$ is a context identifier, and $x, y \in \mathcal{V}$ are vertex variables, and both x and y appear in a body predicate (not necessarily the same predicate), or, of the form

$$\mathsf{result}(x_1, \ldots, x_n),$$

where $n \geq 0$, result is a reserved predicate not in $\mathcal{L}$, $x_1, \ldots, x_n \in \mathcal{V}$, and each x_i appears in a body predicate.

Note that for ease of presentation, in this syntax (and the corresponding semantics we give below) each edge is assumed to have exactly one label. The generalization to finite sets of labels is straightforward and omitted for the sake of clarity.

Given a set of rules R, the *dependency graph* of R is the directed graph having as node set all (and only) those elements of $\mathcal{L}$ appearing in a predicate of a rule of R and with an edge from x to y iff x appears in the head of a rule r and y appears in the body of r. We say R is *recursive* if the dependency graph of R has a cycle; otherwise, we say R is *non-recursive*.

An *RPGLog query* is a finite non-empty non-recursive set of rules such that at least one rule has head predicate result and all result predicates have the same arity.

Example 3.7   Consider the following query q which retrieves the set of all experts which are known after the year 2000, have a salary below \$5000, and are (directly or indirectly) related via knowing or working relationships to someone having a lower salary:

$$
\begin{aligned}
\mathsf{:knownExpert}(y, y) \ \mathtt{IN} \ a \ \ &\leftarrow \ \ \mathsf{:knows}(x, y) \ \mathtt{AS} \ k, \mathsf{:Expert}(z), k.year > 2000, y = z. \\
\mathsf{:related}(x, y) \ \mathtt{IN} \ b \ \ &\leftarrow \ \ \mathsf{:knows}(x, y). \\
\mathsf{:related}(x, y) \ \mathtt{IN} \ b \ \ &\leftarrow \ \ \mathsf{:worksFor}(x, y). \\
\mathsf{result}(x) \ \ &\leftarrow \ \ \mathsf{:knownExpert}(x, x), \mathsf{:related}^*(x, y), \\
& \qquad x.salary < 5000, y.salary < x.salary.
\end{aligned}
$$

For clarity, we omitted "AS e" from a "$p(x, y)$ AS e" in a rule body if e does not appear elsewhere in that rule body. Also, note that the query could be simplified, e.g., by dropping the conjunct "$y = z$" and replacing z by y in the body of the first rule; we include this here simply to illustrate basic features of the language. The context identifier b appearing in the two rules with head ":related(x, y) IN b" explicitly demands that only one :related edge is derived for a particular vertex pair x and y even if both rules with head ":related(x, y)" apply to x and y. Instead, the query demands the derivation of two distinct :related edges for x and y if both rules with head ":related(x, y)" declare a different context identifier.

Semantics

The semantics of *RPGLog* queries follows closely that of non-recursive Datalog [Green et al., 2013].

Let $G = (V, E, \eta, \lambda, \nu)$ be a property graph and $q \in RPGLog$. Consider a rule $r \in q$:

$$head \quad \leftarrow \quad body_1, \ldots, body_n, constraint_1, \ldots, constraint_m.$$

A *mapping* is a function with domain $\mathcal{V} \cup \mathcal{E}$ and range $\mathcal{O}$, i.e., assigning object identifiers to variables. We say mapping μ *satisfies* r in G if μ satisfies each body predicate b of r, where *satisfaction of a predicate in G* is defined as follows.

- If b is of the form "$p(x, y)$ AS e":

  - in the case where $p \in \lambda(E)$, then it holds that there exists an *edge* $\in E$ such that $\mu(e) = edge$, $p \in \lambda(edge)$ and $\eta(edge) = (\mu(x), \mu(y))$; and

  - in the case where $p \notin \lambda(E) \cup \lambda(V)$, then it holds that there exists an *edge* $\in [\![p]\!]_G$ such that $(\mu(x), \mu(y)) \in edge$ and $\mu(e) \in edge$.

- If b is of the form "$p^*(x, y)$" where $p \notin \lambda(V)$, then it holds that $(\mu(x), \mu(y)) \in [\![p^*]\!]_G$.

- If b is of the form "$p(x)$" where $p \in \lambda(V)$, then it holds that $\mu(x) \in V$ and $p \in \lambda(\mu(x))$.

- If b is of the form "$x.p \; \theta \; y.q$", then it holds that $\nu(\mu(x), p) \; \theta \; \nu(\mu(y), q)$.

- If b is of the form "$x.p \; \theta \; val$", then it holds that $\nu(\mu(x), p) \; \theta \; val$.

- If b is of the form "$x = y$", then it holds that $\mu(x) = \mu(y)$.

In all other cases, b is not satisfiable.

We next give the semantics of transitive closure and rule evaluation. We assume we are given a function to provide fresh object identifiers in $\mathcal{O}$, i.e., IDs distinct from the object IDs occurring in G and on which ν is nowhere defined. We denote this function by ω_G, which has domain $\mathcal{O} \times \mathcal{O} \times \mathcal{C}$ and is injective on codomain $\mathcal{O} \setminus (V \cup E)$.[7]

For $p \notin \lambda(E)$, let $\hat{p} \subseteq q$ be the (possibly empty) set of all rules with head predicate p. Then $[\![p]\!]_G = \bigcup_{r \in \hat{p}} [\![r]\!]_G$, where

$$[\![r]\!]_G \quad = \quad \{\{(\mu(x), \mu(y)), \omega_G(\mu(x), \mu(y), c)\} \mid \mu \text{ is a mapping satisfying } r \text{ in } G\}.$$

Here, (x, y) and c are the output variables and context identifier, respectively, appearing in the head of rule r. As p is non-recursively defined and G is finite, $[\![p]\!]_G$ is well-defined and finite.

In the case of a predicate $p^*(x, y)$, if $p \in \lambda(E)$, then

$$[\![p^*]\!]_G \quad = \quad \{(x, x) \mid x \in V\} \cup \left\{(x, y) \mid x, y \in V \text{ and } x \xrightarrow{p,G} y\right\},$$

---

[7]Essentially, ω_G is a skolem function which is parameterized by two node identifiers and a context identifier. For a recent overview of object creation in query languages, see Bonifati et al. [2016b].

where $x \xrightarrow{p,G} y$ denotes that for some $n > 0$, there exists $e_1, \ldots, e_n \in E$ and $v_1, \ldots, v_{n+1} \in V$ such that, $x = v_1$, $y = v_{n+1}$, and, for $1 \le i \le n$, $\lambda(e_i) = p$ and $\eta(e_i) = (v_i, v_{i+1})$. Otherwise, if $p \notin \lambda(E)$, then

$$\llbracket p^* \rrbracket_G \;=\; \{(x, x) \mid x \in V\} \cup \left\{ (x, y) \mid x, y \in V \text{ and } x \xrightarrow{\llbracket p \rrbracket_G} y \right\},$$

where $x \xrightarrow{\llbracket p \rrbracket_G} y$ denotes that for some $n > 0$, there exists $e_1, \ldots, e_n \in \llbracket p \rrbracket_G$ and $v_1, \ldots, v_{n+1} \in V$ such that, $x = v_1$, $y = v_{n+1}$, and, for $1 \le i \le n$, $(v_i, v_{i+1}) \in e_i$. In both cases, as p is non-recursively defined and G is finite, $\llbracket p^* \rrbracket_G$ is well-defined and finite.

Finally, let $\{r_1, \ldots, r_k\} \subseteq q$ be the (non-empty) set of all rules with head predicate result$(x_1, \ldots, x_n)$. The semantics of evaluating q on G is the set

$$\llbracket q \rrbracket_G \;=\; \bigcup_{r \in \{r_1, \ldots, r_k\}} \{(\mu(x_1), \ldots, \mu(x_n)) \mid \mu \text{ is a mapping satisfying } r \text{ in } G\}.$$

Note that if $n = 2$ we could define a standard scheme to construct a property graph from $\llbracket q \rrbracket_G$ as output, if so desired. See Section 3.3.2 for further discussion of this point.

Example 3.8 The query given in Example 3.7 evaluated on the example graph of Figure 2.2 gives us

$$\llbracket q \rrbracket_{G_{ex}} \;=\; \{(11)\}.$$

3.2.2 REGULAR PROPERTY GRAPH ALGEBRA

We next give an algebraic presentation of the queries definable in *RPGLog*. We are motivated in this by (1) the use of the algebra as a tool in the formal study of path query languages, and (2) the use of the algebra in the study of engineering of graph queries (e.g., compilation and execution strategies).

Syntax

The *regular property graph algebra* (RPGA) consists of all and only those expressions constructed over elements of $\mathcal{L}$ using transitive closure, union, and graph join operations. We have the following grammar for the set of *subquery* expressions *subRPGA*:

$$e \;::=\; \ell \mid e^* \mid e \cup e \mid \bowtie_{pos_i, pos_j}^{\Phi, c} (e, \ldots, e),$$

where

- $\ell \in \mathcal{L}$;

- $(e, \ldots, e)$ is of length $n > 0$;

- $c \in \mathcal{C}$ is a context identifier;

- $pos_i, pos_j \in \{\mathrm{src}_1, \mathrm{trg}_1, \ldots, \mathrm{src}_n, \mathrm{trg}_n\}$; and

- Φ is a conjunction of a finite number of terms of the form:

  - $\lambda(pos) = \ell$ for $pos \in \{\mathrm{src}_1, \mathrm{trg}_1, \ldots, \mathrm{src}_n, \mathrm{trg}_n\}$ and $\ell \in \mathcal{L}$,
  - $pos_i.p \quad \theta \quad pos_j.q \quad$ or $\quad pos_i.p \quad \theta \quad val, \quad$ for $\quad pos_i, pos_j \in$ $\{\mathrm{src}_1, \mathrm{trg}_1, \ldots, \mathrm{src}_n, \mathrm{trg}_n, \mathrm{edge}_1, \ldots, \mathrm{edge}_n\}$, $p, q \in \mathcal{K}$, $val \in \mathcal{N}$ and $\theta \in \{=, \neq, <, >, \leq, \geq\}$, or
  - $pos_i = pos_j$ for $pos_i, pos_j \in \{\mathrm{src}_1, \mathrm{trg}_1, \ldots, \mathrm{src}_n, \mathrm{trg}_n\}$.

Then, expressions $e \in RPGA$ are all and only those of the form

$$\bowtie_{\overline{pos}}^{\Phi} (e_1, \ldots, e_n),$$

where $n > 0$, each e_i is a *subRPGA* expression $(1 \leq i \leq n)$, Φ is as above, and $\overline{pos}$ is a list of length zero or more, containing elements of $\{\mathrm{src}_1, \mathrm{trg}_1, \ldots, \mathrm{src}_n, \mathrm{trg}_n\}$.

Note that, as with our exposition of *RPGLog* above, for ease of presentation each edge is assumed to have exactly one label. Again, the generalization to finite sets of labels is straightforward and omitted for the sake of clarity.

Example 3.9   The query given in Example 3.7 can be expressed in *RPGA* as

$$\bowtie_{\mathrm{src}_1}^{\emptyset} (\bowtie_{\mathrm{trg}_1, \mathrm{trg}_1}^{\Phi, x} (\text{:knows}, (\text{:knows} \cup \text{:worksFor})^*)),$$

where Φ is

$\mathrm{edge}_1.year > 2000 \wedge \lambda(\mathrm{trg}_1) = \text{:Expert} \wedge \mathrm{trg}_1.salary < 5000$
$$\wedge \, \mathrm{trg}_1.salary > \mathrm{trg}_2.salary \wedge \mathrm{trg}_1 = \mathrm{src}_2$$

and x is an arbitrary context ID.

Semantics

Let $G = (V, E, \eta, \lambda, \nu)$ be a property graph and $e \in subRPGA$. The semantics of evaluating e on G, denoted as $[\![e]\!]_G$, is defined as follows:

- (case $e = \ell \in \mathcal{L}$). $[\![e]\!]_G = \{\{\eta(edge), edge\} \mid edge \in E \text{ and } \lambda(edge) = \ell\}$;

- (case $e = f \cup g$). $[\![e]\!]_G = [\![f]\!]_G \cup [\![g]\!]_G$;

- (case $e = f^*$). $[\![e]\!]_G = \{(x, x) \mid x \in V\} \cup \{(x, y) \mid x, y \in V \text{ and } x \xrightarrow{[\![f]\!]_G} y\}$, where $x \xrightarrow{[\![f]\!]_G} y$ denotes that for some $n > 0$, there exists $e_1, \ldots, e_n \in [\![f]\!]_G$ and $v_1, \ldots, v_{n+1} \in V$ such that, $x = v_1$, $y = v_{n+1}$, and, for $1 \le i \le n$, $(v_i, v_{i+1}) \in e_i$; and

- (case $e = \bowtie_{pos_i, pos_j}^{\Phi, c} (e_1, \ldots, e_n)$). For $1 \le i \le n$, let $(\mathrm{src}_i, \mathrm{trg}_i, \mathrm{edge}_i)$ be the schema of $[\![e_i]\!]_G$, where for each $t = \{(x, y), z\} \in [\![e_i]\!]_G$, we have $t.\mathrm{src}_i = x$, $t.\mathrm{trg}_i = y$, and $t.\mathrm{edge}_i = z$. Then, we have $[\![e]\!]_G = \{\{(t.pos_i, t.pos_j), \omega_G(t.pos_i, t.pos_j, c)\} \mid t \in \sigma_\Phi([\![e_1]\!]_G \times \cdots \times [\![e_n]\!]_G)\}$, where in evaluating the filter Φ

  – "$\lambda(pos) = \ell$" is true if and only if $\lambda(t.pos) = \ell$,

  – "$pos_i.p \; \theta \; pos_j.q$" is true if and only if $\nu(t.pos_i, p) \; \theta \; \nu(t.pos_j, q)$,

  – "$pos_i.p \; \theta \; val$" is true if and only if $\nu(t.pos_i, p) \; \theta \; val$, and

  – "$pos_i = pos_j$" is true if and only if $t.pos_i = t.pos_j$.

Here, σ is the standard relational algebra selection operator [Ullman, 1988].

Finally, the semantics of evaluating $\bowtie_{pos_1, \ldots, pos_m}^{\Phi} (e_1, \ldots, e_n) \in RPGA$ on G is the set

$$[\![\bowtie_{pos_1, \ldots, pos_m}^{\Phi} (e_1, \ldots, e_n)]\!]_G \;=\; \{(t.pos_1, \ldots, t.pos_m) \mid t \in \sigma_\Phi([\![e_1]\!]_G \times \cdots \times [\![e_n]\!]_G)\}.$$

As with *RPGLog* queries, if $m = 2$ we can construct a property graph from $[\![e]\!]_G$ if so desired. Again, see Section 3.3.2 for further discussion of this point.

A Selection Operator

For predicates Ψ built over terms only of the form $\lambda(pos) = \ell$ or $pos.p \; \theta \; val$, we could introduce a *value selection* operator $\sigma_\Psi(e)$ to *subRPGA*, as a macro for $\bowtie_{\mathrm{src}_1, \mathrm{trg}_1}^{\Psi} (e)$. This would facilitate the standard query optimization heuristic of "pushing down selections" [Ullman, 1989]. Given such an operator, our running example query Q_1 can be rewritten as

$$\bowtie_{\mathrm{src}_1}^{\emptyset} (\bowtie_{\mathrm{trg}_1, \mathrm{trg}_1}^{\Psi_a, x} (\sigma_{\Psi_b}(\text{:knows}), (\text{:knows} \cup \text{:worksFor})^*)),$$

where Ψ_a is "$\mathrm{trg}_1.salary > \mathrm{trg}_2.salary \wedge \mathrm{trg}_1 = \mathrm{src}_2$" and Ψ_b is "$\mathrm{edge}_1.year > 2000 \wedge \lambda(\mathrm{trg}_1) = $:Expert $\wedge \; \mathrm{trg}_1.salary < 5000$."

Note that σ is only applicable to a single (binary) subquery e.

3.2.3   EQUIVALENCE AND COMPLEXITY OF *RPGLog* AND *RPGA*

RPGLog and *RPGA* are two syntaxes for the same query language, in the following sense.

Theorem 3.10

- *Let $q \in RPGLog$. There exists $e \in RPGA$ such that for any property graph G, it holds that $[\![q]\!]_G = [\![e]\!]_G$.*

- *Let $e \in RPGA$. There exists $q \in RPGLog$ such that for any property graph G, it holds that $[\![e]\!]_G = [\![q]\!]_G$.*

The proof of Theorem 3.10 follows by a straightforward induction on the structure of queries/-expressions. Henceforth, we will refer to the family of queries expressible in these languages as the *RPGQ*.

It is easy to demonstrate that the complexity of *RPGQ* evaluation is the same as that of the Regular Queries which they generalize, namely, NP-complete in combined complexity and NLogspace-complete in data complexity.

3.3   *RPGQ* IN CONTEXT

We have introduced *RPGQ* as a vehicle for further study of the design and engineering of core graph query language functionalities. Toward this, we conclude our presentation of graph query languages by putting *RPGQ* in context with its well-known fragments, practical extensions, and relationships to practical graph query languages.

3.3.1   IMPORTANT FRAGMENTS OF *RPGQ*

It can be shown that *UCRPQ* (and hence also each of *RPQ*, *CQ*, and *CRPQ*) is a (strict) subset of *RPGQ*. Likewise, a straightforward structural induction establishes that every expression in the positive *RA* (i.e., the *RA* fragment obtained by replacing the "$-$" operator with the "$\cap$" operator) can be equivalently expressed in *RPGQ*.

A useful capability for path querying is to introduce a unary "path projection" operator $\pi(e)$:

$$[\![\pi(e)]\!]_G \quad = \quad \{(s, s) \mid \exists t \in V \text{ such that } (s, t) \in [\![e]\!]_G\}.$$

Path projection (also known as "nesting") allows us to perform an existential check, filtering out those nodes in the graph which do not have an outgoing path selected by e.

Example 3.11   The query $q = \pi(\text{:knows}^+/\text{:worksFor})$ evaluated on G_{ex} of Figure 2.2 results in $[\![q]\!]_{G_{ex}} = \{(10, 10), (11, 11), (12, 12)\}$. These are the people who have someone in their :knows network who works.

Extending *RPQ* with path projection is known to strictly increase the expressive power of the language. However, since we can express $\pi(e)$ in positive *RA* as $id \cap (e/e^-)$, it follows that *RPGQ* contains *UCRPQ* extended with path projection.

3.3.2   EXTENDING *RPGQ* FOR COMPOSABILITY

In our discussion of *RPGLog* and *RPGA* above, we noted that a standard scheme could be introduced to convert the output of binary queries to the property graph data model. In general, if a property graph is desired as output, it is important to consider ways in which *RPGQ* queries of arbitrary arity can be extended with property graph creation functionality. Queries with a property graph as output are composable, i.e., the output of a query can be used as input of another query. Composability is an important feature in practice. It facilitates database views, which are central for modular query writing, external schemas, fine-grained access control, advanced performance tuning, etc. We discuss property graph creation in three steps based on the *RPGLog* formalism: (1) creating vertices to abstract matched subgraphs into single entities; (2) creating edges to connect new vertices to form new graph structures; and (3) creating property values to populate new graph structures with data.

Creating Vertices

As defined above, *RPGLog* already allows creating edges, where a match of an arbitrary pattern expressed in a rule's body can be abstracted to a connection between two vertices that are part of that match. However, it is not possible to abstract the whole match into a new entity, i.e., into a new vertex. To support this, we extend *RPGLog* with the possibility to create new vertices out of matches. We call the resulting language *RPGLog-V*, defined as follows.

Syntax.   We additionally allow the head predicate *head* to be of the form

$$p() \text{ IN } c,$$

where $p \in \mathcal{L}$, $c \in \mathcal{C}$, and p does not appear in query q in any head predicate of the form "$p(x, y)$ IN c."

Semantics.   The semantics of this new head predicate is defined analogously to what we have in Section 3.2.1. For $p \notin \lambda(V)$, let $\hat{p} \subseteq q$ be the (possibly empty) set of all rules of with a head predicate of the form "p IN $\cdot$". Then $[\![p]\!]_G = \bigcup_{r \in \hat{p}} [\![r]\!]_G$, where

$$[\![r]\!]_G \ = \ \{\omega_G(\mu, c) \mid \mu \text{ is a mapping satisfying } r \text{ in } G\}.$$

Here, c is the context identifier in the head of rule r. As above, we require that p is non-recursively defined and G is finite, so that $[\![p]\!]_G$ is well-defined and finite. Additionally, we extend the satisfaction of a body predicate b in G by: If b is of the form "$p(x)$" where $p \notin \lambda(V)$, then it holds that $\mu(x) \in [\![p]\!]_G$. We generalized the object identifier function ω_G to be parameterized by a pair of mapping μ and context identifier c.

Example 3.12   The following rule r_1 creates a new vertex labeled :TrainingTandem for each pair of apprentice and expert, where the apprentice works for the expert.

$$r_1 : \quad \text{:TrainingTandem() IN } c \quad \leftarrow \quad \text{:Apprentice}(x), \text{:worksFor}(x, y), \text{:Expert}(y).$$

Let us assume the query contains another rule r_2 that creates training tandems for apprentices working for scholars:

$$r_2 : \quad \text{:TrainingTandem() IN } c \quad \leftarrow \quad \text{:Apprentice}(x), \text{:worksFor}(x, y), \text{:Scholar}(y).$$

If the underlying graph contains an apprentice working for someone who is both an expert and a scholar, these pairs of apprentices and expert/scholar matches in r_1 as well as r_2. Since both rule heads have the same context identifier c, only a single training tandem vertex is created for a single pair of apprentices and expert/scholar (instead of two). In contrast, a similar looking rule r_3 creates a new :TrainingTandem vertex for each pair of apprentice and expert, where both know each other:

$$r_3 : \quad \text{:TrainingTandem() IN } d \quad \leftarrow \quad \text{:Apprentice}(x), \text{:knows}(x, y), \text{:knows}(y, x), \text{:Expert}(y).$$

Here, a pair of apprentice and expert that match in r_1 as well as r_3 results in two new :TrainingTandem vertices because the rules have different context identifiers c and d, respectively.

Creating Edges

The creation of isolated vertices is seldom useful. Useful queries typically need to connect new vertices back to (parts of) the match they have been created from. Creating an edge between a new vertex and its original match requires to have the new vertex $\omega_G(\mu, c)$ and the mapping μ side by side. Since rules do not share variables, we need to generalize edge-creating rules and vertex-creating rules of *RPGLog-V* to rules capable of creating multiple graph elements at once, as laid out in the following. We call the resulting language *RPGLog-G*.

Syntax. We change the head predicate *head* to be one of the form H_V, H_E or result$(x_1, \ldots, x_n)$, where:

- H_V is a possibly empty set of simple head predicates h of the form

$$p() \text{ IN } c \text{ AS } v,$$

  where $p \in \mathcal{L}, c \in \mathcal{C}, v \in \mathcal{V}$, and v neither appears in any body predicate nor in any other simple head predicate of the same rule;

- H_E is a possibly empty set of simple head predicates h of the form

$$p(x, y) \text{ IN } c,$$

  where $p \in \mathcal{L}, c \in \mathcal{C}, x, y \in \mathcal{V}$, and both x and y appear in a body predicate (not necessarily the same predicate); and

- result$(x_1, \ldots, x_n)$ is defined as before.

Although not strictly necessary, it is practical to enforce that $H_V \cup H_E \neq \emptyset$ to avoid rules without any output.

Semantics.   For rule r with a head predicate H_V, H_E, we define

$$M_r^0 = \{\mu \mid \mu \text{ is a mapping satisfying } r \text{ in } G\}$$

to be the set of mappings satisfying the body of the rule, and

$$M_r^V = \left(\bowtie_{p \in H_V} M_{p,r}^V\right) \bowtie M_r^0$$

to be the set of mappings satisfying the body of the rule and additionally including the new vertices produced by that rule r.

For $p \notin \lambda(V) \cup \lambda(E)$, let $\hat{p} \subseteq q$ be the (possibly empty) set of all rules with a head predicate H_V, H_E such that $p \in H_V \cup H_E$. Then $[\![p]\!]_G = \bigcup_{r \in \hat{p}} [\![p; r]\!]_G$, where

- if $p \in H_V$

$$[\![p; r]\!]_G = \{\omega_G(\mu, c) \mid \mu \in M_r^0\} \quad \text{and} \quad M_{p,r}^V = \{\mu \cup \{(v \mapsto \omega_G(\mu, c))\} \mid \mu \in M_r^0\};$$

and

- if $p \in H_E$

$$[\![p; r]\!]_G = \{\omega_G(\mu, c) \mid \mu \in M_r^V\}.$$

Here, c and v are the context identifier and the variable in the simple head predicate p of rule r, respectively. We still require that p is non-recursively defined and G is finite, so that $[\![p]\!]_G$ is well defined and finite.

Example 3.13   The following query considers teams of two collaborating experts each with a coworker. The two experts of a team are the heads of the team; the coworkers are simple team members. Now, the query looks for a person p who is a member of two different teams that share at least one head:

:Team() IN c AS t, :head(t, e), :head(t, f), :member(t, x_1), :member(t, x_2)
$\quad\quad \leftarrow$:Expert(e), :Expert(f), :collaboratesWith(e, f),
$\quad\quad\quad$:worksFor(x_1, e), :worksFor(x_2, f).
result(p)
$\quad\quad \leftarrow$:member(p, t_1), :member(p, t_2), :head(t_1, e), :head(t_2, e), $t_1 \neq t_2$.

As this Example 3.13 shows, vertex and edge creation allows the transient introduction of higher-level concepts, such as the team, in the graph and express further query steps with the help of these concepts. The person could be also found without explicitly introducing teams as new vertices, but then the query would list all possible constellations of the two teams to find the wanted person. Instead, the creation functionality allows us to modularize and simplify query writing by making explicit higher-level concepts.

Creating Property Values

Another desirable feature is the possibility to assign property values to newly created vertices and edges. Therefore, we extend *RPGLog-G* to *RPGLog-GP* as described in the following.

Syntax.   First, we extend the language with value variables; hence, let $\mathcal{X}$ be a set of *value variables*.

Second, we additionally allow a body predicate to be of the form

$$o.q \text{ AS } x,$$

where $o \in \mathcal{V} \cup \mathcal{E}, x \in \mathcal{X}$, o appears in one other body predicate, x appears in no other body predicate, and $q \in \mathcal{K}$.

Third, we extend the head predicate of the form H_V, H_E to H_V, H_E, A, where

- H_V is defined as before;

- H_E is a possibility empty set of simple head predicates of the form

$$p(x, y) \text{ IN } c \text{ AS } e,$$

  where $p \in \mathcal{L}, c \in \mathcal{C}, x, y \in \mathcal{V}$, both x and y appear in a body predicate (not necessarily the same predicate), and $e \in \mathcal{E}$ neither appears in any body predicate nor in any other simple head predicate of the same rule; and

- A is a possibly empty set of assignments of the form

$$o.q = exp,$$

  where $o \in \mathcal{V} \cup \mathcal{E}$ appears after the AS keyword in one of simple head predicates in H_V and H_E in the same rule, $q \in \mathcal{K}$, and exp is a function $\mathcal{N}^m \mapsto \mathcal{N}$ with m being the number of value variables appearing in the body of the same rule.

Semantics.   To accommodate the new body predicate in the semantics of the language, we additionally allow a body predicate b to be satisfied in G as follows.

- If b is of the form "$o.q$ AS x", then it holds that $m(x) = v(m(o), p)$.

The semantics of the head predicate H_V, H_E, A in *RPGLog-GP* extends the semantics of H_V, H_E in *RPGLog-G*. Additionally to what we have in that semantics, we define

$$M_r^E = \left(\bowtie_{p \in H_V} M_{p,r}^E \right) \bowtie M_r^V$$

to be the set of mappings satisfying the body of the rule and additionally including the new vertices and new edges produced by that rule r.

For $p \notin \lambda(V) \cup \lambda(E)$, let $\hat{p} \subseteq q$ be the (possibly empty) set of all rules with a head predicate H_V, H_E, A such that $p \in H_V \cup H_E$. Then $[\![p]\!]_G = \bigcup_{r \in \hat{p}} [\![p; r]\!]_G$, where the definition of $[\![p; r]\!]_G$ is extended by

- if $p \in A$

$$[\![p;r]\!]_G = \{((\mu(o),q) \mapsto exp(\mu(\mathcal{X}_r))) \mid \mu \in M_r^E\}.$$

Here, o, q, and exp are the variable, the property key, and the function appearing in the simple head predicate p of rule r, respectively, while $\mathcal{X}_r$ is the set of value variables appearing in the body of rule r.

Example 3.14   The following query considers teams of two persons collaborating with each other. Precisely, the query asks for teams with an average age greater than 30:

:Team() IN c AS t, :member(t, x_1), :member(t, x_2), t.averageAge $= (a_1 + a_2)/2$
$\leftarrow$:collaboratesWith(x_1, x_2), :collaboratesWith(x_2, x_1),
      x_1.age AS a_1, x_2.age AS a_2.
result(t, a)
$\leftarrow$:Team(t), t.averageAge AS $a, a > 30$.

3.3.3   *RPGQ* AND PRACTICAL GRAPH QUERY LANGUAGES

We next illustrate how *RPGQ* captures the core of the contemporary graph query language G-CORE [Angles et al., 2018a]. G-CORE is a practical language developed by an international industry-academia consortium to identify a natural syntax for expressing the most important graph query language features arising in practice. The *RPGQ* query presented in *RPGLog* syntax in Example 3.7 can be written in G-Core as:

```
PATH related = (x)-/<:knows+:worksFor>/->(y)
SELECT x
MATCH (z)-[k:knows]->(x:Expert)-/<:related*>/->(y)
WHERE k.year > 2000 AND x.salary < 5000 AND y.salary < x.salary
```

G-CORE also includes graph creation functionality. As in the Example 3.13, G-CORE allows introducing high-level concepts and queries over those by means of graph creation and composability. Example 3.13 can be written in G-Core as:

```
SELECT id(m)
MATCH (m)-[:member]->(t1:Team)-[:head]->(h),
      (m)-[:member]->(t2:Team)-[:head]->(h)  ON (
    CONSTRUCT (m1)<-[:member]-(t:Team)-[:member]->(m2),
              (h1)<-[:head]-(t:Team)-[:head]->(h2),
    MATCH (h1)-[:teamsUpWith]->(h2),
          (m1)-[:worksFor]->(h1),
          (m2)-[:worksFor]->(h2)
)
WHERE t1!=t2
```

The property creation query of Example 3.14 can be also be expressed in G-Core:

```
SELECT id(t), t.averageAge
MATCH (t:Team) ON (
    CONSTRUCT (x1)<-[:member]-(t:Team)-[:member]->(x2)
            SET t.averageAge := (x1.age+x2.age)/2
    MATCH (x1)-[:teamsUpWith]->(x2)-[:teamsUpWith]->(x1)
)
WHERE a.averageAge > 30
```

Beyond *RPGQ*, G-Core allows querying multiple graphs in a single query and foresees extensions for tabular data input and output to facilitate interoperability with traditional SQL systems.

Other practical query languages do not (yet) support the full power of *RPGQ*. The arguably most prominent property graph query language Cypher, in its current version Cypher 9 [Francis et al., 2018], lacks graph creation, does not allow transitive closure over derived edges, and is not closed and composable over property graphs. Rather, Cypher 9 is comparable to *UCRPQ* but not exactly equivalent. Differences are the matching semantics, which can be described as edge isomorphism, and the path finding semantics, which queries all paths (bag semantics) instead of reachable vertex pairs (set semantics). Furthermore, the language does not support the full power of *RPQ*. Beyond *UCRPQ*, Cypher 9 is composable over tables and provides relational functionality such as selection, projection, grouping and aggregation, and ordering. Note, however, that Cypher is evolving in an open process[8] and Cypher 10 is expected to fill many of the mentioned gaps. Furthermore, a recently started standardization effort[9] around Oracle's PGQL [van Rest et al., 2016], G-Core, and Cypher gives rise to the hope that practical graph query languages in the near future will support the full power of *RPGQ*.

Gremlin,[10] the second prominent query language for property graphs, sets the focus on navigational queries. It can also express *UCRPQ*, however, with bag semantics for paths and a look and feel that is more reminiscent of a programming language interface rather than a declarative query language.

SPARQL [W3C, 2013], the standardized query language for RDF graphs, is comparable to *UCRPQ*. It offers graph creating functionality with a CONSTRUCT clause, hence, it can be considered as closed for RDF graphs. However, the language is not composable, since it does not allow to use the output of a query as input data of another query without persisting the query result; cf. Angles and Gutierrez [2011].

VerDiLog [Bonifati et al., 2018] is a graph query and view maintenance engine for regular queries over dynamic graphs. The underlying query language is based on Regular Datalog, which captures the transitive closure of *UCRPQ* and corresponds to the *RPGQ*-equivalent graph query language for plain RDF-style graph instances. Additionally, the correctness of the engine's output is formally guaranteed by its mechanical certification using the Coq proof assistant [Team, 2018].

---

[8]http://www.opencypher.org/
[9]https://gql.today/ and http://gqlstandards.org/.
[10]http://tinkerpop.apache.org/

3.4   BIBLIOGRAPHIC AND HISTORICAL NOTES

The study of graph query languages goes back to at least the 1940's, with the introduction of *RA* by Tarski [1941]. Our presentation of *RA* follows Surinx et al. [2015]. It is well known that *RA* without the transitive closure operation is equivalent in expressive power to the fragment of first-order logic consisting of all and only those expressions in which at most three distinct variables are used [Fletcher et al., 2015b, Tarski and Givant, 1987].

In the database research community, graph query languages have been a central topic in the investigation of various data models, such as in object-oriented, semi-structured, and XML data management [Abiteboul et al., 1999, Hidders, 2001]. The introduction of *UCRPQ* by Consens, Cruz, Mendelzon, and Wood in the late 1980's and subsequent study of the language has played a fundamental role in these investigations [Consens and Mendelzon, 1990, Cruz et al., 1987, 1988].

Reutter et al. [2017] established the complexity of query evaluation and query containment for the regular queries, and shown that the language contains *UCRPQ*. Barceló et al. [2012b] demonstrated that *RPQ* with path projection is strictly more expressive than *RPQ*. *RPQ* and *UCRPQ* extended with path projection have been introduced and studied in several settings [Barceló et al., 2012b, Bienvenu et al., 2014, Bourhis et al., 2014b, Pérez et al., 2010].

Graph query languages with extended abilities to reason about property values (i.e., data) and comparison of paths have also been proposed and studied; recent work here includes [Barceló and Muñoz, 2017, Barceló et al., 2012a, 2015, Hellings et al., 2013, Libkin et al., 2016, Santini, 2012]. The study of *RPGQ* with respect to these capabilities is an interesting open topic for investigation.

Other extensions to graph query capabilities worth mentioning are inclusion of objectified path [Angles et al., 2018a], objectified subgraph [Junghanns et al., 2016], and RDF*-type hypervertices [Hartig, 2017]. Graph construction for query languages that are composable over graphs has been consider already very early [Cruz et al., 1987] in form of edge construction and has been recently picked up again in the context of property graphs and enriched with aggregation capabilities [Angles et al., 2018a, Voigt, 2017].

An in-depth study of contemporary practical query language syntaxes has been conducted by Angles et al. [2017]. For further details on the rich literature and history of graph query languages, we also recommend several excellent surveys on various aspects of this topic [Angles et al., 2017, 2018b, Arenas et al., 2018, Wood, 2012, Wu and Khan, 2018].

CHAPTER 4

Constraints

Graph-shaped data differs from structured data mainly because of the lack of an underlying schema and metadata. Graph datasets typically blend values with metadata information without a clear distinction among them. An important class of metadata is given by integrity constraints and dependencies, whose goal is to impose the adherence to a specified structure. Constraints and dependencies may serve the need of imposing a limited schema, solving inconsistencies among different parts of the graphs in order to fulfill data cleaning tasks or, in the case of inter-source constraints, aiding the process of exchanging data among different graph data sources. Graphs arising in many applications exhibit inconsistencies and conflicts that are inherent to the processes of graph generation, graph reasoning, and graph data integration and fusion. Indeed, graphs are often obtained by direct translation from other formats and sets of graphs are integrated into a target graph without paying attention to possible conflicts that may arise in the process at hand. Due to these reasons, the data quality of graph datasets needs to be defined in a principled manner in order to be able to detect conflicts and possibly repair them. Graph-to-graph dependencies are also used to guide the process of translating a graph data source into a target data source. These dependencies rely on graph queries to extract data from a source graph and cast it into the format given by a target graph.

In this chapter, we first focus on graph functional dependencies (GFDs), which extend relational functional dependencies and conditional functional dependencies by specifying graph patterns and graph property dependencies (Section 4.2). We then present entity graph dependencies (GEDs), which allow to define keys, (conditional) functional dependencies and even more complex dependencies on graphs (Sections 4.3). Extending relational dependency theory, we recall the static analysis on such dependencies, including satisfiability, implication, and validation of GFDs and GEDs. We then switch to more expressive dependencies for graphs, such as graph denial constraints (GDCs), and outline applications and open challenges for the above families of constraints. We also briefly discuss graph neighborhood constraints along with graph schema mappings as examples of graph-to-graph dependencies as opposed to the intra-graph dependencies illustrated before (Section 4.4).

4.1 PRELIMINARIES

We recall the definition of a *graph pattern*. A graph pattern as defined in Chapter 3 is a *vertex-selecting* graph pattern. We report in the following the definition of an *edge-selecting* graph pattern as drawn from the property graph data model. Let $\mathcal{V}$ be the set of vertex and edge variables.

An *edge-selecting graph pattern* is a directed graph $Q[\bar{x}] = (V_Q, E_Q, \lambda, \mu)$ where

- V_Q is a finite set of pattern vertices;

- E_Q is a finite set of pattern edges;

- $\lambda : V_Q \cup E_Q \to \mathcal{L}$ is a partial function assigning a label to each vertex and edge;

- $\bar{x}$ is a list of variables such that either $\bar{x} \subset \mathcal{V}$ with $|\bar{x}| = |V_Q|$ or $\bar{x} \subset \mathcal{V}$ with $|\bar{x}| = |E_Q|$; and

- $\mu : \bar{x} \to V_Q$ is a bijective function assigning distinct variables in $\bar{x}$ to vertices V_Q; or $\mu : \bar{x} \to E_Q$ is a bijective function assigning distinct variables in $\bar{x}$ to edges in E_Q.

Notice that the binding variables $\bar{x}$ can be defined upon vertices or edges in the graph and this makes the difference between a vertex-selecting graph pattern and an edge-selecting one.

We will rely on this extended definition of graph pattern to define graph constraints in a convenient fashion. For ease of exposition, we call a vertex-selecting (or, edge-selecting) graph pattern simply a graph pattern, as its nature will be clear from the list of binding variables.

4.2   GRAPH FUNCTIONAL DEPENDENCIES

We first present GFDs [Fan et al., 2016], a class of dependencies for property graphs that subsume Functional Dependencies (FDs) and Conditional Functional Dependencies (CFDs). Their expressive power allows to capture inconsistencies on properties of the same vertex (edge, resp.) or across different vertices (edges, resp.). As opposed to relational FDs, that only involve dependencies among properties, GFDs for property graphs allows the specification of two constraints: (1) a topological constraint in terms of a graph pattern Q to identify the graph vertices (or the graph edges, resp.) on which the dependency is defined; and (2) a dependency involving the properties of the vertices (or the properties of the edges, resp.) in each subgraph identified by Q.

4.2.1   SYNTAX

A GFD ϕ is a pair $(Q[\bar{x}], X \to Y)$, where

- $Q[\bar{x}]$ is a graph pattern, called the pattern of ϕ and

- X and Y are two (possibly empty) sets of literals of $\bar{x}$.

A literal of $\bar{x}$ has the form of either $x.A = c$ or $x.A = y.B$, where $x, y \in \bar{x}$, $A, B \in \mathcal{K}$ denote property keys (not specified in Q), and $c \in \mathcal{N}$ is a constant. We refer to $x.A = c$ as a constant literal, and $x.A = y.B$ as a variable literal. Intuitively, GFD ϕ specifies two constraints:

- a topological constraint imposed by the pattern Q and

- a property dependency specified by $X \rightarrow Y$.

We can readily notice the difference between GFDs and relational FDs in terms of their respective scope. While the scope of an FD spans the entire relation R on which it has been defined , a GFD is defined on each subgraph matching the graph pattern Q. Precisely, the dependency $X \rightarrow Y$ is imposed on the properties of the vertices (edges, resp.) of such subgraphs.

Example 4.1   Figure 4.1 illustrates three graph patterns Q_1, Q_2, and Q_3 on which we define GFDs as follows. Their encoding as CQs is as follows:

$$Q_1 = (x, y) \quad \leftarrow \quad :\text{Expert}(x), :\text{Product}(y), :\text{creates}(x, y)$$
$$Q_2 = (x, y) \quad \leftarrow \quad :\text{worksFor}(x, y)$$
$$Q_3 = (x, y) \quad \leftarrow \quad :\text{Expert}(a), :\text{Product}(b), :\text{creates}(a, b) \text{ AS } x, :\text{monitors}(a, b) \text{ AS } y.$$

Then, we have

$$\phi_1 = (Q_1(x, y), x.\text{class} = 1 \rightarrow y.\text{type} = \text{'patent'})$$
$$\phi_2 = (Q_2(x, y), \emptyset \rightarrow x.\text{team} = y.\text{team})$$
$$\phi_3 = (Q_3(x, y), \emptyset \rightarrow x.\text{date} = y.\text{since}).$$

GFD ϕ_1 states that experts of class 1 create products that are patents. GFD ϕ_2 states that people who work together must belong to the same team. GFD ϕ_3 states that a product must be monitored since its creation date.

Notice that Q_1 and Q_2 are defined on variables x, y bound to graph vertices whereas Q_3 is defined on variables x, y bound to graph edges.

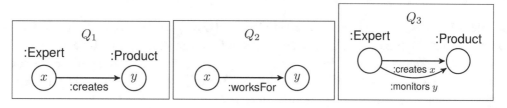

Figure 4.1: The graph patterns Q_1, Q_2, and Q_3 of GFDs ϕ_1, ϕ_2, and ϕ_3, respectively.

4.2.2   SEMANTICS

To define the semantics of GFDs, there exists a match $h(\bar{x})$ of Q in a graph G for a literal $x.A = c$ if there exists a property A at the vertex $v = h(x)$ and $v.A = c$; similarly for literal $x.A = y.B$. We denote by $h(\bar{x}) \models X$ if $h(\bar{x})$ satisfies all the literals in X; similarly for $h(\bar{x}) \models Y$. We assume an isomorphic matching function μ from free variables in $Q(\bar{x})$ to an input graph G, as discussed in Section 3.1.2. We write $h(\mu(x))$ as $h(x)$ whenever it is clear from the context.

A graph G satisfies a GFD ϕ, denoted by $G \models \phi$, if for all matches $h(\bar{x})$ of Q in G, if $h(\bar{x}) \models X$ then $h(\bar{x}) \models Y$. We write $h(\bar{x}) \models X \rightarrow Y$ if $h(\bar{x}) \models Y$ whenever $h(\bar{x}) \models X$.

We have to take into account the following cases.

- For a literal $x.A = c$ in X, if the vertex $v = h(x)$ does not have a property A such that $v.A = c$, then $h(\bar{x}) \models X \rightarrow Y$, and we say that the GFD is trivially satisfied.

- For a literal $x.A = c$ in Y, and $h(\bar{x}) \models Y$, then the vertex $v = h(x)$ must have a property A such that $v.A = c$ by the above definition of the satisfaction of a GFD; similarly for a literal $x.A = y.B$.

- When $X = \emptyset$, $h(\bar{x}) \models X$ for any match $h(\bar{x})$ of Q in G; similarly for $Y = \emptyset$.

The above semantics apply to vertex-selecting graph patterns and the semantics for edge-selecting graph patterns can be similarly drawn by replacing vertices with edges in the above exposition. Notice that the implied definition of subgraph isomorphism readily extends to subgraph edge isomorphism and is more restrictive than the usual subgraph homomorphism semantics of CQs as presented in Chapter 3.

Example 4.2   Let G_1 be the graph reported in Figure 2.2 in Chapter 2. Since experts do not have a property class, the GFD ϕ_1 is trivially satisfied. By contrast, neither $G_1 \models \phi_2$ nor $G_1 \models \phi_3$ since both ϕ_2 and ϕ_3 have an empty left-hand side and none of their right-hand side properties is present in graph G_1.

Special Cases

GFDs can express relational FDs and CFDs. In such cases, the graph pattern is replaced by a relation containing tuples corresponding to vertices and edges in a graph.

Example 4.3   Consider for example a GFD $\phi_4 = (Q_4(x), x.\text{company} = \text{'Twitter'} \rightarrow x.\text{class} = 1)$ on a new graph pattern Q_4 consisting of only the vertex :Expert with variable x. GFD ϕ_4 can be easily seen as a CFD if we consider the vertex :Expert in the graph pattern Q_4 as a relation $E(co, cl)$ and express the CFD as $E([\text{co} = \text{'Twitter'}] \rightarrow [\text{cl} = 1])$ enforcing the fact that in a given company all experts are promoted to class 1.

A GFD $(Q[\bar{x}], X \rightarrow Y)$ is called a *constant* GFD if X and Y consist of constant literals only. It is called a *variable* GFD if X and Y consist of variable literals only. As an example, the aforementioned GFDs ϕ_1 and ϕ_4 are constant GFDs, whereas the GFDs ϕ_2 and ϕ_3 are variable GFDs. Constant GFDs subsume relational CFDs and variable GFDs subsume relational FDs. Transposing vertices or edges in a graph to corresponding relations does not lead to express constraints like the ones in the example above (ϕ_2, ϕ_3, and ϕ_4) since they span multiple vertices and edges in the graph. As a consequence, GFDs are more expressive than CFDs and FDs, the latter being defined on a single relation. At the end of this chapter, we will provide a recapitulative classification of relational and graph dependencies.

4.2.3 SATISFIABILITY

We illustrate the satisfiability problem for GFDs. These problems are common to all kinds of dependencies.

Definition 4.4 A set of GFDs Σ is *satisfiable* if there exists a model G such that (1) $G \models \Sigma$ and (2) for each GFD $(Q[\bar{x}], X \to Y)$ in the set Σ, there exists a match $h(\bar{x})$ of Q in G.

Intuitively, satisfiability is needed to check whether there exists a graph G on which all GFDs in Σ are satisfiable. In other words, satisfiability is to check whether the GFDs in Σ are not conflicting with each other.

Example 4.5 Consider the GFD ϕ_1 presented above. Consider now another GFD ϕ_5 as follows:

$$\phi_5 = (Q_1(x, y), x.\text{class} = 1 \to y.\text{type} = \text{'software release'}).$$

The set of GFDs $\Sigma = \{\phi_1, \phi_5\}$ is not satisfiable as there exists no graph G that includes a vertex :Expert leading via the predicate :creates to a vertex :Product having a property type with distinct values 'patent' and 'software release'.

Theorem 4.6 *The satisfiability problem for GFDs is coNP-complete.*

Crux. The lower bound is proved by reduction from subgraph isomorphism to the complement of GFD satisfiability. For the upper bound, one can give an algorithm that returns "yes" if Σ is *not* satisfiable, corresponding to the complement of GFD satisfiability. (1) Guess a set $\Sigma' \subseteq \Sigma$, a pattern Q such that Q carries labels of Σ and $|Q|$ is at most the size of the largest pattern in Σ, and a mapping from the pattern of each GFD in Σ' to Q. (2) Check whether the mappings are isomorphic to subgraphs of Q. (3) If so, derive the set Σ_Q of GFDs embedded in Q from Σ' and the guessed mappings. (4) Check whether Σ_Q is conflicting; if so, return "yes." The algorithm is in NP as the steps (2), (3), and (4) are in PTIME. Thus, GFD satisfiability is in NP. $\square$

The correctness of the previous algorithm is due to the following Lemma.

Lemma 4.7 *A set Σ of GFDs is satisfiable if and only if Σ is not conflicting.*

In order to prove this lemma, we need auxiliary definitions as follows.

Definition 4.8 Embeddable Graph Pattern. A graph pattern $Q' = \left(V'_Q, E'_Q, \lambda', \mu'\right)$ is embeddable in a graph pattern $Q = (V_Q, E_Q, \lambda, \mu)$ if there exists an isomorphic mapping f from the graph $\left(V'_Q, E'_Q\right)$ to a subgraph of (V_Q, E_Q), which preserves vertex and edge labels.

Definition 4.9 Embedded GFD. Let Q' be an embeddable graph pattern in Q via f. Then for any GFD $\phi' = (Q'[\bar{x}'], X' \rightarrow Y')$, $\phi = (Q[\bar{x}], f(X') \rightarrow f(Y'))$ is an embedded GFD of ϕ' in Q, where $f(X')$ and $f(Y')$ are the application of f to each $x' \in X'$ and $y' \in Y'$, respectively.

Definition 4.10 Embedded and Derived GFD. For a pattern Q and a set Σ of GFDs, a set Σ_Q of GFDs is said to be embedded in Q and derived from Σ if for each $\phi \in \Sigma_Q$, the pattern of ϕ is Q, and there exists $\psi \in \Sigma$, such that ϕ is an embedded GFD of ψ in Q.

Definition 4.11 Literals Enforced by GFDs. The set of literals enforced by GFDs, denoted enforced(Σ_Q), from Σ_Q is computed inductively as follows:

- if $(Q[\bar{x}], \emptyset \rightarrow Y)$ is in Σ_Q, then $Y \subseteq$ enforced(Σ_Q), i.e., all literals of Y are included in enforced(Σ_Q); and

- if $(Q[\bar{x}], X \rightarrow Y)$ is in Σ_Q and if all literals of X can be derived from enforced(Σ_Q) via the transitivity of equality atoms, then $Y \subseteq$ enforced(Σ_Q).

Example 4.12 By considering again the GFDs $\Sigma = \{\phi_1, \phi_5\}$, the set of GFDs enforced(Σ) is given by (y.type, 'patent') and (y.type, 'software release').

Definition 4.13 Conflicting GFDs. Σ_Q is conflicting if there exist $(x.A, a)$ and $(x.A, b)$ in enforced(Σ_Q) such that $a \neq b$.

Example 4.14 As previously observed, the GFDs ϕ_1, ϕ_5 are conflicting.

Definition 4.15 Set of Conflicting GFDs. A set Σ of GFDs is conflicting if there exist a pattern Q and a set Σ_Q of GFDs that are embedded in Q and derived from Σ, such that Σ_Q is conflicting.

The set of conflicting GFDs is used in Lemma 4.7, which is used in the crux of Theorem 4.6.

4.2.4   IMPLICATION

Apart from satisfiability of a set of GFDs, one needs to check the implication of GFDs in order to discover redundant GFDs. Since GFDs for which we check implication need to be satisfiable, we assume that this is the case for all GFDs involved in the implication analysis.

Definition 4.16   A set of GFDs Σ *implies* a GFD $\phi = (Q[\bar{x}], X \to Y)$, where X is a satisfiable set of literals, if for all graphs G such that $G \models \Sigma$ it holds that $G \models \phi$.

Intuitively, implication is needed to check whether ϕ is a logical consequence of Σ.

Theorem 4.17   *The implication problem for GFDs is NP-complete.*

Crux. The lower bound is proved by reduction from subgraph isomorphism to GFD implication. For the upper bound, one can give an algorithm that returns "yes" if $\Sigma \models \phi$. (1) Guess a set $\Sigma' \subseteq \Sigma$ and a mapping from the pattern of each GFD in Σ' to Q. (2) Check whether the mappings are isomorphic to subgraphs of Q. (3) If so, derive the set Σ_Q of GFDs embedded in Q from Σ' and the guessed mappings. (4) Check whether $Y \in \texttt{closure}(\Sigma_Q, X)$; if so, return "yes." The algorithm is in NP as the steps (2), (3), and (4) are in PTIME. Thus, GFD implication is in NP. $\square$

The correctness of the previous algorithm is due to the following Lemma.

Lemma 4.18   *A set of satisfiable GFDs Σ implies a GFD $\phi = (Q[\bar{x}], X \to Y)$, where X is a satisfiable set of literals, if and only if Y is deducible from Σ and X.*

In order to prove this lemma, we need the following auxiliary definitions.

Definition 4.19   GFD in normal form.   A GFD $\phi = (Q[\bar{x}], X \to Y)$ is in *normal form* when Y consists of a single constant or variable literal, which is not a tautology (i.e., of the form $x.A = x.A$).

Definition 4.20   Closure of GFDs.   For a set Σ_Q of GFDs embedded in Q, a set $\texttt{closure}(\Sigma_Q, X)$ of literals is computed inductively as follows:

- $X \subseteq \texttt{closure}(\Sigma_Q, X)$; and

- if $(Q[\bar{x}], X \to Y)$ is in Σ_Q and if all literals of X can be derived from $\texttt{closure}(\Sigma_Q, X)$ via the transitivity of equality atoms, then $Y \subseteq \texttt{closure}(\Sigma_Q, X)$.

Similarly to closure for relational functional dependencies (cf. Abiteboul et al. [1995]), $\texttt{closure}(\Sigma_Q, X)$ can be computed in linear time.

We report in the following an algorithm to compute the $\texttt{closure}(\Sigma_Q, X)$, which uses a GFD at a time and accomplishes the computation in linear time. It suffices to keep track for each unused $(Q[\bar{x}], X \to Y)$ in Σ_Q, the count of the properties in X not yet in $\texttt{closure}(\Sigma_Q, X)$. The algorithm is similar to its relational counterpart and as such quite straightforward.

Algorithm 4.1: Compute the closure of GFDs.

Input: A set Σ_Q of GFDs and a set X of properties
Output: $\texttt{closure}(\Sigma_Q, X)$

1 **for** $(Q[\bar{x}], X \to Y) \in \Sigma_Q$ **do**
2      $count[(Q[\bar{x}], X \to Y) \in \Sigma_Q] := |W|$
3   **for** $A \in W$ **do**
4         $list[A] := list[A] \cup (Q[\bar{x}], X \to Y) \in \Sigma_Q$

5 $closure := X, update := X$
6 **while** $update \neq \emptyset$ **do**
7   Choose $A \in update$
8      $update := update \setminus \{A\}$
9   **for** $(Q[\bar{x}], X \to Y) \in \Sigma_Q \in list[A]$ **do**
10        $count[(Q[\bar{x}], X \to Y) \in \Sigma_Q] := count[(Q[\bar{x}], X \to Y) \in \Sigma_Q] - 1$
11   **if** $count[(Q[\bar{x}], X \to Y) \in \Sigma_Q] = 0$ **then**
12           $update := update \cup (Z \setminus closure)$
13           $closure := closure \cup Z$

14 **return** $closure$

Definition 4.21 Deducible Literal. A literal Y is deducible from Σ if there exists a set Σ_Q of GFDs that are embedded in Q and derived from Σ (cf. Definition 4.10) such that $Y \subseteq \texttt{closure}(\Sigma_Q, X)$.

4.2.5 VALIDATION

As discussed above, satisfiability allows one to check whether a set Σ of GFDs is ill defined and thus not suitable to detect conflicts in the underlying graph. On the other hand, implication lets one verify that there are no redundant GFDs in Σ. Once the set Σ of GFDs has been checked in terms of satisfiability and implication, it still remains to be seen whether a graph G is valid with respect to Σ, that is it does not contain any violation of the GFDs in Σ. Notice that in order to check validation we need the graph G as input to the decision problem, whereas this was not the case in the previous section.

Definition 4.22   Given a set Σ of GFDs and a graph G, the *validation* problem is to decide whether $G \models \Sigma$, i.e., whether for each GFD $\phi \in \Sigma$ such that $\phi = (Q[\bar{x}], X \rightarrow Y)$, no violation $h(\bar{x})$ of Q in G exists such that $G_h \not\models \Sigma$ with G_h being the subgraph induced by $h(\bar{x})$ of Q in G.

Proposition 4.23   *The combined complexity of the validation problem for GFDs is coNP-complete.*

Crux. The lower bound consists of showing that it is NP-hard to check, given G and Σ, whether $G \models \Sigma$, by reduction from subgraph isomorphism. For the upper bound, we give an algorithm that returns "yes" if $G \models \Sigma$: (1) Guess a GFD $(Q[\bar{x}], X \rightarrow Y)$ from Σ and a mapping h from Q to a subgraph of G. (2) Check whether h is isomorphic. (3) If so, check whether $h(\bar{x}) \models X$ but $h(\bar{x}) \not\models Y$; if so, return "yes." This is in NP.   □

We can take advantage of the results obtained in the literature about subgraph isomorphism when Q has at most size k, for a predefined bound k (data complexity). Checking whether Q is a subgraph of G can be done in polynomial time.

Proposition 4.24   *The data complexity of the validation problem for GFDs is in PTIME.*

Crux. The proof follows from the results on subgraph isomorphism to check whether a fixed pattern H of order k is a subgraph of G. In our case, given G and Σ, we take each GFD $(Q[\bar{x}], X \rightarrow Y)$ from Σ where Q has constant size and we look for a mapping h from Q to a subgraph of G. This is in PTIME when Q is fixed.   □

A similar result applies to the problems of satisfiability and implication of a set of GFDs Σ for each GFD in Σ having a graph pattern Q at most size k. The complexity of satisfiability and implication of a set of GFDs Σ is in PTIME for graph patterns of size at most k.

4.3   GRAPH ENTITY DEPENDENCIES

GFDs, as presented in the previous section, do not cover many practical classes of database constraints. As an example, they cannot express key constraints on graphs, imposing that two identical vertices cannot exist and should be merged into one. Graph Entity Dependencies is a class of dependencies that extend GFDs by adding equalities of vertex identities [Fan and Lu, 2017].

4.3.1 DEFINITION AND SPECIAL CASES

A GED ϕ is a pair $(Q[\bar{x}], X \rightarrow Y)$, where

- $Q[\bar{x}]$ is a graph pattern, called the pattern of ϕ and

- X and Y are two (possibly empty) sets of literals of $\bar{x}$.

A literal of $\bar{x}$ has the form of either $x.A = c$ or $x.A = y.B$, where $x, y \in \bar{x}$, $A, B \in \mathcal{K}$ denote property keys (not specified in Q), and $c \in \mathcal{N}$ is a constant. A literal can also be of the form $\mathrm{id}(x) = \mathrm{id}(y)$, where $x, y \in \bar{x}$ and $\mathrm{id}(\cdot)$ denotes the vertex or edge identities. We refer to $x.A = c$ as a constant literal, $x.A = y.B$ as a variable literal and $\mathrm{id}(x) = \mathrm{id}(y)$ as an id literal. Intuitively, GED ϕ specifies two constraints:

- a topological constraint imposed by the pattern Q, and

- an FD $X \rightarrow Y$ to be applied to Q.

An id literal states that x and y denote the same vertex (entity), respectively, the same edge (predicate). In this case, x and y will have the same properties and incident edges, respectively, vertices.

Example 4.25 Figure 4.2 shows the graph pattern Q_1. The GED $\phi_1 = (Q_1(x, y, z), \emptyset \rightarrow \mathrm{id}(y) = \mathrm{id}(z))$ states that if an apprentice x works for two experts y and z, then y and z must be the same person (i.e., y and z are actually the same vertex).

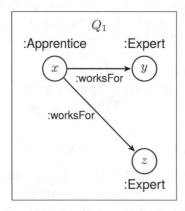

Figure 4.2: The graph pattern Q_1 of a Graph Entity Dependency ϕ_1.

4.3.2   PRELIMINARIES

A homomorphism (also called a match) between a pattern Q and a graph G is a mapping h from $V_Q \cup E_Q$ in Q to $V \cup E$ in G such that: (i) $h(u) = u$ for every vertex $u \in V_Q$ such that $L_Q(u) = L(h(u))$; (ii) for every edge $e = (u, p, u')$ in Q, there exists an edge $e' = (h(u), p', h(u'))$ in G such that $p = p'$. An isomorphism between a pattern Q and a graph G is an injective homomorphism h from Q to G such that h^{-1} is an injective homomorphism from G to Q. The reader may notice in the remainder that for GEDs graph homomorphism is needed to find embeddings of the pattern Q into the graph G, contrarily to what has been presented above for GFDs, where graph isomorphism would suffice. Since GEDs may contain equalities between vertex identities, and equalities between vertex identities may be used in the premises of GEDs, graph homomorphism is indeed needed to map vertices in Q to possibly the same vertex in G.

4.3.3   CHASING GRAPH ENTITY DEPENDENCIES

We start by defining the *chase* of G by Σ, a set of GEDs.

We briefly describe below a chase step for a GED $\phi = (Q[\bar{x}], X \rightarrow Y)$. Let $h(\bar{x})$ be a match of pattern Q on graph G such that $h(\bar{x}) \models X$ and l is a literal in Y.

- **Constant literals.** If l is $x.A = c$ and the value of property A in G is not equal to c, then (a) add property A to vertices in G bound by h to variable x if $h(x).A$ does not exist; (b) add c as value of property A.
- **Variable literals.** If l is $x.A = y.B$ and $h(x).A$ does not match with $h(y).B$, then (a) add property A to vertices in G bound to variable $h(x)$ if $h(x).A$ does not exist; (b) add $h(y).B$ as value of property A.
- **Id literals.** If l is $\mathrm{id}(x) = \mathrm{id}(y)$ and $h(x)$ does not coincide with $h(y)$, then equate $h(x)$ with $h(y)$.

Note that the first two chase steps above lead to create a new property $h(x).A$ in Y if such property does not already exist, as required by $h(\bar{x}) \models Y$, otherwise the result of the chase will not lead to a graph such that $G \models \phi$. This is a substantial departure from chase steps for relational Equality Generating Dependencies (EGDs) in which neither a new property of a relation nor its value is created since existing values are equated.

A *chase sequence* of G by Σ, denoted as $\mathrm{chase}(G_\Sigma, \Sigma)$, is a sequence of chase steps such that each chase step is triggered by a GED $\phi = (Q[\bar{x}], X \rightarrow Y)$ in Σ. A valid terminating chase sequence is a chase sequence that either ends when no GEDs in Σ can be triggered and leaves the graph G in a consistent state (i.e., all dependencies are satisfied); or, it is an undefined chase sequence with result $\perp$ if any of the chase steps leaves the graph in an inconsistent state (at least one dependency is not satisfied).

4.3.4   SATISFIABILITY, IMPLICATION, AND VALIDATION

We now turn our attention to satisfiability of GEDs.

Definition 4.26   A set of GEDs Σ is *satisfiable* if there exists a model G such that (1) $G \models \Sigma$ and (2) for each GED $(Q[\bar{x}], X \to Y)$ in the set Σ, there exists a match $h(\bar{x})$ of Q in G.

Intuitively, satisfiability is needed to check whether there exists a graph G on which all GEDs in Σ are satisfiable, which leads to check whether the chase of the GEDs in Σ ($\texttt{chase}(G_\Sigma, \Sigma)$) is a valid terminating chase sequence.

Theorem 4.27   *A set Σ of GEDs is satisfiable if and only if $\texttt{chase}(G_\Sigma, \Sigma)$ is a valid terminating chase sequence.*

Example 4.28   Figure 4.3 shows graph patterns Q_2 and Q_3. Consider two GEDs ϕ_2 and ϕ_3 as follows:

$$\phi_2 = (Q_2(x, y, z), x.\text{name} = x.\text{twitter} \to \text{id}(y) = \text{id}(z))$$
$$\phi_3 = (Q_3(x_1, y_1, z_1, x_2, y_2, z_2), \emptyset \to x_1.\text{name} = x_1.\text{twitter}) .$$

Despite the fact that a homomorphism exists between Q_1 and Q_2, and the fact that when taken separately ϕ_2 and ϕ_3 are satisfiable, the set of GFDs $\Sigma = \{\phi_2, \phi_3\}$ is not satisfiable as there exists no graph G in which we can merge two vertices y and z with different labels.

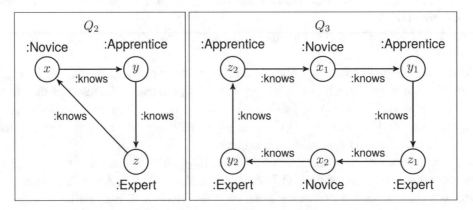

Figure 4.3: The graph patterns Q_2 and Q_3 of GEDs ϕ_2 and ϕ_3.

Theorem 4.29   *The satisfiability problem for GEDs is coNP-complete.*

Crux. The lower bound is proved by reduction from 3-colorability to the complement of GED satisfiability. The reduction is carried out for two subclasses of GEDs, namely the class of GFDs and the class of GKeys [Fan et al., 2015]. The latter class leverages id literals only, whereas the former class leverages constant and variable literals. For the upper bound, one can give an algorithm that returns "yes" if Σ is *not* satisfiable, corresponding to the complement of GED satisfiability. (1) Compute G_Σ. (2) Guess a chasing sequence $\mathrm{chase}(G_\Sigma, \Sigma)$ such that its number of steps is bounded. (3) Check each chase step in $\mathrm{chase}(G_\Sigma, \Sigma)$ such that it leaves G in a consistent state; if not, reject the guess; if yes, continue. (4) Check whether $\mathrm{chase}(G_\Sigma, \Sigma)$ is invalid; if so, return "yes." The algorithm is in NP as steps (2), (3), and (4) are in PTIME. Thus, GED satisfiability is in NP. □

Similarly to what was discussed for GFDs, one can check the implication of a GED from a set of GEDs.

Definition 4.30   A set of GEDs Σ *implies* a GED $\phi = (Q[\bar{x}], X \rightarrow Y)$, where X is a satisfiable set of literals, if for all graphs G such that $G \models \Sigma$ it holds that $G \models \phi$.

Intuitively, implication is needed to check whether ϕ is a logical consequence of Σ.

Theorem 4.31   *The implication problem for GEDs is NP-complete.*

Crux. The lower bound is proved by reduction from 3-colorability to GED implication. The reduction is carried out for two subclasses of GEDs, namely the class of GED_xs and the class of GKeys. The latter class leverages id literals only, whereas the former class leverages variable literals only. For the upper bound, one can give an algorithm that returns "yes" if $\Sigma \models \phi$. (1) Compute the canonical graph G_Q along the same lines as G_Σ. (2) Guess a chasing sequence $\mathrm{chase}(G_Q, \Sigma)$ such that its number of steps is bounded. (3) Check the validity of each chase step in $\mathrm{chase}(G_Q, \Sigma)$; if not, reject the guess; if yes, continue. (4) Check whether $\mathrm{chase}(G_Q, \Sigma)$ is inconsistent; if so, return "yes;" otherwise, continue. (5) Check whether Y can be deduced from $\mathrm{chase}(G_Q, \Sigma)$. The algorithm is in NP as steps (1), (3), (4), and (5) are in PTIME. Thus, GED implication is in NP. □

We now turn our attention to the validation problem for GEDs.

Definition 4.32   Given a set Σ of GEDs and a graph G, the *validation* problem is to decide whether $G \models \Sigma$, i.e., whether for each GED $\phi \in \Sigma$ such that $\phi = (Q[\bar{x}], X \rightarrow Y)$, no violation $h(\bar{x})$ of Q in G exists such that $G_h \not\models \Sigma$, with G_h being the graph induced by $h(\bar{x})$ of Q in G.

Proposition 4.33   *The combined complexity of the Validation problem for GEDs is coNP-complete.*

Crux. The lower bound consists of showing that it is NP-hard to check, given G and Σ, whether $G \models \Sigma$, by reduction from 3-colorability to GED implication. The reduction is carried out for two subclasses of GEDs, namely the class of GED_xs and the class of GKeys. The latter class leverages id literals only, whereas the former class leverages variable literals only. For the upper bound, we give an algorithm that returns "yes" if $G \models \Sigma$. (1) Guess a GED $(Q[\bar{x}], X \rightarrow Y)$ from Σ and a mapping h from Q to G. (2) Check whether h is an homomorphic match. (3) If so, check whether $h(\bar{x}) \models X$ but $h(\bar{x}) \not\models Y$; if so, return "yes." This is in NP.   □

Similarly to what shown for GFDs, one can readily verify that the satisfiability, implication and validation problems for GEDs are in PTIME when graph patterns have a bounded size k. Since these dependencies of bounded size k are of practical interest, we describe in the following their impact in real-world applications.

4.3.5   EXTENSION TO GRAPH DENIAL CONSTRAINTS

Graph Denial Constraints is a class of dependencies that extend GEDs by adding built-in predicates [Fan and Lu, 2017]. As an example, GFDs or GEDs cannot express constraints on graphs in which two values must be different from each other.

Definition and Special Cases

A GDC ϕ is a pair $(Q[\bar{x}], X \rightarrow Y)$, where

- $Q[\bar{x}]$ is a graph pattern, called the pattern of ϕ, and

- X and Y are two (possibly empty) sets of θ-literals of $\bar{x}$.

Empty sets of θ-literals are denoted by $\perp$. A θ-literal of $\bar{x}$ has the form of either $x.A \; \theta \; c$ or $x.A \; \theta \; y.B$, where $x, y \in \bar{x}$, $A, B \in \mathcal{K}$ denote property keys (not specified in Q), $c \in \mathcal{N}$ is a constant and θ is a built-in predicate of the form $=, \neq, >, <, \leq, \geq$. A literal can also be of the form $\text{id}(x) = \text{id}(y)$, where $x, y \in \bar{x}$ and $\text{id}(\cdot)$ denotes the vertex or edge identities. We refer to $x.A \; \theta \; c$ as a constant literal, $x.A \; \theta \; y.B$ as a variable literal and $\text{id}(x) = \text{id}(y)$ as an id literal. Intuitively, GDC ϕ specifies two constraints:

- a topological constraint imposed by the pattern Q, and

- an FD $X \rightarrow Y$ to be applied to Q.

An id literal states that x and y denote the same vertex (entity) respectively the same edge (predicate). In this case, x and y will have the same properties and incident edges (respectively, vertices).

Notice that classical denial constraints can equivalently be expressed as rules of the form $X' \rightarrow \perp$, where X' in such a case corresponds to $X \cup \neg Y$, X and Y being the above sets of literals.

Example 4.34   Recall the graph patterns Q_1, Q_2, and Q_3 in Figure 4.1. We can now rewrite the above GFDs as GDCs as follows.

The GDC $\phi_1 = (Q_1(x, y), x.\text{class} = 1 \wedge y.\text{type} \neq \text{'patent'} \rightarrow \perp)$ states that experts of class equal to 1 and type different from 'patent' cannot co-exist in the graph instance. The GDC $\phi_2 = (Q_2(x, y), x.\text{team} \neq y.\text{team} \rightarrow \perp)$ states that people who work together must belong to the same team.

The GDC $\phi_3 = (Q_3(x, y), x.\text{date} \neq y.\text{since} \rightarrow \perp)$ states that a product must be monitored since its creation date.

4.3.6   APPLICATIONS AND PRACTICAL IMPACT OF GRAPH DEPENDENCIES

Figure 4.4 offers a recapitulative view of the inclusion relations between the various classes of constraints handled in this chapter spanning from GFDs to GDCs and contrasting them with their relational counterparts. Graph Entity Dependencies (GEDs) represent a more expressive class than GFDs and Graph Keys (GKeys). As Figure 4.4 shows, they encompass relational key constraints (RelKeys) along with relational functional dependencies (Rel-FDs) and relational conditional functional dependencies (Rel-CFDs) and also relational equality-generating dependencies (Rel-EGDs). The utility of GFDs relies on the fact that they enable consistency checking on graph databases. GFDs are, however, not yet used in practice and popular commercial graph databases such as Neo4j that has only simple constraints, such as unique node property constraints and node keys.[1] On the other hand, neither GEDs nor GDCs as presented so far in the literature make use of RPQs (also known as property paths in SPARQL) as their underlying graph patterns rely on simple labels on the edges rather than on complex regular expressions. GEDs can also express equalities among vertex identifiers and are also more powerful than Rel-Keys due to the fact that vertex and edge identities can depend on each other and engender a recursive chain of dependencies. The subset of GEDs using id literals corresponds to GKeys and serve the need of deduplicating a graph dataset by purging identical vertices (or, edges). Both GKeys and GFDs can help sanitize real-life knowledge bases, social networks, and scientific databases in the form of graphs.

GEDs (or GFDs) involving constant literals at least in their left-hand sides correspond to the relational counterparts of conditional functional dependencies with a fundamental departure from those in that constant and variable literals in the right-hand sides lead to create properties of vertices or edges whenever these do not exist (as explained in Section 4.3.3). Such

---

[1]Unique constraints in Neo4J guarantee uniqueness of a certain property on nodes with a specific label, while node keys allow to create graph nodes with a mandatory list of properties.

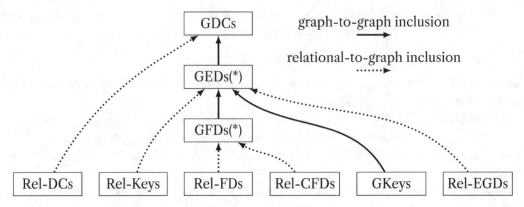

Figure 4.4: Diagram showing the relationships among classes of relational dependencies (DCs, Keys, FDs, CFDs, EGDs) and graph dependencies (GKeys, GFDs, GEDs, GDCs). The classes annotated with (*) are those discussed in depth in this chapter.

dependencies are highly useful in error detection and data cleaning in a similar fashion to their relational counterparts. In particular, their usage for cleaning the graph database, would imply revisiting the chase in order to replace conflicting values with one of those as suggested by external information (i.e., the ground truth) or some special symbol.

As for what concerns the occurrence in practice of graph patterns of bounded size k, we conclude by discussing the graph patterns frequently occurring in real-world SPARQL query logs. Overall, 56.45% of the SELECT and ASK queries in a large corpus [Bonifati et al., 2017] use at most one triple pattern, 90.76% uses at most 6 triple patterns, and 99.32% at most 12 triple patterns. The average number of triple patterns per query for datasets, including DBPedia (across various years from 2009–2016), LGD, BioPortal, and British Museum, range from 1.16–5.47.

4.4   OTHER CONSTRAINTS FOR GRAPH DATA MANAGEMENT

We next briefly discuss two additional classes of constraints arising in graph data management.

4.4.1   GRAPH NEIGHBORHOOD CONSTRAINTS

As indicated in the introduction to this chapter, a major application of dependencies is in data cleaning. Dirty data commonly arises during the creation and the transformation of data sets, e.g., through incorrect data input or errors in data collection. Having explicit constraints specifying classes of allowable graph instances enables us to identify and repair dirty data.

A recent example of graph constraints for graph data cleaning is the *neighborhood constraints*, introduced and studied by Song et al. [2017]. Here, a *constraint* is specified as an undirected vertex labeled graph C. We then say a graph G *satisfies* C if, for each edge (u, v) of G, either (1) u and v have the same label or (2) there is an edge (u', v') of C such that u and u' have the same label and v and v' have the same label. The intuition is that only certain types of vertices are semantically meaningful as neighbors, and the edges of C specify the allowed neighborhoods of each vertex type (i.e., all vertices bearing a particular label).

Example 4.35   Consider a protein interaction network which has been obtained by an international team of researchers, where vertex labels are drawn from Gene Ontology [Song et al., 2017].[2] While collaborating, the scientists have introduced erroneous labels on some vertices of the network. Indeed, the ontology, viewed as a neighborhood constraint C, specifies that :PlasmaMembrane vertices can only have as neighbor vertices with the labels :Cytoplasm, :Cytoskeleton, or :CellularComponent. In the network itself, however, we find that there are many :PlasmaMembrane vertices having edges to vertices labeled :Nucleus.

Satisfaction of a neighborhood constraint is clearly solvable in polynomial time. Finding high-quality repairs of dirty graphs, however, is significantly more expensive. Song et al. [2017] introduce two natural repair models for achieving a satisfactory graph, namely, by a bounded number of (1) vertex label modifications and (2) edge modifications.

Example 4.36   The violations of the neighborhood constraint in our protein interaction network can be repaired by relabeling the vertices of the graph to satisfy the constraint. Note, however, that this is not as simple as relabeling the :PlasmaMembrane vertices or the :Nucleus vertices, as any changes in vertex labels may lead to violations of other neighborhood constraints, cascading through the network. Alternatively, the network can be repaired by removing all edges between :PlasmaMembrane and :Nucleus vertices. Either approach may lead to an unacceptably high number of modifications to the network.

Under either the label-modification or edge-modification models, the cost-bounded repair problem is shown to be NP-complete. Consequently, Song et al. [2017] introduced several high-quality methods for the approximate repair of dirty graphs under neighborhood constraints.

4.4.2   GRAPH-TO-GRAPH CONSTRAINTS

Constraints are also central in the study of data integration and exchange [Arenas et al., 2010]. Although graph data integration and exchange topics are beyond the scope of this book, it is informative to make a connection to the work in this area.

A graph *schema* is a finite subset of the alphabet of labels $\mathcal{L}$. We say a graph G has schema S if every label occurring in G is an element of S. Similarly, we say a query q is defined on graphs of schema S if every label occurring in q is an element of S.

[2]http://www.geneontology.org/

In graph data exchange, we are interested in mapping a graph under a source schema S to a graph under a target schema T [Barceló et al., 2013, Boneva et al., 2015, Bonifati and Ileana, 2018, Calvanese et al., 2000, 2002, 2013, Francis et al., 2015]. In general, a *schema mapping* M is a set of pairs of queries (q, q'), where q is a query over (graphs of schema) S and q' is a query over T, and both queries are of the same arity. M is essentially a constraint between an instance of S and possible instances of T. The instance of S is given as an input to the graph data exchange problem, along with the schemas S and T and the schema mapping M. The possible instances of schema T are instead to be computed by the data exchange problem. In particular, given a graph G with schema S, we say graph G' with schema T is a *solution* for G under M if $[\![q]\!]_G \subseteq [\![q']\!]_{G'}$ for every $(q, q') \in M$.

Example 4.37   Returning to our gene interaction network of Examples 4.35 and 4.36, suppose our research team has been invited to contribute author collaboration information to a bibliographical graph database.

In the team's graph, author information on scientific publications is captured using the Contributor Role Ontology[3] predicates :WritingOriginalDraft (:WritingD) and :WritingReviewAndEditing (:WritingRE). The Contributor Role Ontology is part of the Open Biological and Biomedical Ontology[4] to which the Gene Ontology also belongs. In the bibliographical graph, author collaboration information is captured via the predicate :InNetwork, which links authors who have directly or indirectly authored a paper together.

A schema mapping for exchanging authorship information from the gene graph to the bibliographical graph is given by $\{(q, q')\}$ where q and q' are *RPQ*s with

$$\begin{aligned} q &= \; ((\text{:WritingD} + \text{:WritingRE})^- \,/\, (\text{:WritingD} + \text{:WritingRE}))^+ \\ q' &= \; \text{:InNetwork}. \end{aligned}$$

Query q identifies all pairs of people (x, y) in the gene graph such that x and y have directly or indirectly written a paper together. Query q' indicates that for each such pair (x, y), there should be an edge labeled :InNetwork from x to y in the bibliographical graph.

Graph data exchange under schema mappings has been studied for mappings defined by *RPQ*s (as in our example above) and many of the generalizations of *RPQ* discussed in Chapter 3. Furthermore, the impact of enforcing additional constraints on the target instance has also been explored. We refer the reader to recent work in the area [Francis and Libkin, 2017] for further details.

4.5   BIBLIOGRAPHIC AND HISTORICAL NOTES

The theory of dependencies [Fagin and Vardi, 1984] is one of the oldest and most studied theories in relational databases [Abiteboul et al., 1995]. Relational dependencies include (among

---

[3]http://obofoundry.org/ontology/cro.html
[4]http://obofoundry.org/

others) primary keys (PKs), foreign keys (FKs), and more expressive FDs as examples of intra-relation constraints. A generalization of these constraints is represented by EGDs. Relational inclusion dependencies represent a well-studied class of inter-relation constraints that generalize FKs and whose upper class is given by Tuple-Generating Dependencies (TGDs), which are a class of dependencies more general than Inclusion Dependencies. Extensions of relational FDs with conditions (CFDs) have been considered by Fan et al. [2008] in order to capture inconsistencies in relational data.

Recent influential papers have considered the counterparts of relational dependencies for graphs and RDF data. The pioneering paper was on the definition of graph keys [Fan et al., 2015] that have been studied for the problem of entity matching, i.e., the problem of unifying different entities in graph databases. The problem of scalable parallel algorithms has also been tackled. Keys for graphs exploit vertex and value identities and can be recursively defined. Graph keys have been extended to cover more general graph functional dependencies [Fan et al., 2016] and their static analysis properties (satisfiability, implication, and validation) have been investigated. An axiomatization system similar to its relational counterpart [Armstrong, 1974, Beeri et al., 1977] has been derived. The problem of evaluating such constraints in parallel on multiple processors has also been considered and corroborated by experimental analysis [Fan et al., 2016]. Implication and axiomatization of functional dependencies for RDF graphs have been studied by considering RDF triples as the basic components [Hellings et al., 2016]. The most recent findings about the more expressive classes of GEDs and their extensions to graph denial constraints and GEDs with disjunction have led to study the complexity of the problems of satisfiability, implication, validation and parallel scalability [Fan and Lu, 2017]. A new wave of research is also considering human intervention to guide the repairing process for consistency-detecting dependencies (CDDs), corresponding to graph denial constraints with only equalities [Arioua and Bonifati, 2018]. Finally, graph data exchange has been addressed in many recent influential papers [Barceló et al., 2013, Boneva et al., 2015, Calvanese et al., 2000, 2002, 2013, Francis et al., 2015], in which the problems of existence of solutions, query answering and query rewriting under graph schema mappings are tackled. Their complexity is also studied for different fragments of graph queries.

CHAPTER 5

Query Specification

We describe in this chapter graph query specification techniques to help users formulate path queries from examples provided as input or via graph exploration. This problem amounts to learning queries from examples and reverse-engineering queries starting from examples that users want or do not want. The complexity of these problems has been studied in-depth and practical implementations have appeared already to witness an increasing interest of the community toward these approaches.

We focus on interactive graph query specification, which is a novel paradigm for formulating graph queries that guides the user through the various steps of a workflow, in which he/she is invited to make choices about focusing on a subset of the initial graph (represented or not as a summary of the original graph) and to single out a fragment in which labeling helps specifying what is expected in the query result and what is not, until coming up with a goal query that is sufficiently close to what the user has in mind. Such a workflow is key to the graph query specification process, and involves different problems, such as graph summarization and visualization, that go beyond a data management perspective.

We also describe the exemplar query paradigm devoted to find isomorphic structures in the graphs respecting the original specified exemplar query. We will contrast it with the Graph-Query-By-Example (GQBE) paradigm for graph queries and highlight their differences and similarities.

We conclude by presenting graph exploration techniques that are driven by an input query and take user intentions into account.

5.1   PATH QUERY SPECIFICATION

Query specification is a daunting task for non-expert users who are unfamiliar with the query languages. The problem of query specification is exacerbated for graph databases, that are harder to query than relational tables [Bonifati et al., 2015]. Indeed, knowledge graphs, examples of which are DBPedia [Auer et al., 2007, Bizer et al., 2009],[1] Yago [Suchanek et al., 2007],[2] Freebase [Bollacker et al., 2008],[3] Microsoft Concept Graph,[4] typically contain millions of entities and their relationships. Ordinary users need to inspect these voluminous graphs in order to

---

[1]http://wiki.dbpedia.org/datasets
[2]https://github.com/yago-naga/yago3
[3]https://developers.google.com/freebase/
[4]http://concept.research.microsoft.com/ and https://www.microsoft.com/en-us/research/project/prob ase/.

formulate their queries and they may end up writing queries that do not correspond to their intentions. Graph query specification has led to identify novel methods to aid users formulate their queries. Such methods enable users to specify the expected query results instead of directly tapping into knowledge graphs and searching the nodes and edges to formulate the query. They also entail a substantial breakthrough with respect to conventional query specification methods, such as writing query statements or using query-by-example interfaces. In particular, the problem of reverse-engineering queries from examples has received a great deal of attention recently, and has been carried out successfully for regular languages, regular path queries, relational database queries and XML queries. The common ground of these approaches lies in the definability problem for first-order logic [Arenas and Diaz, 2016], that is to find, given a (relational) database instance I and a relation R, whether there exists a first-order relational query Q (or a relational algebra expression Q) such that $Q(I) = R$ (Q evaluated on the instance I gives R as an answer). The above informal definition holds for relational (algebraic) queries. In the following, we revisit the definability problem and its complexity and we discuss its extensions to *RPGQ* (defined in this book in Chapter 3) . We then present the mainstream approaches for reverse-engineering graph queries that are directly tied to the definability problem. We postpone to the next section the discussion of exemplar query and GQBE approaches relying on a different assumption, that is asking the users to provide an example of what they want and finding similar entities to enlarge the query result set.

5.1.1   THE DEFINABILITY PROBLEM FOR GRAPH QUERIES

The *RPGQ* definability problem is defined as RPGQ-DEF = {(G, res), where G is a graph instance, res is a binary (or unary) relation as query result, and there is a *RPGLog* query Q such that $[\![Q]\!]_G = res$} [Arenas and Diaz, 2016]. In the above, we assume that the query Q does not mention any constants. We call $RPGLog_{noConst}$ the fragment of *RPGLog* that does not contain literals of the form $x.p \; \theta \; val$. Let U be an infinite countable universe. A graph instance is a set of vertex and edge relations, corresponding to the graph vertices and to the graph edges, respectively, with each relation a finite subset of U. Given two graph instances G_1 and G_2 of a graph, a function $f : U \to U$ is an *isomorphism from G_1 to G_2* if and only if (i) f is a bijective function and (ii) for every edge relation (vertex relation,respectively) res in G_1 such that arity(res)=2 (arity(res)=1, resp.), and for every edge $p \in U^2$ (node $e \in U^1$), it is the case that $p \in res^{G_1}$ if and only if $f(p) \in res^{G_2}$, where $f(p)$ is defined as $(f(e_1), f(e_2))$ if $p = (e_1, e_2)$. Given a graph instance G, a function $f : U \to U$ is an *automorphism of G* if f is an isomorphism from G to G itself.

The active domain of G, denoted by $adom(G)$, is the set of elements of U that appear in some relation of a graph instance G (analogously for $adom(res)$). Given a graph instance G and a query result *res*, $(G, res) \in$ RPGLOG-DEF only if (a) *adom(res)* $\subseteq$ *adom(G)* and (ii) *AUT(G)* $\subseteq$ *AUT(res)*, whereas *AUT* is the set of all automorphisms on *G* or on *res*, respectively.

Example 5.1   Let us make an example on the graph schema illustrated in Figure 2.2 in Chapter 2. Let us take a graph instance *G* containing a unary relation Expert$_I$ and a binary relation :knows$_I$. The pair $(G, res) \in$ RPGLOG-DEF, that is, we can find a *RPGQ* query without constants *Q* such that $[\![Q]\!]_G = res$. Such a query is given in *RPGLog* by *result(a, b)* $\leftarrow$:knows(a, b), :knows(b, a). In fact, in this case *AUT(G)* $\subseteq$ *AUT(res)*. Figure 5.1 illustrates the definable graph query result *res*.

Expert$_I$
'Alice'
'Bob'
'Matthew'

:knows$_I$	
'Alice'	'Matthew'
'Matthew'	'Alice'
'Bob'	'Alice'

res	
'Alice'	'Matthew'
'Matthew'	'Alice'

Figure 5.1: A graph instance *G* based on relations Expert and :knows and definable graph query result *res*.

5.1.2   COMPLEXITY OF DEFINABILITY FOR GRAPH QUERIES

The complexity of definability has been studied for several classes of queries, including first-order queries and conjunctive queries, up to considering more sophisticated graph queries. Table 5.1 summarizes the classes of graph queries considered in this book for which the computational complexity of the definability problem is known. FO-definability is GI-complete [Arenas and Diaz, 2016], where GI is the class of polynomially reducible to the graph isomorphism problem. Definability as defined above has been studied for the conjunctive queries (*CQ*s) as well and has been shown to be CONEXPTIME-complete [Willard, 2009]. *RPQ* definability reduces to definability by a finite language and is PSPACE-complete [Antonopoulos et al., 2013]. Definability for chain and linear *CRPQ*s is PSPACE-complete, for acyclic *CRPQ*s is PSPACE-hard and in EXPTIME, and definability is in EXPSPACE for general *CRPQ*s [Antonopoulos et al., 2013]. Finally, definability for *UCRPQ*s is CONP-complete [Antonopoulos et al., 2013], while definability for single-occurrence regular expressions when only concatenation is admitted (SORE(·))[5] is NP-complete [Antonopoulos et al., 2013]. The question about the exact complexity of definability for *RPGLog* remains open.

5.1.3   FROM DEFINABILITY TO LEARNABILITY OF GRAPH QUERIES

The problem of learning a graph query starting from a set of examples has been addressed in the literature for the fragment of Regular Path Queries (*RPQs*) [Bonifati et al., 2015]. There

[5]Regular expressions using only concatenation and where every Σ-symbol can occur at most once.

Table 5.1: Summary of complexity results for definability

Query Class	Complexity	Reference
FO	GI-complete	[Arenas and Diaz, 2016]
CQ	CONEXPTIME-complete	[Willard, 2009]
RPQ	PSPACE-complete	[Antonopoulos et al., 2013]
chain/linear CRPQ	PSPACE-complete	[Antonopoulos et al., 2013]
general CRPQ	EXPSPACE	[Antonopoulos et al., 2013]
UCRPQ	CONP-complete	[Antonopoulos et al., 2013]
SORE(·)	NP-complete	[Antonopoulos et al., 2013]

is a fundamental difference between definability and learnability arising from the assumption about the input examples. While definability requires the query to select nothing else than the set of positive examples and considers all other nodes as implicitly negative, learnability allows the query to select or not the nodes that are not explicitly labeled as positive examples and thus to include them in the set of negative examples. Therefore, in some sense the positive and negative examples must be stated as such at the very beginning of the learning process. Given a set of explicit positive and negative examples starting from which a query needs to be inferred, a problem that we must solve beforehand is the *consistency checking* problem, i.e., deciding whether a query satisfying the aforementioned set exists in the first place.

In the sequel, we focus on node-selecting queries for ease of exposition. The treatment of edge-selecting queries is equivalent and omitted for conciseness. Given a property graph $G = (V, E)$, a *node-selecting example* (abbreviated as *example*) is a pair (v, α), where $v \in V$ and $\alpha \in \{+, -\}$. We say that an example of the form $(v, +)$ is a *positive example* while an example of the form $(v, -)$ is a *negative example*. A *sample* S is a set of examples, i.e., a subset of $V \times \{+, -\}$. Given a sample S, we denote the set of positive examples $\{v \in V \mid (v, +) \in S\}$ by S_+ and the set of negative examples $\{v \in V \mid (v, -) \in S\}$ by S_-. A sample is *consistent* (with the class of *RPQ*) if there exists a (*RPQ*) query that selects all positive examples and none of the negative ones. Formally, given a graph G and a sample S, we say that S is *consistent* if there exists a query q s.t. $S_+ \subseteq q(G)$ and $S_- \cap q(G) = \emptyset$. In this case we say that q is *consistent with* S.

Example 5.2 Consider the graph G_{ex} (cf. Figure 2.2) and the sample S s.t. $S_+ = \{v_{10}, v_{11}, v_{12}, v_{13}\}$ and $S_- = \{v_{15}\}$; S is consistent because there exist queries like :knows/:worksFor/:knows$^+$ that are consistent with (S, G).

Let $RPQ_G(v)$ be the language of all words that match a sequence of nodes from G originating in v.

Lemma 5.3   *Given a graph G and a sample S, S is consistent with (S, G) iff for every $v \in S_+$ it holds that $RPQ_G(v) \not\subseteq RPQ_G(S_-)$*

From this characterization [Bonifati et al., 2015], we can derive that the fundamental problem of consistency checking is PSPACE-complete.

Lemma 5.4   *Given a graph G and a sample S, deciding whether S is consistent with (S, G) is PSPACE-complete.*

Crux. The membership in PSPACE follows from Lemma 5.3 and the known result that decide the inclusion of NFAs is PSPACE-complete [Stockmeyer and Meyer, 1973]. The PSPACE-hardness follows by reduction from the universality of the union problem for DFAs, known as being PSPACE-complete [Kozen, 1977].   □

In the classical framework of language identification in the limit [Gold, 1967, 1978], one of the conditions that a learning algorithm must satisfy is that it should always answer in polynomial time: either it returns a query consistent with the examples given by the user or it outputs a special *null* value if no such query exists. Since consistency checking is intractable, we cannot always find an algorithm able to always answer *null* in polynomial time when the sample is inconsistent. As a consequence, the class of *RPQs* is not learnable in the classical framework. One way to circumvent this intractability is to look at restricted classes of queries. However, as we show next, consistency checking remains intractable (NP-complete) even for the aforementioned "SORE($\cdot$)" fragment. This implies that an algorithm able to always answer *null* in polynomial time when the sample is inconsistent does not exist, hence our class of *RPQ* queries is not learnable in the classical framework of language identification in the limit [Gold, 1967, 1978].

Lemma 5.5   *Given a graph G and a sample S, deciding whether there exists a query of the form $a_1 \cdot \ldots \cdot a_n$ (pairwise distinct symbols) consistent with (S, G) is NP-complete.*

Crux. For the membership of the problem to NP, we point out that a non-deterministic Turing machine guesses a query q that is a concatenation of pairwise distinct symbols (hence of length bounded by $|\Sigma|$) and then checks whether q is consistent with S. The NP-hardness follows by reduction from 3SAT, well known as being NP-complete.   □

The proofs of Lemma 5.4 and 5.5 rely on techniques inspired by the definability problem for graph query languages [Antonopoulos et al., 2013].

Since consistency checking is intractable even for simpler subclasses of *RPQs*, a viable solution is to use a relaxed notion of learnability by trading the soundness condition and relying on learning with *abstain* [Laurence et al., 2014]. The learning algorithm is then allowed to answer a special value *null* whenever it cannot efficiently construct a consistent query. In practice, the *null* value is interpreted as "not enough input examples have been provided." However, the learning algorithm should always return in polynomial time either a consistent query or *null*. In other words, the algorithm should efficiently decide whether it can construct a consistent query or not. As an additional clause, a learning algorithm must also be *complete*, i.e., when the input sample contains a *polynomially sized characteristic sample* [Gold, 1978], the algorithm must return the goal query. The above clauses are summarized in the following definition.

Definition 5.6   A class of queries $\mathcal{Q}$ is *learnable with abstain in polynomial time and data* if there exists a polynomial learning algorithm *learner* that is the following.

1. **Sound with abstain.** For every graph G and sample S over G, the algorithm *learner*(G, S) returns either a query in $\mathcal{Q}$ that is consistent with S, or *null* if no such query exists or it cannot be constructed efficiently.

2. **Complete.** For every query $q \in \mathcal{Q}$, there exists a graph G and a polynomially sized characteristic sample CS on G s.t. for every sample S extending CS consistently with q (i.e., $CS \subseteq S$ and q is consistent with S) the algorithm *learner*(G, S) returns q.

A polynomial learning algorithm adhering to the above definition has been presented in Bonifati et al. [2015], along with the construction of a polynomial characteristic sample to show the learnability of *RPQ*s. Learnability with abstain for the entire fragment of *RPGQ* queries, beyond the simple class of *RPQ*s, is a future direction of investigation.

5.1.4   INTERACTIVE GRAPH QUERY SPECIFICATION

Constructing a characteristic sample S as needed by a learning algorithm or a result set *res* required by an algorithm solving the definability problem is overwhelming for end users especially since they do not have immediate feedback on the effect of their input on the learning or definability process. In this section, we discuss an interactive approach to graph query specification in which the process of building a sample is guided by a minimal number of user interactions. Users can then refine their input based on the provided feedback on the informativeness of the provided samples.

Let us assume a large graph instance G, named I in the subsequent steps of the workflow. We assume that such an instance I is (not mandatorily) equipped with limited schema information expressed for instance as graph constraints (for instance of the kind GKeys, GFDs, or GEDs as presented in Chapter 4). We target non-expert users who are not acquainted with a formal query language and unable to formulate a query on such a large graph instance I. We expect that such users are willing to visualize and label fragments I' of this large instance I depending on whether or not they would like the fragments as part of the query result. These labeled fragments can then be used as positive and negative examples in order to construct the user's goal query, which in particular satisfies the labels provided by the user. We assume that the goal query that the user has in mind belongs to a class of queries Q that is adequate to the model of the instance that she wants to query. In the remainder, we refer to the class of queries Q that contains the user's goal query as the *goal query class*. The goal query class Q can for instance be either the baseline class of regular path queries *RPQ* or the more expressive class *RPGQ* considered in this book.

Given the property graph data model, we assume a *function* that maps a graph instance encoded in that model to the set of all its *fragments*. A fragment F is defined as a small part of the instance that still satisfies the syntax of the property graph data model and that can be visualized and labeled by the end user. For the property graph data model, a fragment boils down to a graph node or a graph edge, or a small subgraph including the surroundings of the node or of the edge in order to let the user inspect the paths and the nodes of interest originating in that node or in that edge, respectively. The simplest possible labeling that the user can provide is a Boolean labeling (*positive* or *negative*), to indicate whether a fragment should or should not be selected by the query that she has in mind. However, more complex labeling can be accommodated such as for instance a confidence degree associated with a fragment or to a portion of a fragment.

The human feedback necessary to provide labeling should be kept minimal all along the process, and should concern a small number of graph fragments.

The steps of the entire interactive workflow are depicted in Figure 5.2.

The workflow bootstraps with a graph instance G and an empty *sample S*. According to Definition 5.6, a query q is *consistent with S* if q selects all positive examples and none of the negative ones contained in S. Initially, since we have an empty sample S, the set of all queries in Q is also empty.[6] The following process is then iterated: starting from I, choose a fragment F, label F as *positive* or *negative*, and update the set of queries Q consistent with S. The iterations are halted when the goal user query is found in the set of queries Q consistent with S. We assume that successive user labeling is sound,[7] meaning that if the user labels as positive a fragment consistently with query q, then q always belongs to the set of queries consistent with the user sample. Of course, the choice of the fragment F is crucial in that it lets the user eliminate a maximal number of candidate queries from the set of all queries Q consistent with S (if labeled as negative) or identifying the minimal set of queries Q to retain (if labeled as positive). To that purpose, candidate fragments can be identified as *uninformative* or *informative*. Given a sample S, we say that a fragment is *uninformative* if labeling it explicitly as a positive or a negative example does not eliminate any query in the set Q consistent with S. Then, a fragment is considered *informative* if neither it has been labeled by the user nor it is uninformative.

Pre-Processing and Exploration of the Input Graph

The workflow in Figure 5.2 takes as *input* a large graph instance I, an empty sample S, and an initially empty set of candidate queries Q consistent with the samples (step 1 in Figure 5.2).

---

[6]The latter is also provided as input to the graph query specification process.

[7]The assumption of soundness translates to considering the user as an oracle, whose provided labels are always consistent from one iteration to the next.

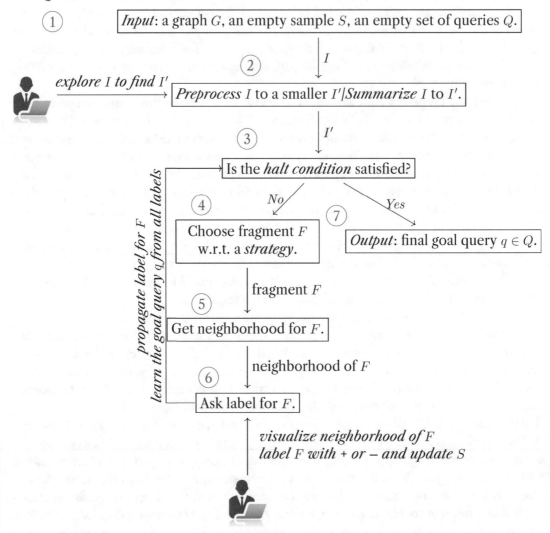

Figure 5.2: Interactive workflow for graph query specification.

Since working on the entire instance would be unfeasible for the end user due to the fact that relevant fragments would have to be exhaustively processed and considered in order to build the set of queries consistent with it, it is desirable to identify subsets of the entire instance that are representative of it. For instance, a simple criterion would be to consider the subgraph of the initial large graph on which we can find the same paths as in the entire graph. This step (corresponding to step 2 in Figure 5.2) has been instantiated with a generic procedure leading to randomly choose a subgraph [Bonifati et al., 2015]. Carefully redesigning this step would mean to rely on suitable data visualization techniques in order to let the users visually explore the subgraphs of interest at an appropriate resolution. Classical data mining tasks such as graph data summarization techniques [Koutra and Faloutsos, 2017, Liu et al., 2018] can be also applied at this stage to let the user work with smaller graph structures and derive actionable insights from them. Graph summarization is especially beneficial in order to facilitate the user's graph exploration and untangle the "hairball" visualization problem, which oftentimes occurs with visualization overlays dedicated to networks.

The number of redundant fragments according to graph isomorphism can be also identified and used to discard some of the candidate fragments. Alternatively, more sophisticated techniques based on algebraic operators could permit to establish the equivalence of subgraphs according to an algebraic visualization design [Kindlmann and Scheidegger, 2014]. To the best of our knowledge, the interplay of visualization equivalences and graph query equivalences is not explored so far in the literature.

Blending Fragmentation, Informativeness, and Visualization

The interactions with the user continue until a *halt condition* is satisfied (step 3 in Figure 5.2). A natural halt condition is to stop the interactions when there is exactly one consistent query with the current sample. In practice, we can imagine weaker conditions e.g., the user may stop the process earlier if she is satisfied by some candidate query q in Q proposed at some intermediary stage during the interactions. The fragments shown to the user are chosen according to a *strategy*, i.e., a function that takes as input an instance I' and a sample S, and returns a fragment F from I' (step 4 in Figure 5.2). Since we want to minimize the number of examples needed to learn the user's goal query, an intelligent strategy should propose to the user only informative fragments. We point out that while it is possible to design an optimal strategy (i.e., that is guaranteed to propose to the user a minimal number of fragments), such a strategy would be based on the minimax algorithm [Aho et al., 1983, Russell and Norvig, 2010], thus being exponential and unfortunately infeasible in practice. Similar to preprocessing, visualization design may turn to be invaluable to help present the examples to the user and navigate the space of all fragments. This motivates us to investigate *practical strategies* (i.e., that efficiently compute the next fragment to propose to the user) since the rationale is to reduce to the minimum the time between successive interactions. This approach leads to defining the *entropy* of a fragment, which intuitively is a measure of the quantity of information that labeling that fragment brings to the learning process. The computation of the entropy of a fragment is related to the actual data model and to the goal query class. Examples of such measures have already been defined for learning relational joins [Bonifati et al., 2014b, 2016a] and for learning path queries on graphs [Bonifati et al., 2015]. In any case, an intelligent strategy proposes to the user a fragment that maximizes the entropy. A fragment by itself does not always carry enough information to allow the user to understand whether the fragment is part of the query result or not. Therefore, it may happen that we have to enhance the information of a fragment by zooming out on the *neighborhood* of such a fragment before actually showing it to the user. The step of constructing the environment of a fragment may become cumbersome in the case of queries on graph databases. Hence, an inherent challenge is to compute a small environment of a node that is easy to visualize by the user and rich enough to permit labeling. Examples of neighborhoods are the surrounding regions of a node or an edge, or, to a certain extent, the remote regions of the graph that are similar to the local region of the node by using some similarity criteria. We will come back to this issue in the next section when presenting the exemplar query and GQBE paradigms.

Label Propagation and Visualization of the Graph Neighborhood

The user visualizes the neighborhood of a given fragment F and labels F w.r.t. the goal query that she has in mind (step 5 in Figure 5.2). The easiest possible fragment labeling that may occur is to add positive "+" or negative "−" labels to the fragments that then become positive and negative samples, respectively (step 6 in Figure 5.2). Then, the label given by the user for F can be propagated to the rest of the instance in order to prune the fragments that become uninformative. At this stage, a *learning algorithm* as described in the previous section (i.e., a function that takes as input an instance and a sample, and outputs a query consistent with the sample) can be invoked in order to propose the "best" query that is consistent with all labels provided until this point. If a learning with abstain algorithm is chosen here, it will lead to return the goal query or null if no query can be found that satisfies the input samples (step 7 in Figure 5.2 can then return null instead of the learned query q). In all the other cases, when the halt condition is satisfied, the latest learned query q is returned to the user. In particular, the halt condition may take into account such an intermediary learned query q e.g., when the user is satisfied by the output of q on the instance and wants to stop the interactions earlier.

5.2   GRAPH SEARCHING FOR QUERYING

In this section, we turn our attention to the problem highlighted in the step 5 of Figure 5.2, i.e., the problem of letting the user find relevant surroundings of an initial fragment under scrutiny in the interactive query specification process. We call this process subgraph searching and underline the fact that it can be guided by an initial user sample. Searching for relevant subgraphs is also used in novel query paradigms, such as the exemplar query paradigm [Mottin et al., 2016]. Two steps are highlighted in the exemplar query specification workflow. The first step is devoted to build the user sample, i.e., to identify in the graph instances the subgraphs that are involved in the initial user sample. In some sense, the first step of the exemplar query paradigm could be adopted as a means to process the entire graph instance and to reduce its scope (step 2 of Figure 5.2). This step leverages existing literature on the topic of query answering and keyword-based search on graphs (Steiner-tree approximations and r-cliques [Kargar and An, 2015, Kasneci et al., 2009]). Steneir-tree approximations of weighted graphs lead to define entities with the closest relationship among each other according to a given cost function, while r-cliques are sets of content nodes that cover all the input keywords, and the distance between each pair of nodes is less than or equal to r. The second step, which is addressed in the exemplar query paradigm [Mottin et al., 2016], is to be able to find starting from the initial user sample, similar samples by leveraging congruence relations based on graph isomorphism and strong simulation. The exemplar queries is a novel paradigm of query answering in which a query is interchangeably treated as a sample of the desired query result set. The final selected query results of the user are the k most relevant ones, which gives a bound to the problem of enumeration of fragments in step 5 of Figure 5.2. The results of the evaluation of an exemplar query are called exemplar answers.

Definition 5.7   Given an *RPGQ* query q and a graph instance G, the set of exemplar answers is defined as $\{res \mid \exists res' \in [\![q]\!]_G$ such that $res \approx res'\}$.

The congruence relation $\approx$ is instantiated with (1) edge-preserving subgraph isomorphism and (2) various notions of simulation [Henzinger et al., 1995]. The congruence relation can be instantiated in its basic case with edge-preserving subgraph isomorphism between a query q and an exemplar answer *res*. It must be interpreted as a bijection h from the nodes of q to the nodes *res* such that for every edge $e = (u, p, u')$ in q, there exists an edge $e' = (h(u), p', h(u'))$ in *res* such that $p = p'$. Besides subgraph isomorphism and simulation, other notions of subgraph matching relations could have been employed here, such as for instance 1-1 homomorphism [Fan et al., 2010], which corresponds to an extended notion of subgraph isomorphism, where edges can be mapped to paths instead of single edges (as is the case in basic edge-preserving subgraph isomorphism).

The difference between the exemplar query paradigm (as illustrated in Figure 5.3) and the interactive graph query specification workflow (as depicted in Figure 5.2) resides in the fact that the former starts from an initial exemplar query (which can be a small subgraph in the graph instance G in Figure 5.2), while the latter bootstraps directly with the entire graph instance, that is then narrowed down to a smaller instance by pre-processing and/or graph summarization techniques. Whereas we can observe that step 2 is significantly different for the two paradigms in Figures 5.2 and 5.3, the search of similar exemplar answers as performed in the exemplar query paradigm can be adopted in step 5 of the interactive graph query specification process depicted in Figure 5.2.

Before concluding this section, we present a brief comparison of the exemplar query paradigm with the Query-By-Example (QBE) [Zloof, 1975] paradigm. While in QBE the user is expected to provide query keywords and query constants (possibly with wildcard) to be used in predicates, in the exemplar query paradigm, the initial exemplar query represents the user intentions toward finding similar results (according to the adopted congruence relation). GQBE [Jayaram et al., 2015] is another paradigm for graph query specification, which is reminiscent of QBE for relational queries and bootstraps with a set of graph entity tuples that are used to compute the Maximal Query Graph (MQG). In a sense, the MQG has its counterpart in the initial exemplar query needed as input for the exemplar query paradigm. In the GQBE paradigm, graph searching is performed in a way to find similar candidate subgraphs in the instance graph by also allowing approximate matching. The query space is modeled as a lattice in which the supremum of the lattice is the MQG and the leaves of the lattice are minimal query trees, that cannot be simplified further. Strategies on the graph permit to compute the possible candidate answer set whereas no strict congruence relation is applied as in the exemplar query paradigm.

The exemplar query paradigm and the GQBE paradigm are exemplified in Figures 5.3 and 5.4, respectively. Notice that both methods mandate the user to provide complex input (explicit query graph or graph entity tuples), whereas the goal of interactive graph query specification as in Figure 5.2 is to limit the user input to positive and negative labels on the nodes and edges of the graph fragments.

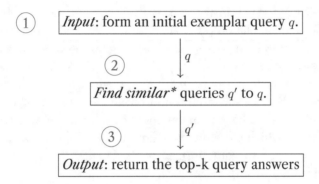

Figure 5.3: Exemplar Query paradigm, with similar* being edge-isomorphic or simulation-equivalent.

5.3   QUERY-DRIVEN GRAPH EXPLORATION

Throughout the aforementioned paradigms, exploring large graph-shaped data may turn out to be overwhelming for the end user. In particular, both methods demand as input a set of entities that must be singled out in the graph and that are to be labeled by the user as positive (or, negative) results of the query to be inferred. The task of graph exploration can be facilitated for end users by providing them with appropriate graph summaries. Several criteria can be adopted in order to steer a given graph summarization technique toward query specification tasks. Grouping-based summarization techniques that leverage the graph semantic structure and topology (by considering categorical or numerical attributes) as well as bit-wise compression techniques can be beneficial to the process of query specification [Liu et al., 2018]. The goal of this section is to provide insights of how a few existing methods could be extended in order to take into account the user intentions in the process of graph query inference. Even though

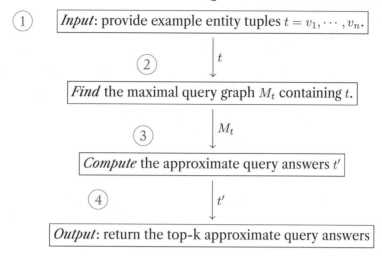

Figure 5.4: Graph Query-By-Example (GQBE) paradigm.

user intentions have started to be taken into account in graph clustering and graph outlier detection [Perozzi et al., 2014], they have not been considered in graph summarization techniques.

While graph sampling could seem a valid option, it is less suited for graph query specification in the pre-processing step of the interactive workflow of Figure 5.2, due to the fact that sampling aims at obtaining a sparsified version of the original graph, where some property of the original graph is enforced (such as diameter, in- and out-degree distribution, size distribution of connected components, PageRank score, and so on) [Liu et al., 2018]. In contrast, the goal of graph summarization is to build groups of nodes that preserve the same connectivity patterns to the rest of the graph. As such, graph summarization allows to obtain a more compact graph that is structurally closer to the initial graph than that obtained by graph sampling and that is more suitable for the upcoming tasks of query specification.

We must also observe that, to the best of our knowledge, very few of the existing methods for graph summarization take the user intentions as parameters. The only work in this direction aims at guiding the users toward a small set of interesting summaries amongst the set of all possible summaries [Zhang et al., 2010]. On the other hand, interestingness is not necessarily guided by the query inference process. A graph summary is defined by adding nodes, called groups, corresponding to partitions of nodes of the original graph, and adding edges, known as group relationships, representing the connections among groups. A group relationship between groups exists if there is at least one edge connecting nodes in the two groups. A group relationship can be *strong* or *weak* depending on the number of edges forming the group relationship. Figure 5.5 shows a possible graph summary that one can obtain from a professional network in which several experts (exemplifying the running example in the book) collaborate with each other. We assume that the groups of nodes of HP (high prolific) experts, P (prolific) experts, and

LP (low prolific) experts have been created by looking at the number of products created by these experts. Moreover, in the original graph the number of edges of type collaboration between HP and P experts is much higher than the number of edges of type collaboration between HP and LP experts, thus creating one strong group relationship in the former case and one weak group relationship in the latter case.

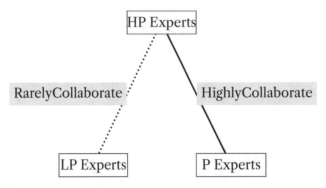

Figure 5.5: An illustration of a group-based graph summary (HP=High Prolific, LP=Low Prolific, P=Prolific).

The interestingness of a graph summary is thus measured by leveraging three distinct metrics: (i) diversity, corresponding to finding groups of nodes that have diverse semantic relationships (encoded as labeled edges); (ii) coverage, corresponding to the number and sizes of groups that participate to the graph summary; and (iii) conciseness, corresponding to the summaries with fewer groups and more semantic relationships, in order to facilitate understandability and visualization.

Interesting graph summaries are then defined as the summaries exhibiting more diversity and coverage with respect to the original graph combined with conciseness, in order to meet the user requirement of being able to display and inspect the graph summary. Given a graph summary S, interestingness can be defined as follows [Zhang et al., 2010]:

$$Interestingness(S) = \frac{Diversity(S) \times Coverage(S)}{Conciseness(S)}. \tag{5.1}$$

The key intuition behind formula 5.1 is that large graph summaries are informative but less usable for end users than small graph summaries. Moreover, the above measure does not take into account the query that the user has in mind. For instance, the above definition of coverage can be adjusted by taking into account the expected graph query answer sets instead of considering the representativeness of the entire input graph. Similarly, the notions of diversity for the obtained graph summary is not necessarily demanded by the user during the query specification process and can be omitted in the above formula leading to the following variation:

$$Interestingness(S) = \frac{CoverageWrt.DesiredQuery(S)}{Conciseness(S)}.$$ (5.2)

Deriving a more precise characterization of the notion of interestingness for a graph summary subject to user inspection in the graph query specification workflow is definitely a future challenge in this area.

5.4   BIBLIOGRAPHIC NOTES

The complexity of the definability problem for several prominent fragments of *UCRPQ*s has been studied in depth [Antonopoulos et al., 2013]. Due to the fact that the complexity is quite high, we are not aware of systems implementing this concept. The complexity of satisfiability and learning of SPJ queries has been tackled in the literature, when the query is, or is not, of bounded size. We leave the discussion of this complexity explicitly out of this chapter and refer the reader to previous work [Weiss and Cohen, 2017]. A comprehensive framework for *RPQ* specification focusing on the problem of learning from positive and negative examples has been proposed in Ciucanu [2015]. A preliminary version of the interactive graph specification workflow presented here appeared in Bonifati et al. [2014a]. In this chapter, we revisit this workflow under the lens of a deeper understanding of the necessary user interactions, and with observations of the necessary techniques (graph instance and graph query visualization, graph summarization) in order to make it feasible in practice. We also contrast it with related graph query paradigms for non-expert users, such as GQBE [Jayaram et al., 2015] and exemplar queries [Mottin et al., 2016]. We observe that these two paradigms require different types of input and lead to obtain different outputs for graph query inference.

Since this chapter focuses on graph query specification, which is the problem of inferring a query from a set of positively or negatively labeled query results or from a set of query keywords (disconnected in the case of QBE and connected in the case of the exemplar query paradigm), we do not cover other problems, such as graph query reformulation [Mottin et al., 2015] and graph query relaxation [Poulovassilis and Wood, 2010]. In the latter problems, a query must be provided as input even though it may occur that is underspecified and/or needs to be generalized (as in query relaxation) since it gives an empty result (as in the empty-answer [Vasilyeva et al., 2015] or too-few or too-many problem [Vasilyeva et al., 2016]). The latter problem has been studied for graph pattern matching queries leveraging the property graph data model, by providing suitable explanations for the cases of why-empty, why-too-few, and why-so-many queries and addressing their modifications [Vasilyeva, 2017]. Non-intrusive user intervention while deriving the preferred query rewritings is expected, which builds on user preference models based on past user choices.

A comprehensive survey of graph summarization techniques spanning static and dynamic graphs has recently appeared [Liu et al., 2018]. Among the techniques for heterogeneous graphs, grouping-based, bit compression-based, and influence-based techniques are worth mentioning. The latter two are less query-oriented than the first and are disregarded in our analysis. Grouping-based summarization for large graphs have focused mainly on the problem of providing graph summaries that stay small and intuitive for the end-users, while permitting classical OLAP operations [Zhang et al., 2010]. None of the available techniques takes into account either the user intentions for subsequent querying of the graph (otherwise known as query specification needs) or possible classes of queries to be executed on the graph. Work on applying compression to graph instances by targeting specific queries (reachability and pattern matching queries, respectively) does not take user intentions for query specification into account [Fan et al., 2012, Fletcher et al., 2015a, Picalausa et al., 2012].

CHAPTER 6

Data Structures and Indexes

A property graph is a complex structure requiring some care to be represented in the linear memory model[1] of computers. A memory representation for property graphs should be: (1) concise, i.e., represent a given graph with a small memory footprint; and (2) access-efficient, i.e., allow queries reading and writing as little data as possible to process a given query as quickly as possible on the given hardware architecture. Due to complexity of the PGM, there is no single data structure that can represent a property graph out of the box. Neither is there a representation that became a de facto standard for PGM. Usually, PGM representations combine multiple ideas and techniques to represent the various parts of a property graph. Some PGM representations differ drastically while other PGM representations differ only in a few aspects. To avoid redundancy and repetition, we structure the discussion of PGM representation into the following main aspects.

1. Conceptual schemas for PGM representation define how the complex PGM structure is split up into a set of conceptual relations that model the structure of PGM storage. Most common conceptual schemas for PGM consist of ternary relations, as we show in Section 6.1.

2. Ternary relations can be represented in various ways using different data structures and encodings. We distinguish two principled approaches. The direct representation is discussed in Section 6.2, while the pivoted representation is discussed in Section 6.3.

3. Adjacency indexing concerns techniques specifically tailored for representing the adjacency of a graph or more generally a binary relation. We present these in Section 6.4.

4. Reachability indexing concerns indexing techniques specifically tailored for operation on the transitive closure of a binary relation. We present these in Section 6.5.

5. Structural indexing concerns indexing techniques specifically tailored for the expressive power of a given query language. We present these in Section 6.6.

Specific implementations and approaches do not always separate these aspects so explicitly and clearly. We use the separation here primarily to structure the discussion. It allows presenting individual techniques in a more generalized way, show orthogonalities, and illustrate the vast space of possible PGM representation formats.

---

[1]Where not explicitly mentioned otherwise, we do not distinguish between volatile memory and persistent storage but instead use the term "memory" indifferently for both.

The discussed data structures and representation techniques have not necessarily been proposed in the context of the PGM. Many techniques proposed, e.g., in the context of RDF, are also relevant for PGM. Likewise, PGM representations often make use of relational or general purpose data structures. We focus the discussion on concepts and techniques that are applicable to PGM representation and have been proposed for or used in graph data management or graph processing systems.

6.1   CONCEPTUAL SCHEMAS OF PGM REPRESENTATION

Out of the five components of a property graph V, E, η, λ, and ν, representing V and E is trivial. Both are merely sets of identities, which can be easily covered implicitly with the representations of η, λ, and ν. Hence, we focus the discussion on η, λ, and ν.

Basic schema.   The most straightforward conceptual schema for representing property graphs mirrors the formal definition of the PGM. The three functions, η, λ, and ν, are represented directly as conceptual relations Adjacency, Label, and Property, respectively.

Labels as property.   A common approach is to treat labels as properties in the storage system. This allows omitting relation Label. Instead labels are represented with a system-reserved property λ in the Property relation.

Edge labels in adjacency.   Edge labels are often the primary filter predicate on the adjacency. To account for that, edge labels can be stored in a four-column Adjacency relation $(E, V_s, V_t, \mathcal{P}(\mathcal{L}_E))$. If the Adjacency relation is meant primarily for forward lookups, i.e., finding an edge and a target vertex for a given source vertex and edge label, then edges and corresponding target vertices can be stored as pairs in a single column, so that Adjacency remains ternary.

Partitioned by object type.   A fourth common conceptual schema is to store adjacency and labels as properties and horizontally partition the Property relation by object type into a Vertex and an Edge relation. The Vertex relation stores all properties and labels of the vertices, while the Edge relation represents all properties and labels as well as the adjacency of the edges. Here, the adjacency is represented as system-reserved properties s and t for the source and the target vertex, respectively.

Universal.   The universal conceptual schema stores adjacency, labels, and properties of all objects, i.e., vertices as well as edges, in a single relation. Obviously, this conceptual schema is more general than the PGM. For instance, it allows vertices to have a source and a target, which is not provided by the PGM. A system using the universal schema has to enforce the full PGM semantics at a higher level of its architecture. The advantage of this schema is its simplicity. The query engine only has to deal with a single base relation.

Table 6.1 shows an overview of these five basic conceptual schemas for the representation of property graphs. For each relation the underlined columns indicate the primary key. The list is not meant to be complete, but to show the most common conceptual approaches.

Table 6.1: Conceptual representation schemas for PGM

Basic Schema	Adjacency			Label			Property		
	$\underline{E}$	V_s	V_t		$\underline{\mathcal{O}}$	$\mathcal{P}$	$(\mathcal{L})$	$\underline{\mathcal{O}}$	$\mathcal{K}$	$\mathcal{N}$

Labels as Property	Adjacency			Property		
	$\underline{E}$	V_s	V_t	$\underline{\mathcal{O}}$	$\underline{\mathcal{K} \cup \{\lambda\}}$	$\mathcal{N} \cup \mathcal{P}(\mathcal{L})$

Edge Labels in Adjacency	Adjacency			Property		
	$\underline{V_s}$	$\mathcal{P}(\mathcal{L}_E)$	$E \times V_t$	$\underline{\mathcal{O}}$	$\underline{\mathcal{K} \cup \{\lambda\}}$	$\mathcal{N} \cup \mathcal{P}(\mathcal{L}_V)$

Partitioned	Vertex			Edge		
	$\underline{V}$	$\underline{\mathcal{K} \cup \{\lambda\}}$	$\mathcal{N} \cup \mathcal{P}(\mathcal{L}_V)$	$\underline{E}$	$\underline{\mathcal{K} \cup \{\lambda, s, t\}}$	$\mathcal{N} \cup \mathcal{P}(\mathcal{L}_E) \cup V$

Universal	Object		
	$\underline{\mathcal{O}}$	$\underline{\mathcal{K} \cup \{\lambda, s, t\}}$	$\mathcal{N} \cup \mathcal{P}(\mathcal{L}) \cup V$

Group elements.   As variations of the conceptual schemas, elements of a domain that are (part of) the primary key can be grouped into sets according to other domains. The other domains in the relation form the primary key of the grouped relation. For instance, in an Adjacency relation (E, V_s, V_t), E is the primary key. By grouping all E into a set per V_s and V_t, the Adjacency relation becomes $(V_s, V_t, \mathcal{P}(E))$ with V_s, V_t as its primary key. The cardinality of a grouped relation is usually lower; the arity remains the same.

Ungroup elements.   The opposite of grouping is possible, too. We can ungroup (or unwind) element sets. In fact, it is a common variation of the aforementioned schemas to ungroup the label set. For that to be possible, the considered element set, e.g., $\mathcal{P}(\mathcal{L})$, must not be part of the relation's primary key. For instance, in the basic schema, the Label relation can be ungrouped to $(\mathcal{O}, \mathcal{L})$, with $\mathcal{O}, \mathcal{L}$ as its primary key. The cardinality of an ungrouped relation is usually higher; the arity remains the same.

It can be seen that the conceptual schema for PGM storage typically consists of binary and ternary relations. Obviously, binary and ternary relations can be stored directly as two-column and three-column tables, so that all generalized table storage structures commonly used in relational database management systems are applicable. However, a fixed limitation to a small number of columns allows for more specialized data structures and representation formats. Most data structures for ternary relations can be simplified to represent binary relations. In the following sections, we concentrate our discussion on data structures for ternary relations.

A ternary relation R of the form (A, B, C) is a set of triples (a, b, c) with $a \in A$, $b \in B$, and $c \in C$. For instance, the ternary relation (E, V_s, V_t) indicates which edge connects which pair of vertices. Access primitives for ternary relations are *lookups*. We denote a lookup on R as a positive atom $R(p_a, p_b, p_c)$, where $\hat{p} = (p_a, p_b, p_c) \in (A \cup \{\aleph\}) \times (B \cup \{\aleph\}) \times (C \cup \{\aleph\})$ and $R(p_a, p_b, p_c) = \{t \in R \mid t[i] = \hat{p}[i] \vee \hat{p}[i] = \aleph\}, i \in [1, 3]$. $\aleph$ serves as a wildcard here, indicating a lookup does not filter on the respective domain. We classify such lookups by naming the domains for which the atom gives a value and not $\aleph$. For instance, (A, B)-lookups are atoms $R(a, b, \aleph)$ with $a \in A$ and $b \in B$.

6.2 DIRECT REPRESENTATION OF TERNARY RELATIONS

Ternary relations can be stored as they are, i.e., as a list of all triples $(a, b, c) \in R$, called a *triple table*. The table can be stored row-wise, i.e., as $|R|$ (a, b, c) tuples, or column-wise, i.e., as three arrays $\pi_A(R)$, $\pi_B(R)$, and $\pi_C(R)$. Triple tables have linear space complexity in the size of R. Without further means, lookups require scanning the whole table. If the table is sorted lexicographically, binary search speeds up lookups that are prefixes of the sort order. A lexicographically sorted triple table can also be stored in tree structure, which maintains the sorting under inserts and deletes, e.g., in a B*-tree [Comer, 1979]. Figure 6.1 shows a lexicographically sorted triple table. It contains an excerpt of the graph shown in Figure 2.1 represented in the universal conceptual schema with ungrouped label set. Vertex and edge ids are prefixed if "v" and "e", respectively, to better visual distinction.

6.2.1 VALUE COMPRESSION

Triple tables involve a lot of redundancy; a single value is stored as often as it appears in the relation. Depending on their domain, individual values may have long and variable-sized byte representations. Hence, triples table quickly becomes very large and are not efficient to read, particularly from the main memory. When sorted, however, triple tables can be compressed, which increases their storage and read efficiency drastically. Feasible compression techniques should improve the read performance not just the storage foot print. Therefore, they have to allow for de- and encoding with only small CPU overhead as well as selectively reading only small parts of a table. Such techniques are typically referred to as lightweight compression. A plethora of lightweight compression techniques have been developed and studied, especially in the context of column-wise table storage for main-memory database management systems. We only outline quickly the most common state-of-the-art compression techniques.

$A = \mathcal{O}$	$B = \mathcal{K} \cup \{\lambda, s, t\}$	$C = \mathcal{N} \cup \mathcal{L} \cup V$
v10	λ	:Novice
v10	born	1995
v10	name	'Jason'
v11	λ	:Expert
v11	λ	:Father
v11	born	1976
v11	name	'Michael'
e20	λ	:knows
e20	s	v10
e20	t	v11
e20	since	2011

Figure 6.1: A lexicographically sorted triple table representing an excerpt of the graph shown in Figure 2.1 in the universal conceptual schema with an ungrouped label set.

Dictionary compression.   Dictionary compression uses a dictionary table to map each element of a given domain to a dense domain of positive integer values. Figure 6.2 shows the triple table from Figure 6.1 dictionary compressed. The dictionary table is typically a lexicographically ordered list of the domain elements, where an element's position in the list is its dense domain encoding. Encoding of a single value takes logarithmic effort to find the element in the sorted list. Decoding is a direct access to the respective list position. The resulting code values can be represented with a fixed number of bytes per code and typically require less bytes than the original elements. In a table, each column can have its own dictionary. If two columns are frequently compared, e.g., in a join, they should share a dictionary to allow a comparison without de- and encoding the values.

Delta encoding.   When a table column is sorted and consists of dense domains, consecutive values in the column have only small differences. Storing only the increment (delta) can allow for even less bytes needed per element, as illustrated in Figure 6.3. Note that only positive increments along the sort order are stored as deltas. If a value x_i is smaller than its preceding value x_{i-1}, then x_i is stored instead of the delta $x_i - x_{i-1}$. Delta encoding requires reading all values from the beginning. To facilitate selective reads, delta encoding is typically applied per block, e.g., per memory page. All deltas in a block are encoded with the number of bytes needed to represent the largest delta in the block. In a table, delta encoding works best in the first column of the sort order. The later a column appears in the sort order, the higher the chance of large differences between consecutive values in that column.

Variable byte encoding.   Variable byte encoding improves delta encoding where a few deltas are large and most are small. It allows encoding each delta with an individual number of bytes,

Dictionary		Dictionary		A	B	C
$A \cup C$		B		9	0	3
:Expert		λ		9	3	5
:Father		s		9	4	7
:knows		t		10	0	0
:Novice		born		10	0	1
1976		name		10	3	4
1995		since		10	4	8
2011				11	0	2
'Jason'				11	1	9
'Michael'				11	2	10
v10				11	5	6
v11						
e20						

Figure 6.2: Triple table from Figure 6.1 dictionary compressed.

so that leading zero bytes can be omitted. One variant uses the high bit of a byte to mark the last byte of a code word. Another variant stores the number of non-zero bytes a code word has. This works particularly well in triple tables since the length information of the three code words of a triple fits in a single byte. This variant is shown in Figure 6.3.

Deltas			Deltas as bytes			Deltas variable length encoded	
A	B	C	A	B	C	length	byte string
9	0	3	00 00 10 01	00 00 00 00	00 00 00 11	2,0,1	10 01 11
0	3	5	00 00 00 00	00 00 00 11	00 00 01 01	0,1,2	11 01 01
0	1	7	00 00 00 00	00 00 00 01	00 00 01 11	0,1,2	01 01 11
1	0	0	00 00 00 01	00 00 00 00	00 00 00 00	1,0,0	01
0	0	1	00 00 00 00	00 00 00 00	00 00 00 01	0,0,1	01
0	3	4	00 00 00 00	00 00 00 11	00 00 01 00	0,1,2	11 01 00
0	1	8	00 00 00 00	00 00 00 01	00 00 10 00	0,1,2	01 10 00
1	0	2	00 00 00 01	00 00 00 00	00 00 00 10	1,0,1	01 00 10
0	1	9	00 00 00 00	00 00 00 01	00 00 10 01	0,1,2	01 10 01
0	1	10	00 00 00 00	00 00 00 01	00 00 10 10	0,1,2	01 10 10
0	3	6	00 00 00 00	00 00 00 11	00 00 01 10	0,1,2	11 01 10

Figure 6.3: Dictionary compressed triple table from Figure 6.1 delta and variable byte encoded. For illustration purposes, we assume a byte consists of just 2 bits.

6.2.2   VALUE INDEXING

While lexicographically sorted triple tables allow efficient lookups on prefixes of the sort order, other lookups still require scanning the whole table. Having additional access paths, i.e., indexes, on the triple table mitigates that. Literature offers a cornucopia of indexing approaches for tabular data. We focus on the principle approaches taken in the context of graph database systems. We discuss three aspects any indexing approaches for triple tables has to decide on: (1) the basic types of indexes that should be used; (2) the columns that should be indexed; and (3) the data structures that are used to store the indexes.

Index Types

First, there are three fundamental index types that can be distinguished, regarding how the index information relates to the data that is indexed.

Primary index.   A lexicographically sorted triple table stored in a tree structure is already a primary index. However, the triple can be stored in a similar fashion according to a different sort order. For instance, if table shown in Figure 6.1 is stored in sort order C, B, A, it would allow efficiently looking up which object has a given property value under a specific key. With the lexicographical sort order ABC such a (C, B)-lookup is, what is described in the sentence before, (looking up an object with a given key-value p) requires scanning the table. in the sentence before, looking up an object with a given key-value p. To efficiently support lookups that require different sort orders, the table can simply be stored redundantly in multiple primary indexes.

Secondary index.   Secondary indexes do not contain the complete triples, but just lookup information and references to the respective triples. For instance, a secondary index for C, B-lookups would store the reference instead of A values. A secondary index adds an access path, while trying to avoid the absolute redundancy of another primary index. However, if compression is heavily used and the actual values can be stored with only very few bytes, the reference may by even larger than the values. Hence, secondary indexes typically only make sense if they index a single column or if the primary representation is uncompressed.

Index column.   A special form of secondary indexing is an index column, which integrates additional index information directly into the table. Therefore, an additional column—the index column—is added to the triple table that stores a pointer with each triple. The pointer points to the physical position of a next triple in the same subset of triples. All pointers in the same triple subset form a circular list. This allows efficient navigation of certain triple subsets not subsequently stored in the primary representation. For instance, column D could store for each triple a pointer to the next triple with the same C and B values, so that from a given tuple all other tuples with the same C and B values can be found easily, independent of the sort order of the primary representation. When used in conjunction with a secondary index, the secondary index needs to store the reference of a single triple only. The remaining triples can be found via navigation. With multiple secondary indexes and multiple indexes columns, each combination of them facilitates an access path.

Index Configuration

For any specific triple table that should be indexed, it needs to be decided which columns and column combinations should be indexed, i.e., which index configuration is used. Triple tables used for graph representation—unlike relations in relational databases—are not tangible to the user of the graph database system, so that most systems deploy a fixed set of indexes on a triple table. The following approaches are common for designing the index set.

Exhaustive indexing.   Exhaustive indexing means that every lookup can be processed with the help of an index, so that scanning the whole table is avoided completely. With only three columns, triple tables have only six possible sort orders. A triple table (A, B, C) can be sorted by ABC, ACB, BAC, BCA, CAB, and CBA. Having an index for each of the six sort orders exhaustively indexes a triple table. Exhaustive indexing not only facilitates efficient lookups but also allows the use of efficient merge join algorithms for joins on any of the columns of the triple table. This is particularly appealing for a conceptual representation schema that represents graphs in a single ternary relation like the universal schema (cf. Table 6.1). Generally, the gain in reading efficiency justifies the six-fold redundancy, particularly when the triples are compressed. If the query engine uses only a certain subset of lookups, even a fewer number of indexes is sufficient to exhaustively index the table. For instance, a triple table (E, V_s, V_t) (cf. basic schema, Table 6.1) might be only accessed with (V_s)-, (V_s, E)-, (V_t)-, and (V_t, E)-lookups, i.e., forward and backward traversal of edges. In this setting, the table is exhaustively indexed by just two indexes, a forward index (V_s, E, V_t) and a backward index (V_t, E, V_s).

Projection indexing.   A projection index does not index all three columns but the projection of a subset of columns, i.e., a partial sort order. A triple table (A, B, C) has nine partial sort orders AB, AC, BA, BC, CA, CB, A, B, and C, hence nine possible projection indexes. Without any further payload, projection indexes can efficiently answer projected lookups where triple values of one or two columns are not of interest. For instance, on a triple table (E, V_s, V_t), a lookup may just ask for all outgoing neighbors of a vertex or whether an edge exists between a given vertex pair. A projection index on (V_s, V_t) can efficiently serve these lookups and, very likely, is considerably smaller than a full index on (V_s, V_t, E), since vertex pairs with multiple edges will have just a single index entry per pair. A typical payload of a projection index is: (1) the number of triples matching the index entry; (2) a pointer to the first triple in the primary representation matching the index entry; or (3) both. With pointers as (part of) the payload, a projection index becomes a secondary index, that can be used in conjunction with index columns. With numbers of triples as (part of) the payload, a projection index can provide useful statistical information to the query planner.

Index Data Structures

Triple tables can be indexed with virtually any index structure for tables. The most common tree-structure is the ubiquitous B^*-tree. Research literature offers a plethora of B^*-tree variants, optimized for cache efficiency or other aspects. The use of such proven data structures has also been proposed in the context of graph database systems.

6.3 PIVOTED REPRESENTATION OF TERNARY RELATIONS

Alternative to direct storage in a triple table, ternary relations can be stored in a *pivoted table*. To do so, the primary key of the relation must consist of two domains. A relation $R(A, B, C)$ with a primary key (A, B) can be presented as a table $P\left(A, C_{b_1}, \ldots, C_{b_{|B|}}\right)$, where $C_b = \pi_C(\sigma_{B=b}R)$. All triples $\sigma_{A=a}R$ are stored in P in a single record $r \in P$, with $r[A] = a$ and $r[C_b] = c$ if $(a, b, c) \in R$ or $r[C_b] = \aleph$ otherwise. For instance, consider the Vertex relation $(V, \mathcal{K} \cup \{\lambda\}, \mathcal{N} \cup \mathcal{P}(\mathcal{L}_V))$ of the partitioned schema, cf. Table 6.1. If represented in a pivoted table, each vertex with all its label set and all of its property values is stored in a single record. An example is shown in Figure 6.4.

V	λ	name	born	class	graduated	middleInitial	twitter
v10	{:Novice}	'Jason'	1995	$\aleph$	$\aleph$	'J.'	'@jj05'
v11	{:Expert, :Father}	'Michael'	1976	$\aleph$	1998	$\aleph$	$\aleph$
v12	{:Apprentice}	'Matthew'	1989	2	$\aleph$	$\aleph$	$\aleph$

Figure 6.4: A pivoted table representing the vertices of the graph shown in Figure 2.1 according to the Vertex relation of the partitioned conceptual schema.

As mentioned, the pivoted table representation is only applicable to ternary relations with a two primary key domains. Relations with three primary key domains can be grouped into having only two primary key domains. Relations with only one primary key domain can be represented in pivoted form, but it is not a very reasonable thing to do. If one of the non-primary key domains is a power set, the relation can be ungrouped into having only two primary key domains.

The main advantage of a pivoted table is that it drastically reduces the number of joins needed to access all C that belong the same A compared to an unsorted triple table representation of the same relation. In the example of Figure 6.4, vertex 10 can be accessed with all its labels and properties by reading a single record, while in an unsorted triple table that would require four join operations. When building on a relational storage engine, the pivoted table representation allows utilizing the full ability of storing a table with an arbitrary number of columns.

The main disadvantage of this approach is that property graphs are schema-flexible and none of the domains are fixed. As a consequence, the record format of the pivoted table is not stable. Further, the pivoted table typically includes many NULL values ($\aleph$), as can be seen in the example of Figure 6.4. As their main effect, an unstable record format and the presence of $\aleph$ values increases the interpretation overhead when reading the table and reduces the efficiency of scans. A number of mitigating techniques are available that stabilize the schema of a pivoted table. The techniques can be categorized as (1) *emerging schemas* and (2) *schema hashing*.

Emerging Schemas

The emerging schemas approach builds on the observation that the data schema of most property graphs is flexible but not arbitrary. Although PGM defines the schema elements (labels and property keys) as merely descriptive, they are used rather strictly on the side of the applications in many use cases. Typically, the schema elements stabilize after a certain time. This can be exploited on the database side to have pivoted tables with a stable record format. Essentially, a pivoted table is partitioned horizontally and vertically, so that some partitions contain only $\aleph$ values. Obviously, these $\aleph$ partitions can be omitted. The remaining partitions have less columns and fewer $\aleph$ values. Figure 6.5 illustrates this idea and its effect for the pivoted table shown in Figure 6.4. The partitioning can be done in a number of ways, which we discuss next.

V	λ	name	born
v10	{:Novice}	'Jason'	1995
v11	{:Expert, :Father}	'Michael'	1976
v12	{:Apprentice}	'Matthew'	1989

V	class	graduated
v11	$\aleph$	1998
v12	2	$\aleph$

V	middleInitial	twitter
v10	'J.'	'@jj05'

Figure 6.5: A pivoted table from Figure 6.4 partitioned based on an emerging schema.

Horizontal partitioning by label sets. A very simple partitioning strategy is to horizontally partition the pivoted table by the label set of each object. Columns not instantiated in a partition are omitted in that partition. Obviously, this strategy is only applicable to tables with a label set column. However, if labels are used by the data modeler to denote classes of objects, this approach works well. Objects of the same class typically have the same properties.

Vertical partitioning by property sets. Another strategy is to vertically partition the pivoted table by sets of properties that typically occur together. Objects that do not instantiate any property in a partition are omitted in that partition. For this approach to work, good property sets have to be identified. Given a pivoted table, good property sets can be found by clustering the property keys. The distance of two property keys, a and b, is the Jaccard distance [Levandowsky and Winter, 1971] between X_a and X_b, where X_a and X_b are the sets of all objects that have the property a and b, respectively.

Horizontal partitioning by property sets. Good property sets can also be found by starting with all distinct property sets of objects and merging infrequent property sets, which likely belong to the same semantical class of objects. In each iteration, the most infrequent property set is merged with the closest one according to the Jaccard distance of the sets. This results in horizontal partitioning of the pivoted table. A refinement of this approach uses the TF/IDF score of the properties among all property sets and computes the distance of two property sets as the normalized scalar product of their TF/IDF score vectors. This way, the properties that are distinctive for a property set, i.e., do not appear in many other property sets, have a higher weight in the distance. The refinement can also be used to merge new property sets introduced by inserts of new entities. In general, this approach assumes a rather static database and has to be rerun if the database significantly changes. To deal with dynamic datasets, the system can fix the maximum size for partitions. New entities are assigned to the closest partition. If a partition is full, it is split into two, using the same distance measure.

Schema Hashing

Schema hashing utilizes hash functions to map a pivoted table to a stable record format. A pivoted table $P\left(A, C_{b_1}, \ldots, C_{b_{|B|}}\right)$ is mapped to a table $P'\left(A, X_1^B, X_1^C, \ldots, X_n^B, X_n^C\right)$, where a pair X_i^B, X_i^C is column group i. The resulting table P' has stable record format consisting of column A and n column groups. Values in columns $C_{b_1}, \ldots, C_{b_{|B|}}$ are mapped to the column groups with a hash function $h : B \to \mathbb{N}$. For each record $r \in P$ in the pivoted table, the value $r[C_b]$ is mapped to $r'[X_i^B, X_i^C] = \left(b, r[C_{b_j}]\right)$ in P', with $i = h(b)$. Obviously, the hash function can result in collisions so that two values of the same tuple r are mapped to the same column group. In this case, one of the two colliding values is stored in r' and the other value is stored in a second record r'^+, called a spill record. Additionally, a list of hash functions can be used to be able to fall back to the next hash function in case of collisions and, therefore, reduce the chance of spill records.

Figure 6.6 shows the pivoted table from Figure 6.4 with schema hashing applied. Here, the collision occurred between twitter and middleInitial on vertex 10. Both are mapped by h to column group 3, so that middleInitial is stored in a spill record. In combination with dictionary compression, schema hashing provides a stable, fixed-length record format for pivoted tables.

with $h(\lambda) = 0, h(\text{name}) = 1, h(\text{born}) = 2,$
$h(\text{class}) = h(\text{twitter}) = h(\text{graduated}) = h(\text{middleInitial}) = 3$

V	0	0	1	1	2	2	3	3
v10	λ	{:Novice}	name	'Jason'	born	1995	twitter	'@jj05'
v10	$\aleph$	$\aleph$	$\aleph$	$\aleph$	$\aleph$	$\aleph$	middleInitial	'J.'
v11	λ	{:Expert, ...}	name	'Michael'	born	1976	graduated	1998
v12	λ	{:Apprentice}	name	'Matthew'	born	1989	class	2

Figure 6.6: Schema hashing applied to pivoted table shown in Figure 6.4.

6.4   ADJACENCY INDEXING

In the following, we discuss data structures designed primarily to represent the adjacency of directed graphs. Such data structures can be used to perform adjacency-centric operations, such as breath-first search (BFS) and depth-first search (DFS) for query processing (cf. Chapter 7), on a concise representation. Two main variants can be distinguished. (1) An *existential adjacency index* stores the existence of an adjacency between a pair of vertices. Conceptually, an existential adjacency index represents a binary relation $R(A, B)$. (2) A *referential adjacency index* stores additional information c, e.g., an edge id or an edge label, for each pair of vertices as typically needed in PGM storage. Conceptually, a referential adjacency index represents a ternary relation $R(A, B, C)$ with A, B as primary key.

Any adjacency index should allow efficient neighborhood lookups for a given vertex, i.e., return all $\{b \mid (a, b) \in R\}$ for a given a (all $\{(b, c) \mid (a, b, c) \in R\}$ for a given a, respectively). When deployed for edge-labeled graphs, an adjacency index is often partitioned by the edge label, i.e., the system maintains one adjacency index per label or label set. For multi-graphs, i.e., when multiple edges can connect a given pair of vertices, referential adjacency indexes have to use c to reference a list of edges instead of a single one. For PGM, adjacency indexes are often used as secondary projection indexes in combination with a pivoted representation of the edges.

In the following, we discuss data structures for existential adjacency indexes. Additionally, we mention how each data structure can be extended for use as referential adjacency index.

6.4.1   UNCOMPRESSED ADJACENCY REPRESENTATION

An uncompressed adjacency representation is invariant of an isomorphism of the represented graph in the sense that its space requirement only depends on graph invariants, such as number of vertices, number of edges, degree, etc. It may utilize a given lexicographical order of the vertices for binary search but does not exploit any particular permutation of the vertices.

Matrix.   A matrix m of size $|A| \times |B|$ stores a 1-bit at $m_{i,j}$ for each pair $(a_i, b_j) \in R$ and a 0-bit otherwise. The matrix is linearized into a bit string with $j + (i \cdot |B|)$ being the string position of $m_{i,j}$. a_i is the i-element in A according to its lexicographical order; the analog holds for b_j. Lookups have to determine the index of an element in the lexicographical order of its domain. To avoid rows and columns containing only 0-bits, A and B have to be dense domains, so that $A = \pi_A(R)$ and $B = \pi_B(R)$ hold, respectively, which can be achieved by dictionary compression of R. Figure 6.7 shows a matrix representation. Here, the binary relation $R(A, B)$ contains all edges of the graph shown in Figure 2.2. As can be seen, for instance, the existence of edge 22 is marked in the matrix with a 1-bit at $m_{v11,v12}$. If R represents the edges of a graph (as in the figure), the two columns of the binary relation typically share a dense domain V. In consequence, the matrix contains 0-bit rows for vertices without an outgoing edge, such as vertex 16, and 0-bit columns for vertices without an incoming edge, such as vertex 10. Also visible in the figure is the matrix cannot directly represent multi-graphs. The fact that vertex 15 and vertex 16 are connected by edge 29 and 30 in the same direction is lost in the single 1-bit at $m_{v15,v16}$. However, many complex graph operations, e.g., the graph isomorphism test, as defined in graph theory for simple graphs, are based on adjacency matrices and can be implemented easily on top of a matrix representation with the help of libraries for linear algebra. The matrix representation has quadratic space complexity of $O(|A| \cdot |B|)$ and is therefore only space efficient for very dense binary relations. In the context of graphs, binary relations are typically sparse, i.e., $|R| \ll |A| \cdot |B|$. When used as a referential adjacency index, the matrix stores c instead of the bit at $m_{i,j}$.

	A	B
edge 20	v10	v11
edge 25	v10	v14
edge 21	v11	v11
edge 22	v11	v12
edge 23	v12	v11
edge 24	v12	v13
edge 26	v12	v15
edge 27	v13	v16
edge 28	v14	v15
edge 29	v15	v16
edge 30	v15	v16

$$
\begin{array}{c|ccccccc}
 & v10 & v11 & v12 & v13 & v14 & v15 & v16 \\
\hline
v10 & 0 & 1 & 0 & 0 & 1 & 0 & 0 \\
v11 & 0 & 1 & 1 & 0 & 0 & 0 & 0 \\
v12 & 0 & 1 & 0 & 1 & 0 & 1 & 0 \\
v13 & 0 & 0 & 0 & 0 & 0 & 0 & 1 \\
v14 & 0 & 0 & 0 & 0 & 0 & 1 & 0 \\
v15 & 0 & 0 & 0 & 0 & 0 & 0 & 1 \\
v16 & 0 & 0 & 0 & 0 & 0 & 0 & 0 \\
\end{array}
$$

Figure 6.7: Matrix representation for a binary relation $R(A, B)$ containing the edges of the graph shown in Figure 2.2.

Compressed sparse row (CSR). CSR is a concise and efficient lookup structure. To store a binary relation $R(A, B)$, it uses an array $\hat{a}$ of size $|A|$ and an array T of size $|R|$. T stores the value of b for each $(a, b) \in R$ in lexicographical order AB. Again, let a_i be the i-element in A according to its lexicographical order with $i \in [1, |A|]$. The array $\hat{a}$ stores at $\hat{a}[i]$ the start index of all tuples $(a_i, \aleph)$, so that $\hat{a}[1] = 1$ and $\hat{a}[i + 1] - \hat{a}[i] = |R(a_i, \aleph)|$.[2] Figure 6.8 shows the edges of the graph from Figure 2.2 encode in a CSR structure. As can be seen, all outgoing neighbors of vertex 12 can be found by looking at $\hat{a}[3]$, which yields 5. Then, $T[5]$ contains the first outgoing neighbors of vertex 12. The $\hat{a}[4] - \hat{a}[3] = 3$ consecutive fields starting with $T[5]$ contain the complete outgoing neighborhood of vertex 12. The pure CSR structure consists only of the arrays $\hat{a}$ and T. The vertex array and the edge array are shown for better illustration. Nevertheless, if a CSR structure is used to store a multi-graph, it is typically accompanied by an edge array (or edge label array) as show in the figure. A CSR structure avoids redundancy by factoring out all as and, in practice, requires less space than the matrix representation, particularly when the

[2]Assuming 1-based array indices.

graph is sparse. To keep $\hat{a}$ minimal in size, A has to be a dense domain. Lookups with a given a_i need a single access to $\hat{a}[i]$ to get the position of a's neighborhood in T. A binary search over the neighborhood efficiently finds a given b. Lookups without a given a_i require scanning the complete structure. A more updated friendly variant of CSR stores a separate T_a for each a and the memory address of T_a in $\hat{a}[i]$. Additionally, delta encoding and variable byte encoding as described in Section 6.2.1 can be applied to each T_a. When used as a referential adjacency index, T stores pairs (b, c).

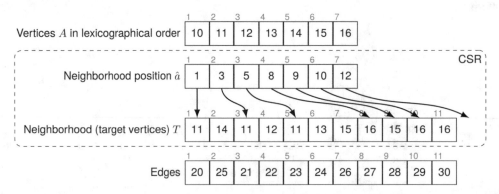

Figure 6.8: CSR structure for a binary relation $R(A, B)$ containing the edges of the graph shown in Figure 2.2.

Density-adaptive CSR.   Graphs often have very dense subgraphs as well as hubs—vertices with very high out-degree. CSR, however, treats all vertices equally. Representing the neighborhood set T_a of vertex a as a list of integers (vertex ids) is suitable for sparse neighborhood sets, i.e., neighborhood sets with low *density*. The density of a neighborhood set is the cardinality of the set divided by the value range of the set. Dense neighborhood sets can be stored more compactly as a bit sequence of length $|B|$, where the b'th bit is set to 1 if b is in the neighborhood set. A system can easily choose the representation for each T_a separately based on collected statistics about the density and the cardinality of the neighborhood set. For neighborhood sets with a non-uniform density, it is possible to divide a neighborhood set into blocks and choose the representation per block. Blocks are either defined individually for each T_a by identifying dense subsets of neighborhood set or globally with fixed range partitioning of B.

Re-pairing.   A CSR representation can be further compacted with an array compression technique called *re-pairing*. Re-pairing replaces frequent pairs in an array with single symbols. Applied to CSR, re-pairing scans over the array T and replaces the most frequent pair xy in T with a new symbol $s \notin B$. It records a rule $s \to xy$ in a dictionary. Only pairs $T[j-1]T[j]$ are considered such that $i \notin \hat{a}$, i.e., $T[j-1]$ and $T[j]$ belong to the adjacency list of the same a. The process is repeated as long as pairs appear more than once in T. Refinements of this basic procedure allow performing the replacement efficiently with a fixed amount of additional space on top of T.

6.4.2 COMPRESSED ADJACENCY REPRESENTATION

Many graphs exhibit *local similarity* in their adjacency structures. Vertices that are adjacent or in proximity share many neighbors. In social graphs, for instance, two persons that are friends typically have a high number of shared friends. Local similarity can be exploited for a more succinct representation of the adjacency. For that, the lexicographical order of vertices (or their ids) has to reflect the locality, i.e., the difference of the order number of two vertices should be small if the two vertices are proximal and share many neighbors. In web graphs, where vertices represent web page URLs and edges represent links, the lexicographical order URLs reflects the locality out of the box. In other graphs, a BFS or label propagation can be used to assign locality-reflecting ids to vertices. With locality-reflecting vertex ids, the adjacency can be compressed in various ways.

Delta encoded adjacency list.   A very simple technique represents the adjacency as a list of triples (a, d_a, B_a) sorted by a, where $B_a = \{b \mid (a, b) \in R\}$ are the outgoing neighbors of a and $d = |B_a|$ is the out degree of a. B_a is also sorted lexicographically. In this representation, two consecutive b in B_a as well as two B_a of consecutive a will have very small deltas because of locality-reflecting vertex ids. The smaller the deltas, the more succinct the representation. Delta encoding (and variable byte encoding), as described in Section 6.2.1, can be applied to each B_a. Compared to the use of delta encoding and variable byte encoding in CSR, the effect is considerably stronger on locality-reflecting vertex ids. Additionally, re-pairing can be applied to delta encoded adjacency lists. Deltas of locality-reflecting vertex ids are mostly small which increases the frequency of a pair of small deltas and by that also increases the compression effect of re-pairing.

Reference compressed adjacency list.   The representation of B_a in an adjacency list can be further compressed by encoding it as the difference to $B_{a'}$ where a' is the direct predecessor of a—a technique called *reference compression*. Therefore, a *copy list* encodes in a sequence of $|B_{a'}|$ bits which elements of $B_{a'}$ are also in B_a and a *list of extras* encodes $B_a \setminus B_{a'}$. Storing the copy list with a variant of run-length encoding makes it more succinct. The run-length encoding only needs to store the length of blocks of consecutive 0 and 1 bits and the number of such blocks, if it assumes the first block always contains 1 bits and may be of length 0. Likewise, the list of extras can be compacted with a variant of delta encoding. Note that a' itself may be encoded similarly as a difference to some a''. A threshold r limits the length of such reference chains.

A generalization of a reference compression encodes the difference to some predecessor a' of a such that the smallest representation of B_a is achieved. The reference to a' is stored as $a - a'$. To limit the number of possible references, $a - a' \leq W$ has to hold for e' where the compression window size W is a parameter for the compression process. Hence, the decompression has to read at most $W \cdot R$ entries for randomly accessing the adjacency of a single a and has to keep a window of $W \cdot R$ entries in memory when scanning the whole adjacency structure.

K^2-trees. k^2-ary tree structures provide a succinct representation of an adjacency matrix. Specifically, they exploit the sparseness of the adjacency matrix and store the adjacency in a compact Quadtree structure [Finkel and Bentley, 1974] of height $\lceil \log_k n \rceil$. Each node in this tree has a single bit assigned indicating whether there is at least one 1-bit in the corresponding sub matrix. A node assigned zero means that all elements in the sub matrix are zeros and the node does not have any children. Formally, for an adjacency matrix m, a node at position i, j in level l is assigned the $\bigvee_{x,y} m_{x,y}$ with $i \cdot k^l \leq x < (i + 1) \cdot k^l$ and $j \cdot k^l \leq y < (j + 1) \cdot k^l$. The tree leaves—nodes at level $l = 0$—correspond to matrix elements. Physically, a k^2-tree is represented by two bit sets, one for the internal nodes (except leaves) and one for the leaves only. Bits are assigned according to a level-wise traversal of the tree, i.e., first all bits of level one, then all bits of level two, and so on. The compression effect stems from the fact that the tree omits all direct and indirect children of nodes assigned zero and hence can represent large all-zero sub matrices by a single bit. Obviously, this technique exploits locality and requires a locality-reflecting vertex order. Empirical studies conducted particularly for the k^2-tree show that BFS ordering generally achieves good compression rates while being affordable. The parameter k allows modifying the height of the tree at the cost of larger internal nodes with more child nodes. Variants allow to set the k per tree level. The k^2-ary tree representation is not designed for a dynamic adjacency with frequent edge insertions/deletions as each of these operations might trigger a rewriting of multiple internal nodes in the tree.

6.5   REACHABILITY INDEXING

In its most generalized form, reachability indexing concerns access operations on the transitive closure of a binary relation. Transitive closure is an essential element of property graph query languages, precisely (conjunctive) regular path queries (cf. Section 3.1) as well as regular property graph queries (cf. Section 3.2), where transitive closure is one operator of the regular property graph algebra. Given a finite binary relation R of graph vertices, the transitive closure operator yields $TC(R)$, which is the transitive closure of R. Note that relation R is not limited to edges of the graph, but can be any binary relation of vertices derived from the graph by means of query operators. In the following, we will interchangeably use R to denote the relation as well as the directed graph described by this relation. Further, let $V(R)$ be the set of all vertices mentioned in R, i.e., $V(R) = \{v \mid \exists x : (v, x) \in R \text{ or } (x, v) \in R\}$. Two fundamental operations may be executed on the top of $TC(R)$.

Reachability check. A reachability check $R.\texttt{reachCheck}(u, v)$ tests whether a vertex v is reachable from another vertex u of a binary relation R, i.e., test whether (u, v) is in the transitive closure of the R, so that $R.\texttt{reachCheck}(u, v) = ((u, v) \in TC(R))$. Generalized to sets, we have $R.\texttt{reachCheck}(P)$, which gives all pairs in $(u,v) \in P$ that are in $TC(R)$, so that $R.\texttt{reachCheck}(P) = \{(u,v) \in P \mid R.\texttt{reachCheck}(u,v)\}$.

Reachability search.   A reachability search $R.\texttt{reachSearch}(u)$ finds all vertices $v \neq u$ that are reachable from vertex u of a binary relation R, i.e., finds all v such that (u,v) is in the transitive closure of the R, so that $R.\texttt{reachSearch}(u) = \{v \mid (u,v) \in TC(R)\}$. Generalized to sets, we have $R.\texttt{reachSearch}(U)$, which finds for all given vertices $u \in U$ all pairs in (u,v) that are in $TC(R)$, so that $R.\texttt{reachSearch}(U) = \{(u,v) \mid u \in U \text{ and } v \in R.\texttt{reachSearch}(u)\}$.

6.5.1   GENERAL CONSIDERATIONS

In a graph database, it is reasonable to assume that set $V(R)$ containing all vertices appearing in R is known. Then, obviously, a reachability search can be answered by reachability checks and vice versa. Precisely, $R.\texttt{reachSearch}(U) = R.\texttt{reachCheck}(U \times V(R))$ and $R.\texttt{reachCheck}(P) = R.\texttt{reachSearch}(\{u \mid (u,\cdot) \in P\}) \cap P$. Which of the two operations is preferable depends on the size of R, $TC(R)$, $V(R)$, U, and P as well as on the complexity of $\texttt{reachCheck}(\cdot)$ and $\texttt{reachSearch}(\cdot)$, respectively.

The main challenge for both kinds of reachability operations is that $TC(R)$ can become very large (at most $|V(R)|^2$) if R is very dense on $V(R)$ or a subset of $V(R)$. Reachability indexing aims at reducing the online processing cost of a reachability operation by investing storage space and offline processing cost. Two extreme cases define the spectrum of this trade-off. Without any indexing, no ($O(1)$) storage space and no ($O(1)$) offline processing cost are invested and reachability operations have an online processing cost of $O(|V(R)| + |R|)$. The most aggressive indexing stores $TC(R)$, which is a storage space investment of $O(|V(R)|^2)$ and an offline processing cost investment of $O(|V(R)| \cdot |R|)$, cf. [Su et al., 2017]. The resulting online processing costs differ for $\texttt{reachCheck}(\cdot)$ and $\texttt{reachSearch}(\cdot)$ and depend on the representation of $TC(R)$. In the best case, $R.\texttt{reachCheck}(u,v)$ can be performed by a single lookup, so that the online processing cost of $R.\texttt{reachCheck}(P)$ is $O(|P|)$. However, in the worst case query plan $|P| = |V(R)|^2$. Also in the best case, $R.\texttt{reachSearch}(u)$ can be performed by a single lookup plus constant delay enumeration of all resulting v, so that the online processing cost of $R.\texttt{reachSearch}(U)$ is $O(|U| \cdot |S|)$, where $|S|$ is the average number of v returned by $R.\texttt{reachSearch}(u)$ for each $u \in U$. Again, in the worst case $|U| \cdot |S| = |V(R)|^2$.

All reachability index structures offer trade-offs between those two extreme cases. The general aim is to accomplish an online processing cost less than $O(|V(R)| + |R|)$ (no indexing) for a storage space and offline processing cost investment less than $O(|V(R)|^2)$ and $O(|V(R)| \cdot |R|)$ (storing $TC(R)$), respectively. All so far proposed reachability index techniques have an offline processing cost of $O(|V(R)| + |R|)$ or more, i.e., require at least one BFS or DFS search over R.

In a general graph database system: (1) R is usually an intermediate result of an individual query and can only be considered constant in a very limited scope; and (2) the query processing typically builds on set-oriented reachability search operations ($R.\texttt{reachSearch}(U)$), cf. Chapter 7. In contrast, reachability indexing techniques proposed in the literature and discussed in the following assume a static R (typically assuming it to be the set of edges of a given graph) and concern single-pair reachability checks (R.reachCheck(u, v)) only. While these methods achieve very good cost trade-offs and their usage appears worthwhile in the considered settings, it is unclear to what extent they are applicable in general graph database systems.

6.5.2   TECHNIQUES

A large body of work concerns index structures supporting reachability checks. Most approaches index R by computing a label (or a code) for each vertex. Do not confuse the reachability index labels with the vertex labels allowed by the property graph model. The reachability index label $L(u)$ of a vertex u encodes the reachability to other vertices in R. Each labeling technique also specifies a predicate $P(u, v)$, which can be evaluated on $L(u)$ and $L(v)$ for a vertex pair u and v. We can distinguish between exact and approximate labeling techniques.

Exact labeling.   With an exact labeling technique, the evaluation of the predicate $P(u, v)$ is sufficient to answer a reachability check R.reachCheck(u, v), so that R.reachCheck$(u, v) = P(u, v)$ no matter if v is reachable from u or not.

Approximate labeling.   By sacrificing exactness, approximate labeling techniques try to achieve smaller index sizes. The first kind of approximation allows false negatives, i.e., R.reachCheck$(u, v) = P(u, v)$ holds only if $P(u, v)$ is true, but if $P(u, v)$ is false we cannot conclude that v is unreachable from u. The second kind of approximation allows false positives, i.e., R.reachCheck$(u, v) = P(u, v)$ holds only if $P(u, v)$ is false, but if $P(u, v)$ is true we cannot conclude that v is reachable from u. In both cases, $P(u, v)$ can answer R.reachCheck(u, v) only for a subset of possible pairs of u and v. The remaining pairs require post processing either on R or on some additional information kept in the index next to the labels.

Three principle labeling approaches have received most consideration: (1) *2-hop labels*, (2) *tree-based labels*, and (3) *approximate transitive closure labels*. Next to these three, other approaches have been proposed for which we refer the interested reader to specialized surveys mentioned in Section 6.7.

2-Hop Labeling

2-hop labeling is an indexing scheme directly applicable to arbitrary directed or undirected graphs. Assuming directed graphs as in PGM, 2-hop labels store for each vertex lists of reachable vertices such that the reachability between any pair of vertices can be determined by a single join of the lists of these two vertices. Therefore, each vertex v is assigned a label $L(v) = (L_{in}(v), L_{out}(v))$ such that $L_{in}(v)$ and $L_{out}(v)$ are sets of vertices from which v can be reached (inbound hop) and a set of vertices that are reachable from v (outbound hop), respectively. The labels are chosen in such a way that each reachability is covered by two hops, i.e., for any given pair of vertices u and v with $u \neq v$, the intersection of u's outbound hops $L_{out}(u)$ and v's inbound hops $L_{in}(v)$ is not empty if and only if u reaches v. Any labeling fulfilling this condition is called a *2-hop cover*. Note that 2-hop labeling does not cover trivial self-reachability over paths of length zero. However, where this is of concern, self-reachability results can be easily added by the surrounding query processing.

Figure 6.9 shows a reachability index based on 2-hop labeling. Edges in the graph may also act as hops in the index. For better visibility, the figure shows in- and outbound hops that are not original edges as dotted and dashed line in red and blue color, respectively. For such an index, we can easily determine, e.g., that vertex 10 reaches vertex 20, since $L_{out}(10) \cap L_{in}(20) = \{15\} \neq \emptyset$. Similarly, vertex 16 does not reach vertex 13, since $L_{out}(16) \cap L_{in}(13) = \emptyset$.

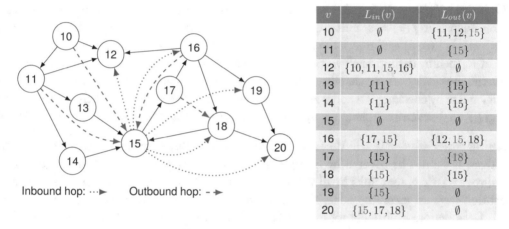

v	$L_{in}(v)$	$L_{out}(v)$
10	$\emptyset$	$\{11, 12, 15\}$
11	$\emptyset$	$\{15\}$
12	$\{10, 11, 15, 16\}$	$\emptyset$
13	$\{11\}$	$\{15\}$
14	$\{11\}$	$\{15\}$
15	$\emptyset$	$\emptyset$
16	$\{17, 15\}$	$\{12, 15, 18\}$
17	$\{15\}$	$\{18\}$
18	$\{15\}$	$\{15\}$
19	$\{15\}$	$\emptyset$
20	$\{15, 17, 18\}$	$\emptyset$

Inbound hop: ···▶   Outbound hop: - ▶

Figure 6.9: Example graph with 2-hop reachability index labels $L_{in}(v)$ and $L_{out}(v)$.

For undirected graphs, 2-hop labeling scheme requires only a single vertex list. The approach can be generalized to distance queries by storing a distance $d(x, v)$ and $d(v, x)$ together with every x in $L_{in}(v)$ and $L_{out}(v)$, respectively, such that the minimum of $d(u, x) + d(x, v)$ among all $x \in L_{out}(u) \cap L_{in}(v)$ is equal to (or sufficiently approximates) the distance between u and v. To facilitate path retrieval, it is possible to store the actual shortest path from v to x and from v to x with every x in $L_{in}(v)$ and $L_{out}(v)$, respectively.

The main challenge is to efficiently compute the *minimal 2-hop cover*, i.e., a minimal set of labels that form a 2-hop cover for a given graph. Finding a minimum 2-hop cover of a directed graph is an NP-hard problem. However, the problem can be cast as an instance of the set cover problem to obtain a 2-hop cover that is larger than the minimal cover at most a factor in $O(\log |V(R)|)$. The index size is in $O(|V(R)| \log |V(R)|)$ with each vertex getting at most $\log |V(R)|$ hops assigned. Hops can be stored in lexicographically sorted order so that the intersection can be computed efficiently.

Tree-Based Labeling

Tree-based labels are derived by depth-first traversal of a spanning tree of R. In general, this is done in four steps. (1) Transform R into a directed acyclic graph (DAG). (2) Ensuring the DAG has a single root vertex. (3) Traverse the DAG of R depth-first to form a spanning tree and compute the labels. (4) Compensate for edges in R not covered by the spanning tree.

DAG transformation.   Let's denote the DAG of R as $\mathrm{dag}(R)$. In case R is not already acyclic, cycles in R constitute strongly connected components (SCCs). There exist efficient algorithms that find the set of all SCCs $\mathrm{scc}(R)$ in R in $O(|V(R)| + |R|)$ time [Slota et al., 2014, Tarjan, 1972]. We can construct $\mathrm{dag}(R)$ by collapsing every SCCs $C_i \in \mathrm{scc}(R)$ into a single vertex, i.e., replacing it by a representative c_i and maintain the connections from and to the SCC. Let $m : V(R) \mapsto V(\mathrm{dag}(R))$ be the mapping from vertices in R to their representatives in $\mathrm{dag}(R)$, such that $f(u) = c_i$ if $\exists C_i \in \mathrm{scc}(R) : u \in V(C_i)$ and else $f(u) = u$. Then, $\mathrm{dag}(R) = \{(m(u), m(v)) \mid (u, v) \in R \wedge m(u) \neq m(v)\}$. Obviously, $|\mathrm{dag}(R)| \leq |R|$. Assume $C \subseteq R$ is a SCC in R, then by definition all vertices in C are pair-wise reachable, such that $\forall u, v \in V(C) :$ $R.\mathrm{reachCheck}(u, v)$. A reachability operation $R.\mathrm{reachCheck}(u, v)$ can be processed over $\mathrm{dag}(R)$ and m by checking if u and v are in the same SCC or their respective SCCs are reachable in $\mathrm{dag}(R)$, so that $R.\mathrm{reachCheck}(u, v) = (m(u) = m(v) \vee \mathrm{dag}(R).\mathrm{reachCheck}(m(u), m(v)))$.

Ensuring single root.   If a DAG is partitioned or has multiple vertices without any incoming edges, it cannot be covered by a single tree. A simple way around that is to introduce a virtual root vertex ρ, that links to all vertices without an incoming edge. In case all vertices of a partition have an incoming edge, the virtual root links to one arbitrary vertex in that partition. Let's denote a virtually rooted DAG of R as $\mathrm{vrdag}(R)$. Assuming $\mathrm{dag}(R) = (V, E)$ and $X = \{v \mid \nexists u, (u, v) \in E\}$, then $\mathrm{vrdag}(R) = (V \cup \{\rho\}, E \cup \{(\rho, v) \mid v \in X\})$ if $|X| > 1$ else $\mathrm{vrdag}(R) = (V, E)$. In case the DAG is not partitioned and all vertices have an incoming edge, an arbitrary vertex is marked as root.

Label computation.   For the label computation, the DAG $\mathrm{vrdag}(R)$ is traversed depth-first (DFS) starting from the root vertex. Multiple labeling schemes have been proposed in this setting, but follow the same principle of numbering the vertices in the spanning tree formed by the DFS. During the DFS a counter c is used to assign the an interval $[v_{min}, v_{max}]$ as reachability index label $L(v)$ to each vertex $v \in V(\mathrm{vrdag}(R))$ with v_{min} and v_{max} being positive numbers and $v_{min} \leq v_{max}$. The DFS starts with $c = 0$. Along the way, v_{max} is the postorder in the traversal, i.e., c is assigned to v and then increased after visiting all children of v and before backtracking to v's parent; v_{min} is set to c when the traversal visits v for the first time, i.e., it is the smallest postorder of all children of v. Given such labels, a vertex v is reachable from a vertex u in the spanning tree if and only if v_{max} is included in the label of u, such that $P(u, v) = v_{max} \in [u_{min}, u_{max}]$. Figure 6.10 shows an example of such labels. The number shown within the vertex denotes the vertex id, while the number shown on top of each vertex indicates the postorder assigned by the DFS used to calculate the labels. The virtual root vertex and its edges are drawn dashed.

The red edges show the route the DFS took. As can be seen, in the spanning tree (only the red edges) rooted at vertex 10, vertex 15 is reachable from vertex 11 but is not reachable from vertex 12. Only considering the reachability labels yield the same: $P(11, 15) = 0 \in [0, 5]$, while $P(12, 15) = 0 \notin [3, 4]$.

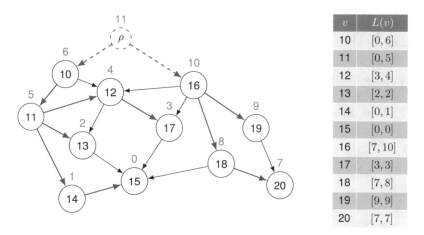

v	$L(v)$
10	$[0, 6]$
11	$[0, 5]$
12	$[3, 4]$
13	$[2, 2]$
14	$[0, 1]$
15	$[0, 0]$
16	$[7, 10]$
17	$[3, 3]$
18	$[7, 8]$
19	$[9, 9]$
20	$[7, 7]$

Figure 6.10: A DAG with spanning trees formed by two DFS and the resulting reachability index labels $L(v)$.

Compensating non-tree edges with link table.   There are multiple ways to take non-tree edges into account. The simplest form is to maintain the transitive closure of all non-tree edges in a table, the *link table*. Therefore a non-tree edge (u, v) is represented using the reachability intervals as $(u_{min}, [v_{max}, v_{max}])$. The transitive closure results from applying the reachability predicate $P(\cdot, \cdot)$. Given two non-tree edges $(u_{min}, [v_{max}, v_{max}])$ and $(w_{min}, [x_{max}, x_{max}])$ with $P(v, w) = w_{max} \in [v_{min}, v_{max}]$, then $(u_{min}, [x_{max}, x_{max}])$ is also in the transitive closure. Obviously, with t non-tree edges in the graph, the size of the link table is in $O(t^2)$. Hence, the link table approach is only feasible for sparse graphs where $t \ll V(\texttt{vrdag}(R))$.

Compensating non-tree edges with tree cover.   Another approach to reflect non-tree edges in the labels is to let each vertex inherit the labels of its outgoing non-tree neighbors. Such labels are also called a tree cover, since a spanning tree is used to cover the whole graph. For a tree cover, a reachability index label for any vertex v is defined as a set of intervals $\{[v_{min_1}, v_{max_1}], [v_{min_2}, v_{max_2}], \dots\}$. Every non-tree edge (u, v) implies that $L(v) \subseteq L(u)$. Such labels can be constructed easily while computing the tree labels as discussed before. During the DFS, each outgoing edge of a vertex u to an already visited neighbor v is a non-tree edge (u, v). Since v has already been visited its label $L(v)$ has already been computed and can be added to the label of u, such that it is updated to $L(u) \cup L(v)$. The label created this way may contain overlapping or adjacent intervals. These can be merged to save space. Given such labels, the reachability check is the same as for the tree-only labels. A vertex v is reachable from a vertex u in the graph if and only if v_{max} is included in the label of u, such that $P(u, v) = \bigvee_i \left(v_{max} \in [u_{min_i}, u_{max_i}] \right)$. Note that outgoing non-tree edges of a vertex v do not change v_{max}. By the definition of non-tree edges, only intervals with an upper bound less than v_{max} are inherited. Figure 6.11 shows the same DAG as in Figure 6.10 with the reachability index labels resulting from the inclusion of non-tree edges. For instance, vertex 13 has a non-tree edge to vertex 15 and hence inherits its label so that $L(15) = \{[0, 0]\} \subseteq L(13) = \{[2, 2], [0, 0]\}$. The merging of overlapping or adjacent intervals can be seen for vertex 12. Here the two adjacent intervals $[2, 2]$ and $[3, 4]$ are merged to $[2, 4]$. In the example graph, vertex 16 reaches vertex 15 but not vertex 14. The reachability index allows deducing the same, since $P(16, 15) = 0 \in \{[7, 10], [2, 4], [0, 0]\}$ while $P(16, 14) = 1 \notin \{[7, 10], [2, 4], [0, 0]\}$.

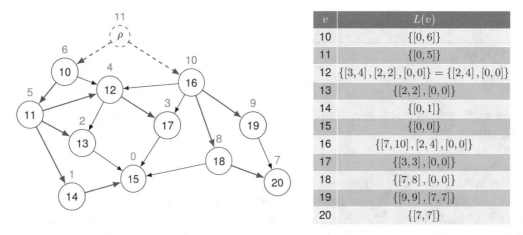

v	$L(v)$
10	$\{[0, 6]\}$
11	$\{[0, 5]\}$
12	$\{[3, 4], [2, 2], [0, 0]\} = \{[2, 4], [0, 0]\}$
13	$\{[2, 2], [0, 0]\}$
14	$\{[0, 1]\}$
15	$\{[0, 0]\}$
16	$\{[7, 10], [2, 4], [0, 0]\}$
17	$\{[3, 3], [0, 0]\}$
18	$\{[7, 8], [0, 0]\}$
19	$\{[9, 9], [7, 7]\}$
20	$\{[7, 7]\}$

Figure 6.11: The DAG from Figure 6.10 with reachability index labels $L(v)$ and compensation for non-tree edges.

Size of tree cover.   As an obvious drawback of the tree-based labeling procedure, the necessary compensation of non-tree edges can lead to a large number of intervals that need to be stored for a single vertex, such that space complexity of a tree-based labeling index is in $O(|V(\text{vrdag}(R))|^2)$. Not considering the possibility of interval merging, the total number of intervals needed in the index depends on which tree cover the DFS selects. The optimal tree cover allows for the fewest intervals to index the graph. However, the optimal tree cover can be found efficiently by considering all vertices in some topological order o and retaining for each vertex only the incoming edge coming from the vertex with the largest number of predecessor vertices in the original DAG according to the topological order o. The possibility to merge intervals depends on the order in which the DFS traverses the children of a vertex in the tree cover. An efficient solution to this combinatorial problem has not been proposed yet.

Approximate Tree-Based Labeling

The space requirements for tree-based labeling index can be reduced further by compressing the index with approximate labels. A simple compression strategy is to merge non-adjacent/non-overlapping intervals. As a consequence, this compression introduces false positives, i.e., pairs of vertices u and v for which $P(u, v) = \top$ although u does not reach v and requires a procedure to handle false positives and still return the correct result for each query. The most aggressive interval compression is to merge all intervals of each label to a single interval. While this efficiently reduces the number of intervals, it also introduces a large number of false positives.

Hence, the challenge is to reduce the space complexity from quadratic to a linear $O(k \cdot |V(\mathtt{vrdag}(R))|)$, while investing a constant factor k with $k \ll |V(\mathtt{vrdag}(R))|$ to significantly reduce the number of false positives. Comparing two random tree covers, single interval compression typically introduces different sets of false positives with only a small overlap. One approach is to utilize this observation by using k random tree covers with a single interval compression to compute labels consisting of exactly k intervals. Another approach builds on the optimal tree cover and directly merges intervals such that each vertex has at most k intervals while minimizing the number of elements appearing in approximate intervals with a dynamic programming procedure.

To deal with remaining false positives, it is important to mark the intervals that resulted from merging as *approximate*. The remaining intervals that have not been merged are marked as *exact*. If $P(u, v) = \top$ and the interval of u providing the positive answer is exact, we can safely conclude that $R.\mathtt{reachCheck}(u, v) = \top$. If $P(u, v) = \top$ and u has only approximate intervals, the query processing performs a guided search through the graph. The guided search exploits the fact that to reach v from u, v has to be also reachable from at least one of outgoing neighbors of u. Hence, the query processing performs a DFS starting from u. For each vertex u' with an outgoing neighbor w, it recursively tests $P(w, v)$ until either w confirms the reachability of v with an exact interval or all outgoing neighbors u' confirm that v is not reachable. Additionally, the DFS can be pruned by exploiting the topological level τ since vertex u cannot reach vertex v if its topological level is less or equal than w, i.e., $\tau(u) \le \tau(v)$.

Figure 6.12 shows approximate labels for the DAG from Figure 6.10. Here, $k = 1$ so that each label consists of exactly one interval. The approximate intervals are marked with *. What can be seen is that the label of vertex 19 indicates that it can reach vertex 18, which is a false positive. Query processing can detect that by looking recursively at the outgoing neighbors of vertex 19. In this case, vertex 20 is the only outgoing neighbor and its label indicates that vertex 18 is not reachable. Consider reachability of vertex 16 to vertex 11, checking all neighbors of vertex 16 can be avoided since $\tau(16) \le \tau(11)$ and hence 16 cannot reach 11.

Approximate Transitive Closure Labeling

As mentioned before, a trivial reachability index is to store the complete transitive closure. In such an index, each vertex u would be assigned with a label $L(u) = L_{out}(u)$ where $L_{out}(u) \subseteq$

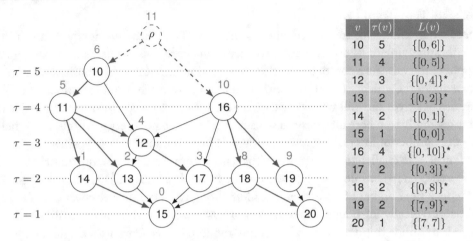

v	$\tau(v)$	$L(v)$
10	5	$\{[0,6]\}$
11	4	$\{[0,5]\}$
12	3	$\{[0,4]\}^*$
13	2	$\{[0,2]\}^*$
14	2	$\{[0,1]\}$
15	1	$\{[0,0]\}$
16	4	$\{[0,10]\}^*$
17	2	$\{[0,3]\}^*$
18	2	$\{[0,8]\}^*$
19	2	$\{[7,9]\}^*$
20	1	$\{[7,7]\}$

Figure 6.12: The DAG from Figure 6.10 drawn in topological levels $\tau(v)$ and with approximative reachability index labels $L(v)$ (approximative labels marked with *).

$V(R)$ is the set of all vertices reached by u including u itself. A vertex u reach v if and only if $P(u, v) = v \in L_{out}(u)$. Naturally, such an index has quadratic space complexity. However, similar to approximate tree-based labeling, it is possible to store a k-sized approximation of $L_{out}(u)$ so that the space complexity reduces to linear $O(k \cdot |V(\text{vrdag}(R))|)$ with k being constant. We call this *approximate transitive closure labeling*. Like tree-based labeling, the approximate transitive closure labeling is assumed to operate on a DAG.

One approximation technique, called *independent permutation labeling*, utilizes a random permutation π of the vertex set $V(\text{vrdag}(R))$ to store the top-k vertices $v \in L_{out}(u)$. The top-k vertices according to π have the k smallest position numbers $\pi(v) \in (1, |V(\text{vrdag}(R))|)$. Another approximation technique, called *Bloom filter labeling*, for such an approximation uses Bloom filters to store a k-bit long representation of $L_{out}(u)$.

Approximate transitive closure labels involve false positives. If the index finds a negative result for $P(u, v) = v \in L_{out}(u)$, it can quickly answer reachability checks in $O(1)$ time. In case of a positive result, a DFS guided by the reachability index is conducted to provide a correct answer. In other words, approximate transitive closure labeling aims at early pruning of negative results and avoiding expensive search for non-reachability. The Bloom filter labeling was shown to have better pruning power than independent permutation labeling while using the same space. Obviously, approximate transitive closure labeling works particularly well for graphs where most vertex pairs are not reachable, i.e., $|TC(R)| \ll |V(\text{vrdag}(R))|^2$. Both approximation techniques have a bounded probability for false positives. This naturally depends on k. The more space one is willing to invest, the higher the pruning power of the index, the better the query performance.

The pruning power of approximate transitive closure labeling can be increased by storing not only an approximation of $L_{out}(u)$ but also of $L_{in}(u)$. Here, $L_{in}(u)$ is the set of all vertices that reach u including u itself. A vertex u can reach v only if $P(u, v) = v \in L_{out}(u) \vee u \in L_{in}(v)$. If either $v \notin L_{out}(u)$ or $u \notin L_{in}(v)$ is false, u does not reach v. Additionally, varying approximation for $L_{out}(\cdot)$ and $L_{in}(\cdot)$ by using a different random permutation or a different hash function in the Bloom filter increases the chances of pruning.

Figure 6.13 shows an example DAG with approximate transitive closure labeling. As approximation technique the example uses a trivial Bloom filter which hashes respective vertices with $h(v) = (v \mod 7)$ and stores the set of resulting hashes. The same hash function is used for $L_{in}(v)$ and $L_{out}(v)$. The number next to a vertex shows the hash value of the vertex. The table shows the resulting labels for each vertex. Consider for example vertex 12 and vertex 18. With the index, we can quickly determine that vertex 12 does not reach vertex 18, since $h(18) = 4$ and $4 \notin L_{out}(12)$. For vertex 10 to vertex 18, however, $h(18) = 4 \in L_{out}(10)$ indicates reachability. However, checking $L_{in}(\cdot)$, reveals truthfully that vertex 10 does not reach vertex 18 since $h(10) = 3$ and $3 \notin L_{in}(18)$. When querying the reachability from vertex 11 to vertex 18, both $L_{out}(\cdot)$ and $L_{in}(\cdot)$ indicate reachability. In such a case the guided DFS starts from vertex 11 and recursively checks the reachability predicate. As can be seen, this allows pruning the DFS at vertex 12 ($h(18) \notin L_{out}(12)$), vertex 13 ($h(18) \notin L_{out}(13)$), and vertex 14 ($h(18) \notin L_{out}(14)$). With no vertices left to explore, it can be correctly concluded that vertex 11 does not reach vertex 18.

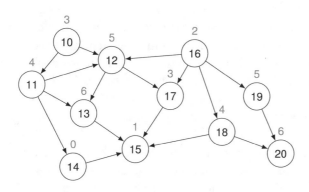

v	$L_{in}(v)$	$L_{out}(v)$
10	$\{3\}$	$\{0, 1, 3, 4, 5, 6\}$
11	$\{3, 4\}$	$\{0, 1, 3, 4, 5, 6\}$
12	$\{2, 3, 4, 5\}$	$\{1, 3, 5, 6\}$
13	$\{3, 4, 5, 6\}$	$\{1, 6\}$
14	$\{0, 3, 4\}$	$\{0, 1\}$
15	$\{0, 1, 2, 3, 4, 5, 6\}$	$\{1\}$
16	$\{2\}$	$\{1, 2, 3, 4, 5, 6\}$
17	$\{2, 3, 4, 5\}$	$\{1, 3\}$
18	$\{2, 4\}$	$\{1, 4, 6\}$
19	$\{2, 5\}$	$\{5, 6\}$
20	$\{2, 4, 5\}$	$\{6\}$

Figure 6.13: Example DAG with approximate transitive closure labeling using Bloom filter labels $L_{in}(v)$ and $L_{out}(v)$ and $h(v) = (v \mod 7)$ as hash function.

6.6 STRUCTURAL INDEXING

Given a query language L and graph G, we can view L as inducing a partitioning of the "objects" in G (depending on L, objects could be nodes, vertices, paths, or more complex graph structures). We can say that objects o_1 and o_2 are L-equivalent (denoted $o_1 \equiv_L o_2$) if and only if for every query in L either both o_1 and o_2 appear in the evaluation of the query on G or neither appears in the query results. In other words, the two objects are indistinguishable as far as L is concerned, and hence can be grouped together during processing queries of L on G. The $\equiv_L$-partition of G is in this sense the ideal basis for constructing data structures for accelerating evaluation of L.

There are two difficulties, however, which could potentially block our way to this ideal situation. First, computing the $\equiv_L$-partition of G might be impractical or even impossible, given that typical query languages have an infinite number of expressions, and the number of possible partitions of a finite set, while still finite, is exponential in the size of G. Second, even if we could efficiently compute the partition, it might be too fine-grained to be of any significant value, i.e., the partition blocks might be too small, to the point that little compression of the graph is obtained by computing the partition. As an example, if we consider first-order logic (i.e., textbook relational algebra) as a query language on graphs, then language equivalence amounts to isomorphism [Libkin, 2004], which is intractable to compute and, furthermore, grouping together isomorphic structures can give us very little compression of graphs in many application domains.

Fortunately, we can successfully overcome both of these difficulties for some expressive graph query languages. To overcome the first hurdle, the general strategy is to identify a fragment L' of L which is rich enough to capture practical classes of queries, while still permitting an efficient construction of $\equiv_{L'}$. This is typically achieved by identifying a tractable "structural" characterization $\equiv$ of $\equiv_{L'}$, purely in terms of the structure of the fixed instance G (i.e., $\equiv$ is independent of L' in the sense that the $\equiv$-partition can be constructed based on the graph structure of G alone). A query $Q' \in L'$ can then be rewritten and evaluated in terms of (an index data structure I on) the $\equiv$-partition of G, perhaps with post-processing to materialize the results of the query. Given a query Q in the full language L, the strategy is then to: (1) decompose Q into subqueries $Q_1, ..., Q_n$, each in L'; (2) evaluate each Q_i directly on the structural index I; and (3) further process the results of the subqueries to obtain the final result of evaluating Q on G.

As an example, consider structural indexing for CQ. In general, CQ does not have a tractable structural characterization [Rossman, 2008]. Fortunately, we can identify large fragments of CQ which do, such as classes of acyclic CQ's where language equivalence is characterized precisely by variations of the structural notion of graph simulation which are computable in polynomial time [Picalausa et al., 2014]. Given a cyclic CQ query Q, we can then decompose it into acyclic subqueries $Q_1, \ldots, Q_n$ which we answer directly on the structural index, and then join and post-process these intermediate results to obtain the full evaluation result of Q [Picalausa et al., 2012].

Structural characterizations of language equivalence in terms of language-independent notions of bisimulation and simulation equivalence have been identified for large practical fragments of subgraph pattern matching queries and navigational path queries [Fletcher et al., 2015a, Picalausa et al., 2014]. Furthermore, graph simulation and bisimulation partitioning have been shown to be efficiently computable not only in main memory settings but also in external memory and distributed environments [Hellings et al., 2012, Luo et al., 2013a,c, van Heeswijk et al., 2016].

Concerning the second hurdle, it has been observed on data arising in practical applications that (bi)simulation-based structural indexing can lead to orders of magnitude size compression of database instances [Agterdenbos et al., 2016, Luo et al., 2013b, Picalausa, 2013].

6.7   BIBLIOGRAPHIC AND HISTORICAL NOTES

The representation of ternary relations is an obvious problem for RDF, since the RDF data model defines RDF as ternary relations. Early RDF management systems, so-called triple stores, used a triple table in conjunction with dictionary compression based on a relational database engine. Examples are Jena [McBride, 2001], Jena2 [Wilkinson et al., 2003], Oracle [Chong et al., 2005], and Virtuoso [Erling and Mikhailov, 2007]. Later this approach was refined with additional compression and exhaustive indexing. Seminal works in this respect are Hexastore [Weiss et al., 2008] and RDF-3X [Neumann and Weikum, 2008, 2010a,b]. RDF-3X used a combination of exhaustive indexing with six primary indexes, projection indexes, delta and variable byte encoding as shown in Figure 6.3, and still represents the state of the art for RDF representation. The more recent system RDFox [Motik et al., 2014, Nenov et al., 2015] varied the RDF-3X concept by using a combination of three index columns added to a triple table and three secondary projection indexes.

Neo4j, the graph database system that made PGM popular, uses a set of fixed-length record tables. Similar to dictionary compressed triple tables, Neo4j leverages the fact that fixed-length records are easily byte addressable. It maintains a set of vertex records, a set of edge records, and property records. All three record types include index columns. Particularly, the edge records make heavy use of index columns, pointing to the source and target vertex, double-linking edges with the same source vertex, and double-linking edges with the same target vertex.

Pivoted tables are appealing because they allow to fully utilize the power of a relational engine. First, pivoted tables have been discussed in the context of RDF including a consideration of the different partitioning schemes based on emerging schemas to deal with schema flexibility of a pivoted table [Abadi et al., 2007, Wilkinson, 2006]. Emerging schemas can be found automatically, using (1) a standard clustering algorithm [Chu et al., 2007], (2) starting from every distinct property set and merging infrequent ones [Pham et al., 2015], or (3) partitioning entities on-the-fly based on their schema similarity [Herrmann et al., 2014a,b]. In combination with a column store engine, pivoted tables are feasible without partitioning along emerging schemas, since the column store vertically partitions the pivoted table by property [Abadi et al., 2007]. SAP HANA Graph follows this approach and represents a property graph with two pivoted tables, one for vertices and one for edges [Paradies et al., 2015, Rudolf et al., 2013]. For efficient traversals, SAP HANA Graph additionally exhaustively indexes the adjacency with CSR data structures [Hauck et al., 2015]. Exhaustive adjacency indexing was also proposed for graph processing systems [Shun and Blelloch, 2013]. Pivoted tables with schema hashing is a technique developed and used by IBM for RDF [Bornea et al., 2013] as well as PGM [Sun et al., 2015].

Adjacency matrices [Cormen et al., 2009] and CSR [Gustavson, 1978] are well-established concepts in computer science. They received new consideration with interest in management and processing of graph data, which lead to refinements such as density-adaptive CSR [Aberger et al., 2016] and re-pairing [Claude and Navarro, 2010a,b]. Also detailed experimental comparison of different adjacency representations have been conducted [Blandford et al., 2004]. The development of adjacency compression techniques such as reference compression [Boldi and Vigna, 2004] and K^2-trees [Brisaboa et al., 2009] has been mainly motivated by the need to analyze Web graphs. However, Apostolico and Drovandi [2009] showed that BFS provides a reasonable method to generate locality-reflecting vertex ids for any graph so that these compression techniques are applicable to any adjacency structure. Other approaches on adjacency compression not discussed in this chapter but worth mentioning are Boldi et al. [2011] and Grabowski and Bieniecki [2011]. There is even work that tries to build a complete PGM storage solely on K^2-trees [Álvarez-García et al., 2010]. Adjacency compression can also be used for simple reachability indexing by storing the transitive closure in a compressing data structure. Particularly, for read-heavy workloads of regular path queries, which can be expensive but do not necessarily have a large result set, this is a promising approach [Tetzel et al., 2017].

Reachability indexing is a well-studied topic, too. Tree-based labeling is the classic approach in this domain [Agrawal et al., 1989] but received new consideration in form of approximate tree-based labeling proposals such as GRAIL [Yildirim et al., 2012] and FER-RARI [Seufert et al., 2013]. The appeal of the 2-hop-cover approach [Cohen et al., 2003] stems from the fact that it can be also used for distance queries and was more influential in that domain. Distance queries are important for route planning, which is typically done outside of database system in specialized systems. Hence, we excluded them from the discussion in this chapter. Recent surveys on distance indexing are provided by Sommer [2014] and Bast et al. [2016]. The latest research on reachability indexing focused on approximate transitive closure labeling approaches, such as independent permutation labeling [Wei et al., 2014] and Bloom filter labeling [Su et al., 2017]. Surveys on reachability indexing are given by Yu and Cheng [2010] and Su et al. [2017].

The methodology for structural index design and use discussed in this chapter was first developed in the context of navigational pattern matching queries on semi-structured data [Fletcher et al., 2009, 2016, Milo and Suciu, 1999]. An alternative strategy based on weakening the query semantics (instead of considering weaker fragments of a given query language, as we have done here) to obtain tractable structural characterizations of language equivalence for graph compression and indexing has been studied by Fan et al. [2012]. A query language-agnostic approach based on hashing has been presented by Zou et al. [2014]. Čebirić et al. [2015] studied lossy structural summaries for *CQ* queries.

A short overview of graph data representation can also be found in Paradies and Voigt [2017, 2018].

CHAPTER 7

Query Processing

The diversity of applications in which graphs are used as primary data models led to a prolif-eration of a variety of graph processing tasks. For example, in social networks, one might be interested in looking for simple patterns in relationships between people such as finding persons with shared interests or discovering common friends. On the other hand, in the Web, one can run a completely different graph algorithm such as PageRank to identify web pages of impor-tance. Similarly, other application domains dictate their own requirements and graph processing methods. Hence, a graph query might be as simple as finding person's neighbors in a social net-work, or as complex as tracking bugs in a evolving software codebase by utilizing sophisticated graph exploration algorithms.

In this chapter, we provide an overview of processing of graph queries in the order of their perceived complexity: starting from the simplest and concluding with the hardest. Specifically, we structure our discussion as follows.

1. *Query pipeline* is the standard abstraction mechanism used in the processing of declarative queries. In this chapter, we guide our discussion of the processing of different classes of declarative graph queries in the context of a generic query pipeline which is described in Section 7.1.

2. Section 7.2 presents the processing of *subgraph matching queries* (i.e., *conjunctive graph queries (CQs)*).

3. The evaluation strategies of the core class of queries which deal with *reachability* in the graph (i.e., *regular path queries (RPQs)*) are presented in Section 7.3.

4. Finally, in Section 7.4, we briefly discuss the evaluation of the broader class of *unions of conjunctive regular path queries (UCRPQs)*.

Note that, in this chapter, we specifically focus on processing of commonly used types of *declara-tive* graph queries and omit the discussion of other types of graph-specific queries such as *shortest path queries*, *path retrieving queries*, and others. Further, we do not discuss processing of *procedu-ral* queries or algorithmic APIs such as PageRank and other general graph algorithms. Finally, we do not consider query processing in a distributed or parallel setting and in vertex-centric environments.

7.1   QUERY PIPELINE

In general, a declarative query can be executed in many different ways by a database engine. The strategy that is used by a database during query execution is encoded in a *query plan*. Often, the *costs* of such plans can vary by orders of magnitude, which motivates the problem of choosing the plan with the lowest possible execution cost. *Query optimization* is a large research area in the database field which attempts to find answers to this problem.

At the heart of a standard query processing pipeline (as shown in Figure 7.1) lies a *query planner*, the module responsible for examining all possible execution plans for each query and selecting a *cheapest* plan to be executed. Candidate plans are considered in a certain order as provided by the *enumerator* module. Often, the space of candidate plans grows exponentially with respect to the size of the given query, making it infeasible to consider every single plan. Hence, it is the task of the enumerator to provide a sufficient number of candidate plans so that a plan close to optimal can be found, while pruning those candidate plans which are unlikely to have the lowest cost.

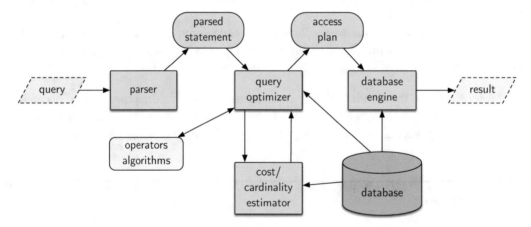

Figure 7.1: Standard query processing pipeline.

The plan space which is considered by the enumerator is determined by its *logical* and *physical* components. Given the formula which is obtained by parsing the query, the logical space contains all different execution orders of the formula's operators which can be followed to answer the query. This is called a *logical* plan. Given a logical plan, the concrete implementation choices for each of the operators are determined by the physical space, to produce a collection of *physical* plans.

A cost of a physical plan is estimated by a *cost model* module. This module specifies the cost formulas which are used to estimate the cost of execution strategies used to evaluate operators in a physical plan. These cost formulas take into account the execution method used, the amount of resources available (such as processor, memory buffer pool, and disk space), the catalog information (such as available indexes and tuple sizes), and the statistical estimates gathered from participating datasets.

This query processing pipeline showcases a typical *life of a declarative query* in a database engine. A variant of this pipeline is used across all types of database engines: relational, document, graph, and others.

7.2   SUBGRAPH MATCHING QUERIES

Subgraph matching is the basic functionality found at the core of many graph query languages. Given a graph G and a conjunctive query (*CQ*, cf. Section 3.1.2) r, the goal of a subgraph query is to return all subgraphs of G that are isomorphic or homomorphic to r. Each such subgraph is encoded by a *mapping* μ of r on G. The algorithms for finding all mappings of r on G are generally based on finding, extending, and combining corresponding *partial mappings* of r on G. Note that r can also be a subquery of a more complex query such as an *RPGQ*.

Definition 7.1   Given a graph pattern $r[z_1, \ldots, z_m]$, a graph G, and $k \geq 0$, a *partial mapping* m_k of r on G is a sequence of pairs $\langle (v_1, \mu(v_1)), \ldots, (v_k, \mu(v_k)) \rangle$ such that $\langle v_1, \ldots, v_k \rangle$ is a sequence of distinct vertices of r, and μ is a mapping of r on G. We call k the *length* of the partial mapping m_k.

In general, subgraph matching algorithms are based on two types of search in a graph: depth-first search (DFS) and breadth-first search (BFS). We briefly discuss both from the perspective of a generic query pipeline.

7.2.1   DFS-BASED ALGORITHMS

The DFS-based algorithms for subgraph isomorphism are based on the *backtracking* principle. Specifically, given a set of query vertices, the partial solutions are constructed one query vertex at-a-time. Then, if a partial solution (computed for a subset of query vertices) cannot be extended, it is discarded from the remainder of the search.

Recall that traditional implementations of depth-first search are recursive in their nature. However, in high-performance query pipelines, recursion is not typically used since it complicates the control flow and does not work well on large graphs if not used carefully. Hence, the DFS-style recursion is typically emulated by *guided*, *stateful*, and iterative graph search. An example of a generic iterative DFS-based subgraph matching algorithm is shown in Algorithm 7.1.

The organization of a *state* of a graph search which is executed in a query pipeline serves two purposes. First, the state stores the intermediate partial mappings (represented by *tuples*) which are extended by performing *operations* during each iteration of a graph search. Second, the state is organized in a way such that it defines the *flow* of the tuples between the operations of the search. For example, in DFS-based search, the state is based on a stack data structure

---

Algorithm 7.1: Generic iterative DFS-based subgraph matching.

Input: Graph $G = (V_G, E_G)$ and query graph pattern $r = (V_r, E_r)$
Output: set of mappings M of r into G

1 $M := \emptyset$
2 $V_r^o := \text{order}(V_r)$ `// ordering query vertices`
3 **for** *each* $v_r \in V_r^o$ **do**
4      $C_{v_r}^{stat} := \text{refine}(G, r, v_r)$ `// static refinement`
5 $S := \emptyset$ `// initialize the search state`
6 $m.\text{init}()$ `// initialize the candidate mapping`
7 $S.\text{push}(V_r^o.\text{next}(), m, 0)$
8 **while** S *is not empty* **do**
9      $v_r, m, n := S.\text{peek}()$
10   **if** $n = 0$ **then**
11        $C_{v_r,m}^{dyn} := \text{refine}(G, v_r, C_{v_r}^{stat}, m)$ `// dynamic refinement`
12     $v_g := C_{v_r,m}^{dyn}.\text{get}(n)$ `// get candidate graph vertex`
13   **if** $v_g \neq \emptyset$ **then**
14        $m_c := m.\text{copy}()$
15        $m_c.\text{add}(v_r, v_g)$
16   **if** *isIsomorphic(*m_c, G, r*)* **then**
17           $v_r^{next} := V_r^o.\text{next}()$ `// get next query vertex`
18   **if** $v_r^{next} \neq \emptyset$ **then**
19              $S.\text{pop}()$
20              $S.\text{push}(v_r, m, n + 1)$ `// update the search state for` v_r
21              $S.\text{push}(v_r^{next}, m_c, 0)$ `// add next query vertex for DFS`
22   **else**
23              $M.\text{add}(m_c)$
24   **else**
25        $S.\text{pop}()$ `// done processing this query vertex`
26 **return** set of mappings M

S provided either by recursive program execution or by the search algorithm itself in order to emulate a recursion (as is done in Algorithm 7.1, cf. Line 5).

The search itself is guided by an evaluation *plan*. The plan defines the *order* (cf. Line 2) in which the query vertices are assigned to graph vertices during the search and which optimization techniques are used to further *refine* the search. These refinements, in general, can be either *static* or *dynamic*. Static refinements are performed based on a graph and a corresponding subgraph query, before the actual search starts. Dynamic refinements, on the other hand, depend on the partial matching(s) obtained so far and are performed *during* the search.

The implementation of a generic DFS-based subgraph matching presented in Algorithm 7.1 depends on many factors such as algorithms used for refinements and isomorphism checks and data structures which are used to represent graphs and intermediate mappings. Here, we give an example of a *matrix-based* DFS subgraph matching.

Matrix-based DFS subgraph matching.   Consider a snippet of a Dutch and English DBPedia graph shown in Figure 7.2 and a query Q_1 over G_{DBP} as follows:

$$Q_1 = (p_1, p_2, p_3) \leftarrow \text{:isLocatedIn}(p_1, p_2), \text{:sameAs}(p_2, p_3).$$

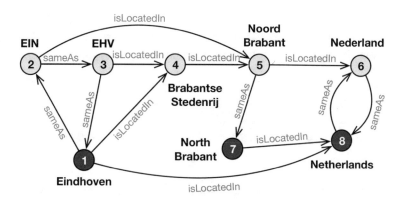

Figure 7.2: Example of an interlinked English and Dutch DBPedia graph G_{DBP}.

Figure 7.3a shows query Q_1 as directed labeled graph. Both data and query graphs can be represented as referential adjacency matrices A_G and A_Q, respectively (as discussed in Section 6.4.1). Example matrices for G_{DBP} and Q_1 are shown in Figures 7.3b and 7.3c.

Given adjacency matrices A_G and A_Q, the assignment of values from vertices in the data graph to vertices in the query graph is encoded by a *permutation* matrix P of size $|V_Q| \times |V_G|$. A permutation matrix enforces the assignment of each query vertex to exactly one graph vertex and vice versa.

The following simple check can be used to verify whether permutation matrix P encodes an isomorphic mapping of query Q in graph G:

$$A_Q = PA_GP^T. \tag{7.1}$$

For example, Figure 7.4 shows permutation matrices for three (out of five) mappings of Q_1 in G_{DBP}.

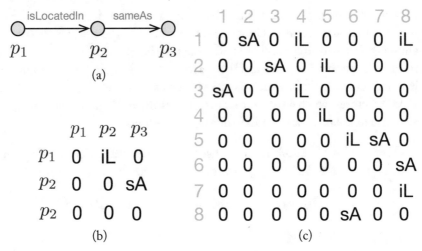

Figure 7.3: Graph and query adjacency matrices: (a) shows graph representation of Q_1; (b) shows query adjacency matrix A_{Q_1}; and graph adjacency matrix $A_{G_{DBP}}$ is shown in (c).

	1	2	3	4	5	6	7	8
p_1	0	0	0	1	0	0	0	0
p_2	0	0	0	0	1	0	0	0
p_3	0	0	0	0	0	0	1	0

P_1

	1	2	3	4	5	6	7	8
p_1	0	0	0	0	1	0	0	0
p_2	0	0	0	0	0	1	0	0
p_3	0	0	0	0	0	0	0	1

P_2

	1	2	3	4	5	6	7	8
p_1	0	0	0	0	0	0	1	0
p_2	0	0	0	0	0	0	0	1
p_3	0	0	0	0	0	1	0	0

P_3

Figure 7.4: Permutation matrices which correspond to some mappings of Q_1 in G_{DBP}.

In order to find all mappings of Q in G, one needs to find all corresponding permutation matrices P for which the isomorphism condition holds. Each mapping can be computed *progressively* by finding permutation matrices $P(i, |V_G|)^1$ of size $i \times |V_G|$ which correspond to *partial* mappings of the first i vertices of Q onto some vertices of G. For the partial mapping to be valid, the graph isomorphism condition (7.1) for the partial permutation matrix must hold

$$A_Q(i,i) = P(i, |V_G|) A_G P(i, |V_G|)^T. \tag{7.2}$$

A naïve recursive backtracking subgraph matching algorithm finds partial mappings by gradually setting a candidate permutation matrix row by row. From the definition of permutation matrix P, it follows that each row k in P contains exactly one *singleton* entry $p_{k,i} = 1$ while all other entries $p_{k,j} = 0$ for $j \neq i$. The recursive procedure starts by setting the first element $p'_{1,1}$ of the first row of the candidate permutation P' to 1 and all other elements to 0. If the partial matching obtained by candidate permutation $P(1, |V_G|)$ satisfies the subgraph isomorphism

---

[1]Here, $A(k, l)$ denotes a submatrix of A which contains the first k rows and first l columns of A.

requirement (7.2) then the procedure is called recursively to set the next row of the candidate permutation matrix. The procedure continues until $|V_Q|$ rows have been set (or all query vertices have been matched to some graph vertices) and the mapping has been found or the subgraph isomorphism requirement is not satisfied. In this case, the procedure backtracks to the previous row and tries the next setting of the singleton entry in that row.

It is easy to see that this backtracking algorithm indeed produces all possible mappings of Q in G. The subgraph isomorphism check is executed in a recursive procedure which is called for each candidate singleton element in all rows of a candidate permutation matrix. The time complexity of the isomorphism check (which is a simple matrix multiplication) is $\Omega(|V_G|^2)$. Since there are $|V_G|$ potential singletons in each of the $|V_Q|$ rows, the worst-case time complexity of this naïve algorithm is very high at $O(|V_G|^2 \cdot |V_G|^{|V_Q|}) = O(|V_G|^{|V_Q|})$.

Refinements.   The time complexity of the naïve algorithm can be reduced significantly by introducing a number of refinements which aim to cut down the number of recursive calls of the algorithm. Recall that refinements can either be static or dynamic. Here, we give a few examples of each type.

A simple static refinement is based on pruning of candidate singletons which can be performed based on the *neighborhood structure* of both query and data graphs. The most shallow neighborhood filter is based on the compatibility of degrees of matching query and graph vertices. For example, consider a matching of query vertex q to graph vertex v and we know that degree of q is greater than the degree of g. Observe that this matching cannot be completed since there are more vertices in a query (neighbors of q) than available vertices in a graph (neighbors of v). Hence, all such candidate matchings (q, v) can be discarded immediately before the construction of any of the mappings.

A simple dynamic refinement in a matrix-based subgraph matching involves a validity check which is employed to verify whether at each step of recursion the partial matrix P' constructed so far is indeed a permutation matrix. Specifically, each candidate singleton $p'_{k,l}$ is checked whether there already exists a singleton $p'_{i,l}$ in one of the previous rows ($i < k$) which were already set in P'. If such a singleton exists then setting $p'_{k,l}$ to 1 violates the definition of the permutation matrix and, therefore, the corresponding recursive call can then be safely skipped. In more general terms, this check ensures that all query vertices in a mapping are matched to distinct graph vertices and vice versa. This is a necessary (but not sufficient) requirement for the mapping to be isomorphic.

More intricate dynamic refinements are based on neighborhood filters which can be employed to ensure that each partial mapping is locally consistent with potential future assignments. Again, consider a matching of q to v in a partial mapping of Q to G. We can easily verify if any of the neighbors of q have been already assigned to some vertices in G. If yes, then all such neighbors of q should be assigned to some neighbors of v. If a violation can be found, i.e., there exists an assignment (q', v') such that q' is a neighbor of q, but v' is not a neighbor of v then the matching of q to v is not locally consistent and cannot lead to an isomorphic mapping.

7.2.2 BFS-BASED ALGORITHMS

Algorithm 7.2: Generic iterative BFS-based subgraph matching.

Input: Graph $G = (V_G, E_G)$ and query graph pattern $r = (V_r, E_r)$

Output: set of mappings M of r into G

1 $M := \emptyset$

2 $V_r^o := \text{order}(V_r)$ `// ordering query vertices`

3 **for** *each* $v_r \in V_r^o$ **do**

4     $C_{v_r}^{stat} := \text{refine}(G, r, v_r)$ `// static refinement`

5 $S := \emptyset$ `// initialize the search state`

6 $m.\text{init}()$ `// initialize the candidate mapping`

7 $S.\text{enqueue}(V_r^o.\text{next}(), m)$

8 **while** S *is not empty* **do**

9     $v_r, m := S.\text{dequeue}()$

10     $C_{v_r,m}^{dyn} := \text{refine}(G, v_r, C_{v_r}^{stat}, m)$ `// dynamic refinement`

11   **for** $v_g \in C_{v_r,m}^{dyn}$ **do**

12       $m_c := m.\text{copy}()$

13       $m_c.\text{add}(v_r, v_g)$

14   **if** *isIsomorphic(*m_c*, G, r)* **then**

15         $v_r^{next} := V_r^o.\text{next}()$ `// get next query vertex`

16   **if** $v_r^{next} \neq \emptyset$ **then**

17           $S.\text{enqueue}(v_r^{next}, m_c)$ `// add next query vertex for BFS`

18   **else**

19           $M.\text{add}(m_c)$

20 **return** set of mappings M

Many subgraph matching algorithms follow a variation of a breadth-first search as their underlying evaluation mechanism. An example of a generic iterative BFS-based subgraph matching algorithm is shown in Algorithm 7.2. Like DFS-style matching algorithms, BFS subgraph matching can be modeled as a guided stateful graph search. However, in contrast to DFS, breadth-first search does not use recursion as it is purely iterative in its nature. Therefore, the state in a generic BFS-based subgraph matching is less complex than in DFS and is based on a queue data structure.

An important feature of BFS-based algorithms for subgraph isomorphism is the fact that they can be optimized by utilizing the *dynamic programming* (DP) approach. Specifically, a given query can be broken down into smaller subqueries which can then be processed independently. Then, the *memoized* solutions to each of the smaller subqueries are eventually combined to produce the answer set of subgraph mappings. Relational evaluation of subgraph queries is the classical example of dynamic programming in BFS-style subgraph matching.

Relational BFS subgraph matching.   Assuming relational representation of a graph as a table G of (s, p, o) *triples*, every subgraph query

$$Q : (z_1, \ldots, z_m) \quad \leftarrow \quad a_1(x_1, y_1), \ldots, a_n(x_n, y_n)$$

can be translated into a semantically equivalent relational SPJR (select-project-join-rename) expression as follows:

$$R_{hSGM} \leftarrow \pi_{z_1, \ldots, z_m} (\bowtie_{\mathcal{V}_Q} (\rho_{s \to x_i, o \to y_i} (\sigma_{p = a_i} (G)))), \tag{7.3}$$

where $\bowtie_{\mathcal{V}_Q}$ denotes zero or more relational joins defined by the composition of vertex variables ($\mathcal{V}_Q$) in Q. Note that the relational algebra expression in (7.3) produces homomorphic mappings, i.e., different query vertices are allowed to map to the same graph vertices. To obtain mappings which are isomorphic, the additional filter needs to be added which explicitly disallows that:

$$R_{iSGM} \leftarrow \sigma_{\bigwedge_{z_i, z_j \in \mathcal{V}_Q, i \neq j} z_i \neq z_j} (R_{hSGM}). \tag{7.4}$$

The relational expression in (7.4) can then be evaluated by any relational database engine. If joins in $\bowtie_{\mathcal{V}_Q}$ are processed pairwise with standard join algorithms and the engine utilizes *push-based* query processing this evaluation method is equivalent to a BFS-style subgraph matching with dynamic programming optimization.[2] An example of this approach for query Q_1 on graph G_{DBP} is shown in Figure 7.5.

7.2.3   DISCUSSION

DFS-based SGM advantages.   Depth-first-search-based subgraph matching (SGM) algorithms are attractive because of their low memory consumption, pipelined results, and efficient refinements through advanced pruning of partial mappings.

DFS's low memory consumption results from the limited number of partial mappings of query-to-graph vertices which are cached in the state during the search. Specifically, the overall memory consumption of a DFS-based search corresponds to storing partial mappings along paths in a graph which are traversed depth-first. Since diameters of real graphs are often small, the overall memory consumption of a DFS-based subgraph matching is also relatively low.

---

[2]This does not mean that relational processing of subgraph matching queries is limited to a BFS-style search. Depending on the query execution model adopted by the corresponding relational engine, any graph search paradigm (BFS, DFS, and others) can be used.

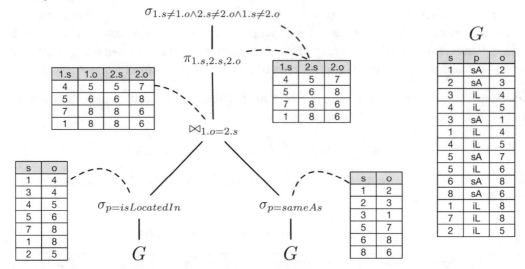

Figure 7.5: BFS-style subgraph matching using relational algebra operators in which both graph and intermediate embeddings are represented as tables.

Further, since mappings are generated depth-first, the query answers can be pipelined to the end-consumer. This behavior is desirable in exploratory and top-k query workloads.

Finally, the majority of advanced pruning strategies have been studied and implemented in the context of DFS-based subgraph matching algorithms. While some of these refinements are applicable in the BFS setting as well, the effectiveness of these strategies for BFS is yet to be confirmed.

DFS-based SGM weaknesses.   Main weaknesses of DFS-based matching result from its complex tuple flow, suboptimal IO patterns, and ineffectiveness of some common refinement strategies.

Complex tuple flow results from the recursive nature of a depth-first search. Recursion has lower performance than an equivalent iterative program typically due to the overhead introduced by function calls and stack maintenance. Even when converted to an iterative stateful graph search, DFS-based matching still has more complex state than its BFS counterpart.

Tuple-by-tuple processing of partial mappings during depth-first search generates IO patterns which are often suboptimal. On typical graph storage clustered by edge labels or properties, DFS would not exploit the locality and would incur significant overhead due to buffer pool misses. Further, tuple-based processing becomes expensive in main-memory setting (when disk IOs are no longer the significant bottleneck) due to excessive function calls and heavy random memory access.

Finally, since only a limited number of partial mappings are kept in the search state, some common refinement strategies are not as effective as in BFS-style matching. For example, in dense and/or cyclic graphs, the same vertex may be discovered by the search multiple times. Clearly, following paths from such vertex is a wasted effort as these paths have already been explored. Due to limited cache in the search state, DFS-based algorithms are not as efficient at detecting such vertices and timely pruning them out from the remainder of the search.

BFS-based SGM advantages.   BFS-based subgraph matching is attractive because of its uncomplicated and adaptable tuple flow, easy parallelization, and sequential IO patterns.

The state in BFS subgraph matching can be simplified thanks to the fundamental iterative nature of the breadth-first search. Furthermore, the lack of backtracking (as in DFS) allows for much simpler tuple flow throughout the execution of a graph search. Adaptable tuple flow, in turn, facilitates powerful optimizations based on dynamic programming which enable faster, parallelized query evaluation which splits up the original query and evaluates each of the resulting subqueries concurrently.

Finally, breadth-first graph exploration produces IO patterns which exploit data locality better than the DFS-based SGM. For example, standard graph indexes clustered on edge labels are perfect for BFS-based SGM since mappings are produced label by label and, hence, result in sequential reads of the storage device. The same configuration will result in more expensive random accesses in a DFS-based setting.

BFS-based SGM weaknesses.   The main disadvantage of breadth-first subgraph matching is its excessive memory consumption. Unlike depth-first exploration, in the naive implementation of BFS-based SGM, partial mappings for each query vertex are fully materialized in the search state before attempting to match the next query vertex specified by the evaluation plan. The space complexity (i.e., the maximum size of the search state during the search) of BFS-based SGM is bounded by the average fan-out of the graph edges and is exponential in the diameter of the matched subgraph.

7.3   REGULAR PATH QUERIES

Regular path queries (*RPQs*) extend subgraph matching queries with non-trivial navigation on a graph. This navigation is performed by returning pairs of vertices in a graph such that paths between the vertices in a pair match a given regular expression.

In the following subsections, we give an overview of different methods used in evaluation of regular path queries. In the literature, we identify three main groups of approaches: relational algebra-based, Datalog-based, and automata-based *RPQ* evaluation methods.

As a running example, consider the graph shown in Figure 7.2 and a query Q_{DBP} as follows:

$$Q_{DBP} = \left(\text{:sameAs}^*/\text{:isLocatedIn}\right)^+/\text{:sameAs}^*.$$

Here, graph G_{DBP} contains information from both English and Dutch DBPedia datasets. Query Q_{DBP} aims to find all places p in both Dutch and English datasets in which a city is located in. This query demonstrates the usefulness of *RPQ*s in navigation of unknown graphs, as it uses succinct but non-trivial Kleene transitive expressions to concurrently resolve both equivalence and geographical closures without prior knowledge of an underlying graph.

7.3.1   RELATIONAL ALGEBRA AND DATALOG-BASED APPROACHES

The simple relational algebra-based *RPQ* evaluation approach can be modeled by the *relational algebra* extended by an additional operator α which computes the *transitive closure* of a given binary relation. This algebra, called α-RA, can be then used to construct an α-RA expression tree (e.g., see Figure 7.6b) based on the bottom-up traversal of a parse tree of the regular expression (Figure 7.6a) in a given query.

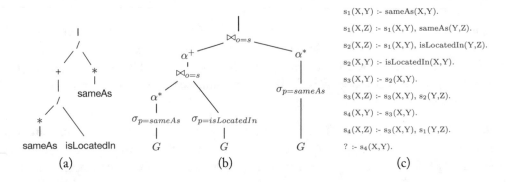

Figure 7.6: A parse tree for a regular expression in Q_{DBP} (a), an α-RA tree (b), and a Datalog program for Q_{DBP} (c).

Many GDBMSes implement *RPQ* evaluation by adapting the α-RA approach since it models relational techniques well and, thus, can be easily and efficiently implemented in most relational databases which support SQL-style recursion.

Native support of recursion makes Datalog a suitable language to express regular path queries. For example, a simple strategy can be used to convert an α-RA tree into a Datalog program (e.g., as shown in Figure 7.6). Then, this program can be submitted to any Datalog-compliant engine (e.g., LogicBlox) in order to evaluate a given *RPQ*.

Note, however, that both α-RA tree and a corresponding Datalog program obtained by the translation procedure are not necessarily the most efficient as all the issues related to query planning apply to the tree and its translation as well (e.g., translation methods, join orders, query rewrites, sideways information passing, and many others).

7.3.2 FINITE AUTOMATA-BASED APPROACHES

Research on regular expressions, of course, well precedes the introduction of regular path queries. Specifically, regular expressions have been introduced in formal languages theory as a notation for patterns which *generate* words over a given alphabet. The dual problem to generation is *recognition*—and *finite state automata* (FA) are the recognizers for regular expressions. Specifically, given a regular expression r, there exists a number of methods to construct a corresponding automaton which recognizes the language of r.

Note that there exist infinitely many FAs which can recognize r, and many approaches exist which aim to construct an automaton deemed efficient for a particular scenario, e.g., finite automata obtained by using *minimization*.

The simplest method which uses an FA for evaluation of regular path queries on graphs works as follows. First, an automaton AQ_{DBP} (e.g., see Figure 7.7a) which recognizes given regular expression r is constructed by using standard methods and then, optionally, minimized (Figure 7.7b). Then, a graph database G_{DBP} is converted into finite automaton AG_{DBP} with graph vertices becoming automaton states and graph edges becoming automaton transitions in AG_{DBP}. Given AQ_{DBP} and AG_{DBP}, a product automaton $P_{DBP} = AQ_{DBP} \times AG_{DBP}$ (Figure 7.7c) is constructed. Finally, automaton P_{DBP} is then tested for non-emptiness by checking whether any accepting state(s) can be reached from the starting state(s). Then, pairs of starting and corresponding reachable accepting states in P_{DBP} form the answer pairs for Q_{DBP}.

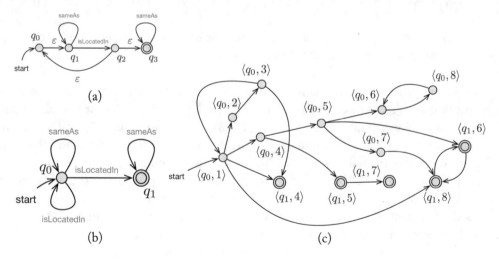

Figure 7.7: An ε-NFA for Q_{DBP} (a), a corresponding minimized NFA (b), and a snippet of a product automaton with a starting state in Eindhoven (vertex 1) (c).

To avoid a construction of a full product automaton, evaluation of *RPQ*s can be performed by running a bidirectional breadth-first search (biBFS) in the graph. Specifically, given a *reachability* query (i.e., an *RPQ* where variables are bound to constants on both ends), two FAs are constructed. The first automaton recognizes the regular language defined by the original expression, and the second automaton accepts the reversed language, which is also regular. The algorithm uses the steps of the biBFS to expand the search frontiers and to connect paths. Before each vertex in a graph is placed on the search frontier for the next expansion, the check is performed whether the partial path leading up to this vertex is not rejected by the appropriate (direct or reverse) automaton. This guarantees that partial results which are not accepted by either automaton are not included in the next iteration of a search.

As an optimization, an *RPQ* evaluation method which executes the search *simultaneously* in the graph and the automaton can be employed. This is achieved by exploring the graph using a BFS while marking the vertices in the graph with the corresponding states in the automaton. Essentially, in this method, edges in the graph are traversed only if the corresponding transition in the automaton allows it. This way, the construction of a full product automaton is avoided and the automaton essentially acts as an evaluation plan for a given *RPQ*.

The idea of using an FA as an evaluation plan can be taken further. It can be shown that effective plan spaces that result from FA-based and α-RA-based approaches are, in fact, incomparable. Hence, to find the best plan, both implicit plan spaces have to be considered. With this in mind, a cost-based optimizer for *RPQ*s which subsumes and extends FA- and α-RA-based approaches can be designed.

7.4   UNIONS OF CONJUNCTIVE REGULAR PATH QUERIES

Unions of conjunctive regular path queries combine the basic core features of graph query languages: subgraph matching (as discussed in Section 7.2) and reachability (as discussed in Section 7.3).

A naive implementation of evaluation of *UCRPQ*s is based on relational algebra extended with α operator (α-RA). As discussed in Section 7.3.1, α-RA is able to evaluate the full fragment of *RPQ*s, albeit possibly not efficiently. Similarly, as discussed in Section 7.2.2, SPJRU algebra is also able to evaluate the full fragment of conjunctive queries. Hence, it can be shown that α-RA is sufficient to evaluate the full fragment of *UCRPQ*s which combines *CQ*s and *RPQ*s.

While α-RA can indeed be used to answer *UCRPQ*s, as we have demonstrated in previous sections, this type of evaluation misses many powerful optimization opportunities, e.g., elaborate DFS-based refinement strategies or rich plan space offered by automata-based *RPQ* evaluation methods. Few of the current graph processing systems are able to optimize across unions of conjunctive regular path queries. This topic remains at the forefront of current research on efficient graph query evaluation, planning, and optimization.

7.5   BIBLIOGRAPHIC AND HISTORICAL NOTES

Query optimization is an established research topic in the database community and has been surveyed extensively [Ioannidis, 1996].

Subgraph pattern matching is a classic problem with an extensive and rich literature across several research areas [Gallagher, 2006]. For a view on the current state of the art, see Bi et al. [2016], Han et al. [2013], Kim et al. [2016, 2015], and Lee et al. [2012].

Losemann and Martens [2012] proposed an *RPQ* evaluation algorithm based on a dynamic programming paradigm. The α-RA algebra was proposed by Agrawal [1988]. Many GDBMSes implement *RPQ* evaluation by adapting the α-RA approach since it models relational techniques well and, thus, can be easily and efficiently implemented in most relational databases which support SQL-style recursion (e.g., PostgreSQL, Oracle, IBM DB2, and others) and relational triple stores (e.g., Virtuoso [Erling and Mikhailov, 2007], IBM DB2 RDF store [Briggs et al., 2012a,b], Oracle [Chong et al., 2005], and others [Sakr et al., 2012]). Evaluation based on α-extended relational algebra is also considered [Dey et al., 2013, Yakovets et al., 2013].

Consens et al. [1995] propose a simple strategy to convert an α-RA tree into a Datalog program (e.g., as shown in Figure 7.6c).

The idea of using FA in evaluation of *RPQ*s is used in various works [Kochut and Janik, 2007, Koschmieder and Leser, 2012, Mendelzon and Wood, 1995, Pérez et al., 2010, Sarwat et al., 2013, Yakovets et al., 2016, Zauner et al., 2010]. Implementation of a **G+** query language [Mendelzon and Wood, 1995] includes the first method which uses FA for evaluation of regular path queries on graphs. Kochut and Janik [2007] propose to evaluate *RPQ*s by running a bidirectional breadth-first search (biBFS) in the graph. Koschmieder and Leser [2012] present an *RPQ* evaluation method which executes the search simultaneously in the graph and the automaton. The WaveGuide system [Yakovets et al., 2016] takes the idea of using an FA as an evaluation plan further. Query plans in WaveGuide are based on the notion of *wavefronts*—stratified automata extended with seeds, append, prepend, and view transitions.

Benchmarking tools are crucial in the experimental design and study of query processing methods. For an overview of benchmarking and synthetic graph and workload generation frameworks, we refer the reader to recent progress in the area [Bagan et al., 2017, Erling et al., 2015, Zhang and Tay, 2016].

CHAPTER 8

Physical Operators

This chapter discusses how graph-centric features used in the graph query languages of Chapter 3 introduce new challenges in physical query evaluation. We focus particularly on the design and implementation of operators used in physical query plans for declarative graph queries.

- Evaluation strategies for computation of transitive closure are presented in Section 8.1.

- Section 8.2 discusses efficient algorithms for multi-way joins.

- Cardinality estimation of operator results is presented in Section 8.3.

- Finally, further physical optimizations such as efficient handling of large intermediate results and sideways information passing are discussed in Section 8.4.

8.1 TRANSITIVE CLOSURE

As described in Chapter 3, one of the core functionalities of modern practical graph query languages involves querying *reachability*. In Chapter 7, we have shown that parts of the query which involve reachability constructs can be evaluated by computing a form of a *transitive closure* over corresponding subgraphs participating in the query.

Let $G = (V, E, \eta, \lambda, \nu)$ be a property graph and $R \subseteq V \times V$ be a *binary* relation which contains pairs of vertices of G. We call R *transitive* on a set of graph vertices V if for all graph vertices s, v, and t in V if $(s, v) \in R$ and $(v, t) \in R$ then $(s, t) \in R$. Then, the transitive closure R^+ of relation R over set V is the *smallest* binary relation on V that contains R and is transitive.

We call relation B a *base* relation over which transitive closure B^+ is computed. Depending on how B is defined over graph G, the transitive closure of B can be used to represent various reachability patterns in a graph. For example, if relation B contains all pairs of vertices which are connected by an edge in G, B^+ would contain all pairs of vertices (s, t) such that vertex t can be reached by following one or more edges from vertex s. An example of this scenario for graph G_{DBP} (shown in Figure 7.2) and the base relation formed by selection of edges with label `isLocatedIn` is presented in Figure 8.1.

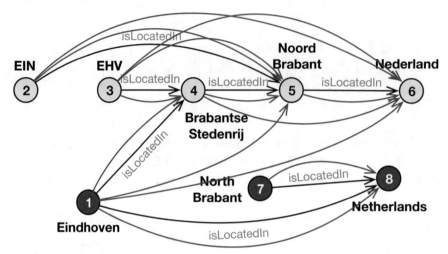

Figure 8.1: Transitive closure (shown as red edges) over base relation defined by selection of isLocatedIn edges in graph G_{DBP}.

Algorithm 8.1: Naive TC.	**Algorithm 8.2:** Semi-naive TC with cycle elimination.
1 $C_0 := B$	
2 $C_1 := \text{join}(B, C_0)$	1 $C_0 := \emptyset$
3 $i := 0$	2 $\Delta_0^R := B$
4 **while** $C_{i+1} \setminus C_i \neq \emptyset$ **do**	3 $i := 0$
5 $\quad$ $i := i + 1$	4 **while** $\Delta_i^R \neq \emptyset$ **do**
6 $\quad$ $C_{i+1} := \text{extend}(C_i, B)$	5 $\quad$ $C_{i+1} := \text{cache}(C_i, \Delta_i^R)$
7 **return** $B^+ = C_{i+1}$	6 $\quad$ $\Delta_{i+1} := \text{crank}(B, \Delta_i^R)$
	7 $\quad$ $\Delta_{i+1}^R := \text{reduce}(\Delta_{i+1}, C_{i+1})$
	8 $\quad$ $i := i + 1$
	9 **return** $B^+ = C_i$

Naive TC.   Given a base relation, its transitive closure can be computed by performing an iterative bottom-up *fixpoint* evaluation. A naive fixpoint strategy is presented in Algorithm 8.1. This strategy is based on iterative breadth-first computation of the transitive closure. During the computation, a partial closure is stored in a binary cache relation (denoted by C_i at the ith iteration). At each iteration, the current cache is *extended* by joining tuples in the cache with tuples from the base relation. If both cache and base are stored in binary relations $C(s, t)$ and $B(s, t)$, respectively, then the extend operation can be represented by the following relational expression:

$$C_{i+1} \leftarrow C_i \cup \pi_{C_i.s, B.t}(C_i \bowtie_{C_i.t = B.s} B).$$ (8.1)

Here, the partial transitive closure is incrementally extended breadth-first by tuples from the base relation until no new tuples are produced, i.e., a fixpoint is reached.

While the naive fixpoint evaluation strategy is extremely simple, it suffers from several serious shortcomings. First, since the partial closure is extended incrementally and assuming the fixpoint is reached after n iterations, we can show monotonic inclusion $C_i \subseteq C_{i+1}$ for any iteration $0 \leq i \leq n$. Therefore, a join in expression (8.1) for cache C_{i+1} is redundant for all tuples of C_i included in C_{i+1} which were already joined with B in the previous iteration. Second, assuming default bag-based semantics of operations in the expression (8.1), the naive fixpoint strategy does not explicitly deal with duplicate tuples at any point during the evaluation. Hence, in addition to a potentially large amount of redundant work caused by processing of duplicate vertex pairs, naive fixpoint evaluation will lead to potentially unbounded computation on cyclic graphs.

Semi-naive TC.   The *semi-naive* fixpoint evaluation strategy (its variant with additional optimizations is presented in Algorithm 8.2) aims to address some of these shortcomings. The key idea of the semi-naive strategy is to use a cache's *differential* relation (denoted by Δ) instead of the whole cache relation to compute the extension of the partial closure at each iteration. Hence, the redundant computation caused by the monotonic inclusion of cache instances between iterations is avoided since the join is performed only for the "new" tuples contained in the differential, i.e., $\Delta_i = C_{i+1} \setminus C_i$.

It is worth noting that to aid the cost analysis of the computation of transitive closure, the extend operation can be broken down into three separate operations crank, reduce, and cache, as shown in Algorithm 8.2. Here, crank performs the breadth-first extension of the current partial transitive closure with tuples from the base relation and can be represented by the following relational expression:

$$\Delta_{i+1} \leftarrow \pi_{\Delta_i^R.s, B.t}(\Delta_i^R \bowtie_{\Delta_i^R.t = B.s} B).$$ (8.2)

Operation reduce removes duplicate pairs of tuples from the differential which are already there (reduce against Δ) and/or in the current partial transitive closure (reduce against C) to produce a *reduced* differential Δ_i^R. Finally, cache integrates the newly discovered and reduced tuples Δ_i^R into the cached closure C_i.

SMART TC.   The SMART transitive closure algorithm aims to obtain the closure in significantly fewer iterations than the semi-naive approach. In the semi-naive transitive closure computation, crank joins the differential Δ_i with the base relation B to produce the *new* differential Δ_{i+1}. The idea of the SMART approach is to join a part of a differential with the whole partial closure produced up to this point.

To showcase this idea, consider the notion of a *closure depth* $d_{s,t}$ which is associated with each pair of vertices in transitive closure B^+ of a binary base relation B. Closure depth is defined recursively as follows.

- For all pairs of vertices (s, t) in the base relation B the depth $d_{s,t}$ is 1.

- For all vertices s, v, t in V, if $d_{s,v} = k$ and $d_{v,t} = l$, then $d_{s,t} = k + l$.

Tuples in SMART's cache are triples $\langle s, t, d \rangle$, where (s, t) is the pair of vertices in the partial closure and d is their corresponding closure depth. Then, the crank operation in the SMART algorithm is defined as follows:

$$\Delta_{i+1} \leftarrow \pi_{C_i.s, \Delta_i.t}(C_i \bowtie_{C_i.t = \Delta_i.s} \sigma_{d=2^i}(\Delta_i)). \tag{8.3}$$

Intuitively, the SMART algorithm extends the partial closure by self-joining the entire partial closure so far with a part of itself, specifically, with those pairs of nodes which have the highest closure depth. For example, during the second iteration ($i = 2$) of the algorithm, the entire closure C_2 (which by now contains pairs with $d = 1, 2, 3$, and 4) is self-joined with its part ($\sigma_{d=4}(C_2)$) to obtain the differential which contains pairs with closure depths $5, 6, 7$, and 8, respectively.

Let n be the number of iterations it takes the semi-naive algorithm to reach a fixpoint. From expression (8.2), it follows that each crank in a semi-naive iteration extends the closure depth by 1. On the other hand, it follows from expression (8.3) that SMART essentially *doubles* the closure depth of discovered vertex pairs with each iteration. Hence, it will take SMART $\log_2 n$ iterations to compute the whole closure compared to n iterations of the semi-naive approach (example shown in Figure 8.2).

Algorithm 8.3: SMART TC.	Algorithm 8.4: WAVEGUIDE TC.
1 $\Delta_0^R := \text{init}(B)$	1 $\Delta_0^R := \text{seed}(G)$
2 $C_0 := \Delta_0$	2 $i := 0$
3 $i := 0$	3 **while** $\Delta_i^R \neq \emptyset$ **do**
4 **while** $\Delta_i^R \neq \emptyset$ **do**	4 $\quad \Delta_{i+1}^S := \text{seed}(\Delta_i^R)$
5 $\quad \Delta_{i+1} := \text{crank}(\Delta_i^R, C_i)$	5 $\quad \Delta^{i+1} := \text{crank}(\Delta_{i+1}^S, \Delta_i^R, G, C_i, P_Q)$
6 $\quad \Delta_{i+1}^R := \text{reduce}(\Delta_{i+1}, C_i)$	6 $\quad \Delta_{i+1}^R := \text{reduce}(\Delta_{i+1}, \Delta_i^R, C_i)$
7 $\quad C_{i+1} := \text{cache}(C_i, \Delta_i^R)$	7 $\quad C_{i+1} := \text{cache}(\Delta_{i+1}^R, C_i)$
8 $\quad i := i + 1$	8 $\quad i := i + 1$
9 **return** $B^+ = C_i$	9 **return** extract(C_i)

Semi-naive vs. SMART.   It is not immediately clear whether SMART is more *efficient* than the semi-naive approach in computing transitive closure of a given relation. Intuitively, SMART makes significantly fewer iterations but each iteration joins larger relations. Further, the way

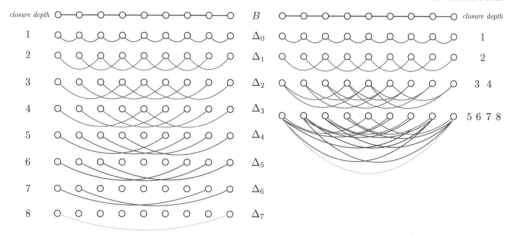

Figure 8.2: Evaluation of simple transitive closure with semi-naive fixpoint (left) vs. SMART fixpoint (right).

vertex pairs of certain depths are obtained can dictate how many tuples were reduced at each iteration. To illustrate this, consider computations of the transitive closure of two base relations B_1 and B_2 by the semi-naive and SMART algorithms shown in Figure 8.3. In this example, B_1 and B_2 exhibit *lensing*, a property characterized by having the majority of vertices with low in/out degrees along with a few *lenses*, vertices with high in/out degrees. The lensing example allows us to easily construct a graph (B_1) for which the semi-naive algorithm produces fewer intermediate tuples (characterized by the sum of all Δ_i's) and shifting the focal points produces a graph (B_2) for which the SMART algorithm is better. This demonstrates that deciding which approach is more efficient depends on the *structure* of the base relation itself and, ultimately, this decision needs to be *cost-based*.

WAVEGUIDE TC. The semi-naive and SMART algorithms showcase the need for *planning* of the evaluation of transitive closure. However, by themselves, these algorithms are too rigid and do *not* explore the full plan space possible for the computation of transitive closure. For example, to compute vertex pairs with closure depth 6, the semi-naive algorithm would join vertex pairs with depths 5 and 1. Similarly, the SMART algorithm would join depths 2 and 4. However, there might be a *better* plan which joins depths 3 and 3, and which neither of the two algorithms considers.

Algorithm 8.4 shows transitive closure powered by a WAVEGUIDE *RPQ* optimizer which subsumes and extends both semi-naive and SMART algorithms by introducing planning for the evaluation of transitive closure. Specifically, if a base relation is defined as a query Q (e.g., an *RPQ*), WAVEGUIDE chooses the optimal plan (P_Q) according to a cost model which takes into account the structure of the base relation and costs associated with physical implementations of

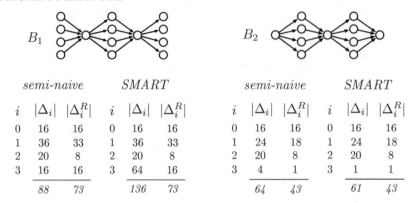

	B_1								B_2						
	semi-naive			*SMART*					*semi-naive*			*SMART*		
i	$|\Delta_i|$	$|\Delta_i^R|$		i	$|\Delta_i|$	$|\Delta_i^R|$		i	$|\Delta_i|$	$|\Delta_i^R|$		i	$|\Delta_i|$	$|\Delta_i^R|$
0	16	16		0	16	16		0	16	16		0	16	16
1	36	33		1	36	33		1	24	18		1	24	18
2	20	8		2	20	8		2	20	8		2	20	8
3	16	16		3	64	16		3	4	1		3	1	1
	88	*73*			*136*	*73*			*64*	*43*			*61*	*43*

Figure 8.3: Analysis of cardinalities of differentials (Δ_i) and reduced differentials (Δ_i^R) for two runs of the semi-naive and SMART algorithms on base relations B_1 (left) and B_2 (right).

the algorithm's operations. Example implementations and their corresponding costs are shown in Table 8.1.

An important feature of a transitive closure algorithm is the ability to *push down* the processing of constraints imposed on the results of the closure. The classes of possible constraints range from simple selections on closure source(s) based on the conjuncts specified in the query to more complex conditions such as aggregates on paths. For example, WAVEGUIDE TC handles the conjunctive selections via a *seeding* construct (line 1 of Algorithm 8.4) used in its evaluation plans and its search algorithm, which uses knowledge of the complete graph G. Further discussion of efficient processing of constrained closures can be found in the bibliography section of this chapter.

Table 8.1: Processing costs associated with typical implementations of operations involved in the computation of transitive closure

Step	Generalized Cost	Example Implementation	Complexity of f (per iter.)
C_{crank}	$\sum_{i=0}^{n} f_1(|\Delta_i^R|, |G|, |C_i|)$	Index-nested loop joins: $\Delta_i^R \bowtie_{P_Q} G$ and $\Delta_i^R \bowtie_{P_Q} C_i$.	$O(|\Delta_i^R| \cdot (\log|G| + \log|C_i|))$
$C_{\text{reduce}}^{\Delta}$	$\sum_{i=1}^{n} f_2(|\Delta_i|)$	Sort Δ_i, remove duplicates.	$O(|\Delta_i| \cdot \log|\Delta_i^C|)$
C_{reduce}^{C}	$\sum_{i=1}^{n} f_3(|\Delta_i|, |C_i|)$	Scan Δ_i, probe C_i's index.	$O(|\Delta_i| \cdot \log|C_i|)$
C_{cache}	$\sum_{i=1}^{n} f_4(|\Delta_i^R|, |C_i|)$	Scan Δ_i^R, insert into C_i's index.	$O(|\Delta_i^R| \cdot \log|C_i|)$

8.2   MULTI-WAY JOINS

As we have seen in Chapter 7, the cardinality of a query result often dominates the query running time since *any* algorithm which evaluates the query has to, *at the very least*, enumerate through all of its result tuples. Hence, in order to obtain a worst-case running time for a given query, it is useful to provide a good upper bound on its output size.

As a running example, consider a query Q_{tri} which finds all triangles of entities connected with sameAs edges in an encyclopedic network such as DBPedia:

$$Q_{tri} : (p_1, p_2, p_3) \quad \leftarrow \quad sameAs(p_1, p_2), sameAs(p_2, p_3), sameAs(p_3, p_1).$$

A graph representation of the triangle pattern in Q_{tri} is given in Figure 8.4. This query pattern can be used to find clusters of equivalent entities in a given network.

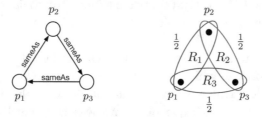

Figure 8.4: A graph representation (left) and a fractional edge cover (right) of a triangle query Q_{tri}.

Given a relational representation of a graph as a table G of (s, p, o) triples, a first naive attempt to establish an upper bound on the cardinality of the result of query Q_{tri} is:

$$|Q_{tri}| < |\sigma_{p=sameAs(G)}|^3. \tag{8.4}$$

This bound is based on the size of the Cartesian product of all relations participating in the query. It is easy to see that this bound is not tight. A tighter bound is obtained by realizing that the query is, in fact, a triangle in which two relations join and the third acts merely as a *filter* of the results of the first join:

$$|Q_{tri}| < |\sigma_{p=sameAs(G)}|^2. \tag{8.5}$$

An even tighter bound on the cardinality of query results can be obtained by using the *AGM bound*, a bound based on a concept of a *fractional edge cover* of a conjunctive query. In essence, a fractional edge cover is an assignment of a weight (u_j) to each relation $(R_j$, represented as hyperedges) participating in the query such that each query variable is "covered" by a total weight greater or equal to 1. Figure 8.4 shows an example of a cover for Q_{tri} where $R_1 = R_2 = R_3 = \sigma_{p=sameAs}(G)$. Given a fractional edge cover for a conjunctive query Q, the AGM theorem provides a bound on the cardinality of Q:

$$|Q| \leq \prod_{i=1}^{n} |R_i|^{u_i}. \tag{8.6}$$

If we plug a *minimal* edge cover in (8.6), i.e., a fractional cover with the lowest total weight, we would obtain a *tight* bound on $|Q|$. For example, for Q_{tri}, a minimal edge cover is obtained by assigning equal $\frac{1}{2}$ weights to all relations. From the AGM theorem, we obtain a bound on $|Q_{tri}|$ which is tighter than (8.4) and (8.5):

$$|Q_{tri}| < |\sigma_{p=sameAs(G)}|^{\frac{3}{2}}. \qquad (8.7)$$

Observe that a typical evaluation of Q_{tri} based on a relational SPJR expression processed with *pairwise* joins would have at least quadratic complexity (as in bound (8.5)) which is not optimal with respect to the bound (8.7). Intuitively, while a join of multiple relations can be selective, with pairwise joins, we are forced to join at most two relations at once which might not be as selective.

This observation motivated the study of a new class of join algorithms, the *worst-case optimal* multi-way join algorithms which exploit the high selectivity of multi-way joins. Leapfrog Triejoin (LTJ) is a simple example of such an algorithm. To evaluate a complex conjunctive query, instead of constructing a tree expression of pairwise joins which can produce large intermediate results, the LTJ algorithm joins all relations at once without producing *any* intermediate results.

A basic building block of the LTJ algorithm is a *leapfrog join*, a variant of a sort-merge join which simultaneously processes k unary relations $A_1(x), \ldots, A_k(x)$. Leapfrog join provides a linear iterator for the intersection $A_1(x) \cap \ldots \cap A_k(x)$.

Algorithm 8.5: lf-init().

1 **if** *any iterator is atEnd()* **then**
2 $\quad$ $atEnd$:= true
3 **else**
4 $\quad$ $atEnd$:= false
5 $\quad$ **sort**(Iter$[0 \ldots k - 1]$)
6 $\quad$ p := 0
7 $\quad$ **lf-search**()

Algorithm 8.6: lf-next().

1 Iter$[p]$.next()
2 **if** *Iter$[p]$.atEnd()* **then**
3 $\quad$ $atEnd$:= true
4 **else**
5 $\quad$ p := $p + 1$ mod k
6 $\quad$ **lf-search**()

Algorithm 8.7: lf-search().

1 x' := Iter$[(p - 1)$ mod $k]$.key()
2 **while** *true* **do**
3 $\quad$ x := Iter$[p]$.key()
4 $\quad$ **if** $x = x'$ **then**
5 $\quad\quad$ key := x
6 $\quad\quad$ return
7 $\quad$ **else**
8 $\quad\quad$ Iter$[p]$.**seek**(x')
9 $\quad\quad$ **if** *Iter$[p]$.atEnd()* **then**
10 $\quad\quad\quad$ $atEnd$:= true
11 $\quad\quad\quad$ return
12 $\quad\quad$ **else**
13 $\quad\quad\quad$ x' := Iter$[p]$.key()
14 $\quad\quad\quad$ p := $p + 1$ mod k

Internally, the LTJ algorithm keeps an array Iter$[0 \ldots (k-1)]$ of k iterators, one for each relation participating in the join. During the search, the Iter[] array is kept sorted according to the current keys at which iterators are positioned, where the first iterator in the array has the smallest current key, and the last iterator has the largest current key (sort() method, line 5, Algorithm 8.5). The smallest and largest keys at which the iterators are positioned are continuously tracked by the algorithm. The iterator with the smallest current key is repeatedly repositioned to an upper bound of the largest key, thus *leapfrogging* the iterators of other relations (seek() method, line 8, Algorithm 8.7). An example run of the leapfrog algorithm for unary relations $A = \{0, 1, 3, 4, 5, 6, 7, 8, 9, 11\}$, $B = \{0, 2, 6, 7, 8, 9\}$, and $C = \{2, 4, 5, 8, 10\}$ is shown in Figure 8.5 (left).

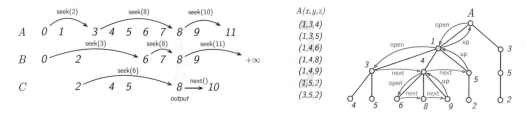

Figure 8.5: An example run of the leapfrog algorithm evaluating the multi-way join of three unary relations A, B, and C (left) and an example traversal of a relation represented as a trie (right).

Given the complexities of the internal methods as presented in Table 8.2, the overall complexity of the leapfrog join is $O(n_{min} \log(n_{max}/n_{min}))$, where n_{min} and n_{max} are the cardinalities of the smallest and the largest relations participating in the join, respectively.

Table 8.2: Methods used in the leapfrog join (top) and leapfrog triejoin (bottom) and their corresponding complexities which are possible with good bookkeeping and using standard data structures such as B-trees

Method	Description	Complexity
int key()	Returns the value of a key at current iterator position	$O(1)$
next()	Process the next key	$O(\log n)$
seek(int where)	Seek the iterator to a value *key* such that *key* $\geq$ *where*, or move to $+\infty$ if no such value exists	$O(\log n)$
bool atEnd()	True if iterator is at end ($+\infty$)	$O(1)$
void open()	Proceeds to the first key at the next depth of a trie	$O(\log n)$
void up()	Returns to the parent key at the previous depth of a trie	$O(\log n)$

To handle relations of higher arity, the LFTJ algorithm uses *tries* to traverse the relations efficiently. Each tuple in a relation corresponds to a unique path from the root to a leaf in a trie. LFTJ's trie iterators support three traversal operations on a given trie efficiently: open(), up(), and next(). The descriptions and complexities of these operations are given in Table 8.2. Figure 8.5 (right) shows an example traversal of a trie of a relation.

The LFTJ algorithm assigns an instance of a leapfrog join for each variable, in turn. A good *variable ordering* chosen by the query optimizer is vital for the performance of the join. Consider an example multi-way join defined by query Q_{tri} presented in Figure 8.4. Suppose the optimizer chooses $[p_1, p_2, p_3]$ as the optimal variable ordering for this join. Then, the topmost leapfrog join LFJ_1 iterates over p_1 values in projections $sameAs(p_1, \_)$ and $sameAs(\_, p_1)$. When LFJ_1 emits a binding for p_1, it is passed to the next level join LFJ_2 which seeks bindings for p_2 for $sameAs_{p_1}(p_2)$ and $sameAs(p_2, \_)$. Once these bindings are found, the final LFJ_3 joins on p_3 in $sameAs_{p_1}(p_3)$, $sameAs_{p_2}(p_3)$. When bindings are exhausted at any level, the join is backtracked to a previous level to seek another binding for a previous variable.

Given the complexities of the LFTJ's basic operations as presented in Table 8.2, it can be shown that the running time of the LFTJ is bounded by the fractional edge cover bound $q(n)$, up to a log factor: $O(q(n) \log n)$. Hence, the runtime complexity of the LFTJ algorithm for Q_{tri} is $O(n^{\frac{3}{2}} \log n)$ which is asymptotically better than any approach which uses pairwise joins and has the runtime complexity of at least $O(n^2)$.

8.3   CARDINALITY ESTIMATION

As we mentioned in Chapter 7, a cardinality estimator is a component of a query pipeline which is *essential* for picking optimal query evaluation plans. Cardinality estimation in relational databases is a well-studied topic. Yet, as we will show in this chapter, many of the assumptions used in the relational world are not directly applicable to graph databases. In our discussion, we focus specifically on estimation of two types of constructs used in graph query processing: *paths* and more complex *patterns*.

There are five main methods used in cardinality estimation: synopses, sketches, histograms, sampling, and wavelets. We discuss simple cardinality estimation methods based on compact synopses and refer the reader to the bibliographic notes for a short overview of other cardinality estimation techniques.

8.3.1   CARDINALITY OF PATHS

As shown in Chapter 3, a basic feature of most graph query languages is querying vertex pairs $[\![g]\!]_G \subseteq V \times V$ connected by *paths* in a graph G which conform to a user-specified *RPQ* g.

A cardinality estimator should be able to produce an estimate of $|[\![g]\!]_G|$ for a given path query g and graph G. One common way to produce this estimate is to recursively break down g into smaller sub-expressions according to the *RPQ* path algebra and use the estimates of sub-expressions to obtain a cardinality estimate for g. This requires the definition of cardinality estimation methods for graph edges, concatenations, unions, inverses, and transitive closures as defined in the algebra. In this section, we briefly discuss cardinality estimation of a *bag* of vertex pairs $[\![g_1/g_2]\!]_G$ which are connected by a path obtained by concatenating two given labels g_1 and g_2.

In general, a cardinality estimate of a concatenation $[\![g_1/g_2]\!]_G$ can be computed as follows:

$$|[\![g_1/g_2]\!]_G| = \sum_{j \in \mathcal{J}_{g_1.g_2}} |\sigma_{t=j}([\![g_1]\!]_G)| \cdot |\sigma_{s=j}([\![g_2]\!]_G)|. \tag{8.8}$$

Here, *join set* $\mathcal{J}_{T_1,T_2}$ (shown in Figure 8.6) denotes the set of nodes which match the concatenation predicate $[\![g_1]\!]_G.t = [\![g_2]\!]_G.s$, where $[\![g]\!]_G.s$ is a shorthand notation for all source vertices $s \in V : \exists(s,t) \in [\![g]\!]_G$ and $[\![g]\!]_G.t$ is a notation for all target vertices $t \in V : \exists(s,t) \in [\![g]\!]_G$. For each such vertex $j \in \mathcal{J}_{g_1,g_2}$, the number of paths which go through j from $[\![g_1]\!]_G.s$ to $[\![g_2]\!]_G.t$ is the product $|\sigma_{t=j}([\![g_1]\!]_G)| \cdot |\sigma_{s=j}([\![g_1]\!]_G.t)|$. Hence, the total cardinality of a join is computed as a sum of cardinalities (numbers of paths) over all $j \in \mathcal{J}_{g_1,g_2}$.

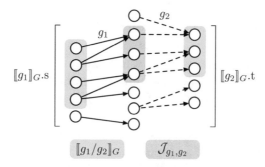

Figure 8.6: Cardinality estimation of a concatenation of graph edges.

In order to estimate the cardinality of a concatenation of two arbitrary labels g_1 and g_2, we should keep the statistics about the corresponding join set $\mathcal{J}_{g_1,g_2}$. Further, cardinalities $|\sigma_{t=j}([\![g_1]\!]_G)|$ and $|\sigma_{s=j}([\![g_1]\!]_G.t)|$ should be maintained for each node $j \in \mathcal{J}_{g_1,g_2}$. In large graph databases, maintaining accurate statistics for these is often not feasible. To reduce the size of statistical information which is kept in the database, the following three assumptions can be made.

1. **Uniformity.** All nodes j in a join set $\mathcal{J}_{g_1,g_2}$ have the same number of tuples associated with them in both $[\![g_1]\!]_G$ and $[\![g_2]\!]_G$.

2. **Independence.** Predicates on sources (s) and targets (t) in $[\![g]\!]_G$ are mutually independent.

3. **Inclusion.** The domain of targets (t) in $[\![g_1]\!]_G$ fully overlaps with the domain of sources (s) in $[\![g_2]\!]_G$, or vice versa.

Let $d(x, [\![g]\!]_G)$ denote the column cardinality of attribute x in $[\![g]\!]_G$, i.e., the number of distinct values of x in $[\![g]\!]_G$. Then, from uniformity assumption, for each vertex $j \in \mathcal{J}_{g_1,g_2}$, we have:

$$|\sigma_{t=j}([\![g_1]\!]_G)| = \frac{|[\![g_1]\!]_G|}{d(t, [\![g_1]\!]_G)} \quad \text{and} \quad |\sigma_{s=j}([\![g_2]\!]_G)| = \frac{|[\![g_2]\!]_G|}{d(s, [\![g_2]\!]_G)}. \tag{8.9}$$

Hence, formula (8.8) becomes:

$$|[\![g_1/g_2]\!]_G| = |\mathcal{J}_{g_1,g_2}| \cdot \frac{|[\![g_1]\!]_G|}{d(t, [\![g_1]\!]_G)} \cdot \frac{|[\![g_2]\!]_G|}{d(s, [\![g_2]\!]_G)}. \tag{8.10}$$

Further, from inclusion assumption, we derive a naive estimation formula for estimating the cardinality of concatenation:

$$|[\![g_1/g_2]\!]_G| = min(d(t, [\![g_1]\!]_G), d(s, [\![g_2]\!]_G)) \cdot \frac{|[\![g_1]\!]_G|}{d(t, [\![g_1]\!]_G)} \cdot \frac{|[\![g_2]\!]_G|}{d(s, [\![g_2]\!]_G)}. \tag{8.11}$$

Synopsis statistics.   Formula (8.11) corresponds to a classical cardinality estimation of a join of two arbitrary tables used in most relational databases today. In queries with joins on foreign keys which are often used in a relational database setting, this formula provides acceptable cardinality estimates. On the other hand, graph databases deal with edge traversals in which intermediate path endpoints in $[\![g_1]\!]_G$ and $[\![g_2]\!]_G$ are joined to produce longer paths in $[\![g_1/g_2]\!]_G$. In this scenario, the inclusion assumption will almost always significantly overestimate the cardinality due to the join set $\mathcal{J}_{g_1,g_2}$ being significantly smaller than both column cardinalities $d(t, [\![g_1]\!]_G)$ and $d(s, [\![g_2]\!]_G)$.

A compact collection of graph label statistics, called *synopsis*, can be used in order to provide a better estimation of the size of a concatenation in a graph. As shown in Figure 8.7 (left), for each edge label l in graph G, synopsis SYN1 stores the statistics presented at the top of Table 8.3.

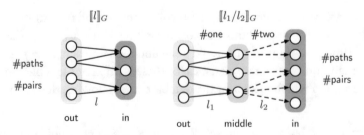

Figure 8.7: Synopsis statistics for graph label frequencies: frequency synopsis SYN1 (left) and joint-frequency synopsis SYN2 (right).

Similarly, as shown in Figure 8.7 (right), synopsis SYN2 stores join-frequency statistics for paths labeled l_1/l_2 in G for pairs of labels l_1, l_2 (see the bottom part of Table 8.3). Let $[\![r/l_1]\!]_G$

Table 8.3: Statistical information stored in (joint-)frequency synopses SYN1 and SYN2

Synopis	Name	Description`
SYN1	out	The number of nodes in G which have outgoing edge labeled with l
	in	The number of nodes in G which have incoming edge labeled with l
	#paths	The number of paths in G labeled with l
	#pairs	The number of distinct node pairs connected with paths labeled with l
SYN2	out	The number of nodes in G which have outgoing path labeled with l_1/l_2
	in	The number of nodes in G which have incoming path labeled with l_1/l_2
	middle	The number of nodes in G which have incoming edge labeled l_1 and outgoing edge labeled l_2
	#paths	The number of paths in G labeled with l_1/l_2
	#pairs	The number of distinct node pairs connected with paths labeled with l_1/l_2
	#one	The number of paths labeled l_1 from nodes in out to nodes in middle
	#two	The number of paths labeled l_2 from nodes in middle to nodes in in

denote vertex pairs (s, t) such that path between s and t in G conforms to regular expression r/l_1. Similarly, let $[\![l_2]\!]_G$ denote all node pairs in G such that a path between them conforms to l_2. Here, r is an arbitrary regular expression, and l_1 and l_2 are edge labels in G.

Using both SYN1 and SYN2, we can estimate the cardinality of concatenation $[\![r/l_1/l_2]\!]_G$ as follows. As shown in Figure 8.8, let S_{l_1} denote the set of all nodes with incoming l_1 edges in G. Then, a subset $S_{r/l_1} \subseteq S_{l_1}$ will have incoming r/l_1 paths. Another subset $S_{l_1/l_2} \subseteq S_{l_1}$ are nodes with incoming l_1 edges and outgoing l_2 edges. The intersection of S_{r/l_1} and S_{l_1/l_2} are those nodes which have incoming r/l_1 paths and outgoing l_2 edges. Therefore, the join set $\mathcal{J}$ is exactly this intersection $S_{r/l_1} \cap S_{l_1/l_2}$.

Consider node x in set S_{l_1}. Assuming independence, the probability that x is in the join set $\mathcal{J}$ is:

$$P[x \in \mathcal{J}] = P[x \in S_{r/l_1} \cap S_{l_1/l_2}] = P[x \in S_{r/l_1}] \cdot P[x \in S_{l_1/l_2}] = \frac{|S_{r/l_1}|}{|S_{l_1}|} \cdot \frac{|S_{l_1/l_2}|}{|S_{l_1}|}. \quad (8.12)$$

Consider a Bernoulli trial in which success means node x is in the join set, and failure otherwise. Then, the probability distribution of the cardinality of a join set $|\mathcal{J}|$ follows a binomial distribution $B(n, p)$ with parameters $n = |S_{l_1}|$ and $p = P[x \in \mathcal{J}]$. Therefore, we can derive the *expected* value of the cardinality of a join set:

$$E[|\mathcal{J}|] = n \cdot p = |S_{l_1}| \cdot \frac{|S_{r/l_1}|}{|S_{l_1}|} \cdot \frac{|S_{l_1/l_2}|}{|S_{l_1}|} = \frac{|S_{r/l_1}| \cdot |S_{l_1/l_2}|}{|S_{l_1}|}. \quad (8.13)$$

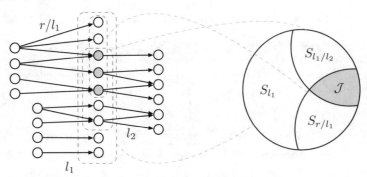

Figure 8.8: Estimating concatenation cardinality using compact label-frequency synopsis. A partition of join-candidate nodes for concatenation $[\![r/l_1/l_2]\!]_G$ is shown.

Observe that $|S_{r/l_1}|$ is the column cardinality $d(o, T_{r/l_1})$ of objects o in table T_{r/l_1}. Further, from synopsis SYN2, we obtain $|S_{l_1/l_2}| = l_1/l_2.\text{middle}$ and, from synopsis SYN1, we obtain $|S_{l_1}| = l_1.\text{in}$. Hence, (8.13) becomes:

$$|\mathcal{J}| \approx E[|\mathcal{J}|] = \frac{d(t, [\![r/l_1]\!]_G) \cdot l_1/l_2.\text{middle}}{l_1.\text{in}}. \tag{8.14}$$

Above, we approximate the cardinality $|\mathcal{J}|$ of a join set by its expected value $E[|\mathcal{J}|]$.

If we keep the independence and uniformity assumptions, but *not* inclusion assumptions, we can estimate the cardinality of a concatenation of two tables $[\![r/l_1/l_2]\!]_G$ by using (8.10, 8.14) and synopses SYN1, SYN2 as follows:

$$|[\![r/l_1/l_2]\!]_G| = \frac{d(t, [\![r/l_1]\!]_G) \cdot l_1/l_2.\text{middle}}{l_1.\text{in}} \cdot \frac{|[\![r/l_1]\!]_G|}{d(t, [\![r/l_1]\!]_G)} \cdot \frac{|[\![l_1/l_2]\!]_G|}{d(s, [\![l_1/l_2]\!]_G)}$$

$$= |[\![r/l_1]\!]_G| \cdot \frac{l_1/l_2.\#\text{two}}{l_1.\text{in}}. \tag{8.15}$$

Further, from uniformity assumption, we can estimate column cardinalities of both sources (s) and targets (t) of the join:

$$d(s, [\![r/l_1/l_2]\!]_G) = d(s, [\![r/l_1]\!]_G) \cdot \frac{l_1/l_2.\text{middle}}{l_1.\text{in}} \tag{8.16}$$

$$d(t, [\![r/l_1/l_2]\!]_G) = d(t, [\![r/l_1]\!]_G) \cdot \frac{l_1/l_2.\text{in}}{l_1.\text{in}}. \tag{8.17}$$

Given these formulas, the cardinality of an arbitrary path g which consists of edge label concatenations can be estimated by breaking g into a left-deep sequence of pairwise concatenations and applying the formulas (8.15), (8.16), and (8.17) repeatedly in a bottom-up fashion until the final cardinality for g is produced.

8.3.2   CARDINALITY OF PATTERNS

The estimation formulas presented in the previous section are sufficient to estimate the cardinality of simple paths in a graph. More elaborate techniques are required to accurately estimate the cardinality of complex graph patterns, e.g., stars, twigs, and other arbitrary subgraphs. In this section, we briefly discuss two synopsis-based approaches which aim to accurately estimate the cardinality of subgraph patterns: *characteristic sets* and *graph summaries*.

Characteristic sets.   A common type of a graph query found in many workloads is a *star* query. As follows from its name, a star query resembles a star when represented as a query graph, with one relation in the center with join predicates to a number of other relations around it. An example of a typical star query Q_{star} describing a book entity is shown in Figure 8.9 (left).

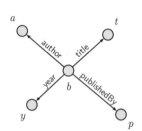
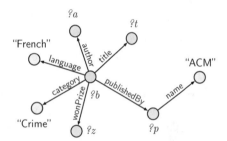

$Q_{star} : (b) \leftarrow author(b, a), year(b, y),$
$\qquad title(b, t), publishedBy(b, p)$

$Q_{cstar} : (a, t) \leftarrow author(b, a), title(b, t), language(b, \mathsf{French}),$
$\qquad category(b, \mathsf{Crime}), wonPrize(b, z),$
$\qquad publishedBy(b, p), name(p, \mathsf{ACM})$

Figure 8.9: Graph representation of typical pattern queries in graph databases. An example of a star query (left) and an example of more complex query which contains a star query (right). Adapted from Neumann and Weikum [2009].

If we estimate the cardinality of a star query by assuming the *independence* of the participating join conjuncts, we will obtain a cardinality which is, in most real graphs, severely underestimated. This is explained by the *correlation* between the join predicates which is almost always present in real-world graphs. For example, books of certain authors are likely to be published by publishers with whom these authors have a contract. Hence, multiplying the corresponding selectivities of author and publishedBy join predicates in Q_{star}, we will obtain a cardinality which is far lower than the actual selectivity of a conjunction of these predicates.

Characteristic sets (CSs) are a type of a compact graph synopsis which aims to capture the correlations between the join predicates in a given query. CSs exploit the fact that edges emitting from vertices can be used to describe the entities encoded in these vertices well. For example, in real graphs, a book entity would almost always be associated with author and title edges. Hence, the emitting edges can be often used to *characterize* the entities. A characteristic set for an entity s in a simple labeled digraph G is defined as a set of edge labels which characterize s in graph

G. This definition can be extended to property graphs by including the labels associated with entity's vertices and its emitting edges.

The *exact* cardinalities of certain queries can be computed by CSs by counting the number of occurrences of the CSs which satisfy the query's join predicates. Note that this can only be done when the query returns *distinct* bindings as CSs do not account for duplicate bindings for the same query variable. To increase the estimation accuracy and *cover* more query types, CSs can be enriched with additional statistical information. For example, to estimate the number of duplicate bindings for a specific entity, each predicate in the CS can be annotated with the number of occurrences of this predicate in entities characterized by this CS.

Precomputed CSs can be used to provide better cardinality estimation for general classes of graph queries with complex arbitrary structure and join predicates bound to constants, e.g., see query Q_{cstar} shown in Figure 8.9. This can be done by *covering* a given query graph by CSs which have been precomputed in the database synopsis. When the maximal statistical cover is found, the resulting cardinality can be computed by using simple estimation formulas which use the correlation information in the covered parts of the query and fall back to using the independence assumption in the uncovered parts of the query.

Obviously, the more CSs are stored in the synopsis, the more queries it can potentially cover. This results in a classical space vs. accuracy trade-off. Many approaches exist describing how to handle this trade-off. For example, a bounded number of *useful* CSs can be kept in the synopsis. The usefulness of a given CS will depend on the query workload and amount of information this CS carries relative to other CSs.

Graph summaries.   Another type of cardinality estimation approach which aims to go beyond estimating the cardinalities of simple paths is based on using *graph summaries* as defined in Section 5.3 of this book. The general idea is, given a graph, to compute its summary and then perform the cardinality estimation on this summary and not on the graph itself. A large number of methods exist on how to obtain a summary of a given graph. Typically, the construction of a summary involves collapsing fragments of a graph (vertices, edges, subgraphs) into a single vertex or an edge in the summary graph. Since graph summaries can capture arbitrarily complex graph structures, summary-based cardinality approaches conceptually subsume other simpler graph synopses such as (joint-)frequency edge label statistics and characteristic sets.

For example, consider a graph of single and married persons and types of cars they own shown in Figure 8.10a. A summary can be computed over this graph by merging the vertices of the same *type*, e.g., all married persons m_i are represented by a single m vertex in the summary. Similarly, the edges in the summary condense the edges in the original graph by assigning weights to edges in the summary which correspond to the counts of the number of edges in the original graph between corresponding entity types. In this example, 2 manages edges between single and married persons translate into weight 2 assigned to the corresponding summary edge.

An interesting challenge in itself is developing mathematically sound cardinality estimation formulas on a graph summary which generalize well to the whole family of graph instances

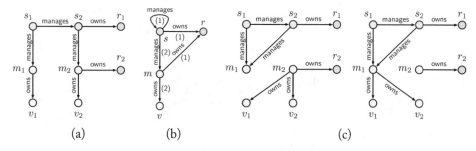

Figure 8.10: An example graph of married (m) and single persons (s) who own vans (v) and/or roadsters (r) (a); a summary of this graph (b); and example graphs which also summarize to this summary (c). Adapted from Stefanoni et al. [2018].

represented by this summary. For example, consider a graph summary s shown in Figure 8.10b and a corresponding family of graph instances shown in Figure 8.10c which summarize to s. One approach is to interpret a summary using a *possible world semantics* as a family of graphs represented by this summary. Then, a cardinality estimation problem reduces to computation of an *expected value* of the query cardinality across the represented family. This approach has the additional benefit of providing statistical guarantees on cardinality estimates for arbitrary queries.

It should be noted that space vs. accuracy trade-off and efficient synopsis update handling which are common problems affecting synopses-based cardinality estimation techniques and are even more challenging for summary-based approaches due to the increased structural complexity of the stored synopsis.

8.4   FURTHER OPTIMIZATIONS

In this section, we briefly discuss two classes of impactful query runtime optimization methods used in graph databases today: *sideways information passing* and *compression of intermediate results*.

Sideways information passing.   As described in Chapter 7, a given graph query is evaluated by executing a physical query evaluation plan, a tree-like structure in which tuples are passed from operator to operator by following logical pipelines. Typically, the tuples which hold a query's intermediate results flow vertically bottom-up in the physical execution plan, i.e., tuples *produced* by the operators at the bottom of the tree are *consumed* by their parent operators up the tree. For example, see the fragment of the physical execution plan for query Q_{cstar} shown in Figure 8.11. In this example, tuples from scan operators are consumed by the merge join 1, and tuples produced by this merge join are consumed by the next merge join upstream (merge join 2). This bottom-up tuple flow continues until the query result is produced.

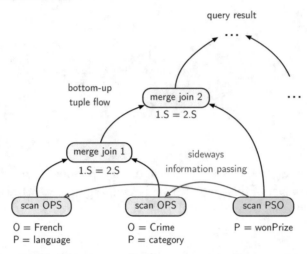

Figure 8.11: An example fragment of a physical execution plan for query Q_{cstar} which utilizes several sideways information passing pipelines to efficiently compute a star fragment of a query. Adapted from Neumann and Weikum [2009].

Most query optimization techniques operate *along* the tuple pipelines, e.g., "pushing down" the selection operators down the join tree. In this scenario, an operator is only "aware" of the operators that generate its input relations, hence restricting the possible optimizations to be *local* to its ancestors or descendants in the operator tree. However, in many cases, operators can benefit greatly by exchanging information with other operators *across* the tree. The optimization strategies that operate across the tuple pipelines are called *sideways information passing* (SIP) strategies.

Broadly speaking, SIP strategies are classified into two types: *cost-based* compile-time methods and *adaptive* run-time methods. Both SIP types aim to create *filters* based on the local information an operator is observing and then sending (or streaming) these filters across the tree to operators for which they may be useful. Compile-time SIP methods include *magic set* rewrites and *semi-join* reducers. Both semi-joins and magic set rewrites precompute the filters which can be then used by other operators during query run-time. Note that it can be expensive to precompute such SIP filters, so, in case a particular filter turns out not to be selective enough to offset the cost of its creation, the overall performance of a plan may suffer from applying this SIP optimization! Hence, this type of SIP strategy needs to be carefully considered at compile-time by the query optimizer which, in turn, is responsible for making a cost-based decision whether to apply a particular SIP strategy or not.

Another type of SIP optimization is based on *lightweight* and adaptive runtime filtering strategies. These strategies are more limited in their applicability and might not be as selective as compile-time SIP filters, but they are designed to be very lightweight so that these optimizations can be "always-on" and do not require any complex cost-based decisions. Again, consider the fragment of an execution plan for query Q_{cstar} shown in Figure 8.11. In this plan, three clustered (sorted) indexes are used to answer a fragment of a star query in Q_{cstar}. Specifically, a book is being matched against three different selection predicates, whether the book has won a prize (1), the book is written in the French language (2), and the book is in the crime category (3). In the absence of SIP, predicates (2) and (3) are evaluated first and then predicate (1) is applied to the result. However, we can use the fact that all participating base relations are sorted and all the joins are merge joins. Specifically, a simple lightweight adaptive SIP filter can be based on occasionally exchanging observed S (subject) values when a certain condition is met. For example, the PSO scan which finds books which won prizes is naturally very selective. Hence, as this scan progresses, it can share its observed S values with other, less selective OPS scans when it detects large gaps in its S values. Since all of the relations are sorted, other operators can use these gaps to *skip* through scanning of some of their respective tuples and thus potentially significantly reduce the intermediate results pipelined up the operator tree.

Compact intermediate results.   The performance of graph query evaluation is often dominated by the sum of the sizes of its output and intermediate results (IR). However, it is a common occurrence in real-world queries, that even while the query itself is very selective and produces a small output, the size of the intermediate tuples which have been processed during the evaluation of this query can be still very large.

Unlike relational databases where most of the joins are foreign-key one-to-one or one-to-many joins which do not drastically increase the size of the intermediate results, in graph databases path traversals can grow the size of the intermediate results exponentially due to compound many-to-many *multiplicity* effect. Consider, for example, *lensing* as shown in Figure 8.12. Suppose each focal vertex has m incoming a-labeled edges and n outgoing b-labeled edges. Then, the number of vertex pairs (x, z) which satisfy (a/b) path pattern is given by a multiplication $m \cdot n$. This multiplicity effect is compounded further if more vertex variables are projected by the query and the more lenses (or similar structures) there are in the underlying graph.

Broadly speaking, the size of intermediate query results can be controlled either by their timely *disposal* or by their *compression*. Some of the intermediate query results can be efficiently discarded by utilizing *pipelining* through the execution plan. In this scenario, once the intermediate result has been consumed it is effectively "forgotten" by its producing operator. While pipelining is extremely effective at reducing the intermediate result sizes, it needs to be used with extreme caution. First, in many execution plans, pipelining can be blocked by certain operators, e.g., during sorting. Second, in certain graphs, pipelining can severely cripple some of the refinement strategies and introduce lots of unnecessary computation. For example, in cyclic graphs, disposal of the intermediate results which contain already visited vertices in the graph can effectively lead to unbounded computation. Similarly, in dense graphs, the same vertex can be processed multiple times due to a "short-term" memory of the corresponding refinement strategy caused by pipelining. Hence, the disposal of the intermediate results should be based

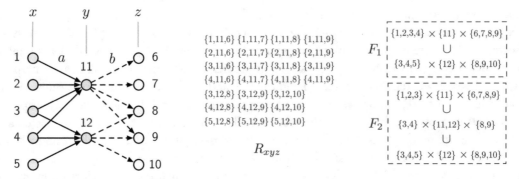

Figure 8.12: Example factorizations F_1 and F_2 of a graph which exhibits lensing and their corresponding enumeration R_{xyz}.

on a cost-based decision of the query optimizer which takes into account the available memory, current execution plan, and the structure of the given query and the graph.

Another option to reduce the size of the IR is to utilize the structural compression of the graph. Akin to graph summaries, the compression of the intermediate query bindings can be performed in many ways. One effective compression technique which works very well in graph databases is based on computing *factorizations* of the result set. Again, consider the lensing graph shown in Figure 8.12 and query $Q(x, y, z) : a(x, y), b(y, z)$. Due to multiplicity introduced by focal nodes in the graph, the cardinality of the query result $|Q(x, y, z)| = |R_{xyz}|$ is 25 triples. Assuming 4-byte `integer` representation for each node ID, the total size of the query result can be estimated as $25 \cdot 3 \cdot 4 = 300$ bytes. The factorization works by detecting common patterns in the set of tuples and factorizing them out to obtain a compact representation of this set as a union of Cartesian products of these common patterns. Naturally, many different factorizations for the same tuple set exist. For example, tuple set R_{xyz} can be represented by factorizations F_1 or F_2 as shown in Figure 8.12. Observe that F_1 stores 16 integers consuming a total of 64 bytes which is more compact than F_2 which stores 21 integers and consumes 84 bytes. Still, both of these factorizations take significantly less space than the original tuple set.

In general, like all compression techniques, IR compression faces the challenge of finding the balance between the size of the compressed representation and its efficient decompression, or *enumeration* of the IR. Ultimately, like many other decisions in the database, this balance needs to be based on a careful cost-based choice of the query optimizer.

8.5   BIBLIOGRAPHIC AND HISTORICAL NOTES

The evaluation of transitive closure is a well-studied topic. Dar and Ramakrishnan [1994] present a good overview of the early evaluation approaches which include naive and semi-naive methods. The SMART approach is introduced in Ioannidis [1986] and Valduriez and

Boral [1986]. The mixed evaluation strategy is presented in Jakobsson [1991]. Jakobsson [1992] presents a tree-based technique for TC evaluation. Yang and Zaniolo [2014] is a more recent work on hybrid SMART and semi-naive approaches in the context of a main-memory multi-core setting. Planning for evaluation of transitive closure on complex base relations is a part of a general-purpose *RPQ* WAVEGUIDE query optimizer [Yakovets et al., 2016].

The study of the worst-case optimal multi-way joins is motivated by the AGM bound which is introduced in Atserias et al. [2013]. Leapfrog Triejoin [Veldhuizen, 2014] is used in LogicBlox, a popular deductive database system. NPRR [Ngo et al., 2018] and Minesweeper [Nguyen et al., 2015] are examples of other recently developed worst-case optimal join algorithms.

Cardinality estimation is one of the most intensively studied areas in the database research community. Most of the research has been done in the context of relational databases: there exist a multitude of cardinality estimation methods based on synopses, sampling, sketches, histograms, and wavelets. A good overview of these methods is presented in Cormode et al. [2012]. Cardinality estimation in graph databases is much less studied. Gubichev and Neumann [2014] and Yakovets et al. [2016] demonstrate that estimation techniques developed for relational databases do not translate well to graphs due to their unrealistic assumptions. Cardinality estimation on tree-like data structures (XML) is studied in various schemes such as synopses, sampling, and sketches in Polyzotis et al. [2004], Zhang et al. [2006], and Luo et al. [2009]. Simple estimation for cardinality of paths in graphs by using (joint-)frequency synopses is presented by Yakovets et al. [2016]. Cardinality estimation with the help of characteristic sets is used in the high-performance triplestore RDF-3X [Neumann and Moerkotte, 2011]. Stefanoni et al. [2018] is a recent work which uses graph summaries to provide statistically sound cardinality estimates with confidence intervals.

Sideways information passing techniques were introduced as complex cost-based magic set transformations [Mumick and Pirahesh, 1994, Seshadri et al., 1996] and semi-join reducers [Bernstein and Chiu, 1981, Stocker et al., 2001]. A holistic SIP strategy based on adaptive exchanging of lightweight filters is used in RDF-3X and is described by Neumann and Weikum [2009]. A hybrid relational-based SIP strategy in which compile-time cost model is used alongside runtime benefit estimation is proposed by Ives and Taylor [2008].

Compression of intermediate results during query evaluation is a relatively unexplored topic. Factorization-based compression of the IR is closely related to the notion of factorized databases [Olteanu and Schleich, 2016]. WIREFRAME is a two-phase cost-based optimizer which compresses the IR into a factorized answer graph [Godfrey et al., 2017]. SEED [Lai et al., 2016] is a scalable subgraph enumeration approach which performs clique compression in order to minimize the IR. Qiao et al. [2017] performed a recent study that aims to find the ideal compression for a given IR.

CHAPTER 9

Research Challenges

Throughout the book we have highlighted open research challenges. In this final chapter we collect and consolidate these challenges, providing an overview of what we see as important open problems for the graph query processing research community, toward a shared research agenda for next-generation graph database systems.

We present the research challenges independently of the chapter organization and we expose them by topic. For each challenge, we pinpoint the chapters and corresponding problems addressed in this book.

Formal properties and efficient execution strategies for *RPGQ*. While the worst-case complexity of *RPGQ* query evaluation is understood, the impact of the novel property graph features of the language is not as well understood. Initial progress has been made in this direction (e.g., Angles et al. [2017, 2018a] and Francis et al. [2018]), however there still remain many open questions, e.g., static analysis of the language and the impact of graph aggregation functionality (Section 3.3.3) and extending the language with paths as first-class citizens. Progress on these questions is vital for the practical realization of efficient and scalable solutions for property graph query processing.

Schema definition for property graphs. Apart from the graph dependencies considered in Chapter 4, other constraints such as graph schemas make sense for property graphs. Currently lacking, however, is a common formalism for property graph schemas. Defining a schema for traditional graph-shaped data has mainly followed two methods, one of which relies on Datalog and the other builds on bisimulation [Abiteboul et al., 1999]. A schema graph can be defined by specifying which incoming and outcoming edges are required, or by specifying which outgoing edges are permitted. The definition can be combined with corresponding declarations of in-degree and out-degree edge distributions [Bagan et al., 2017]. The connection between the above two methods (resulting in dual schema graphs [Abiteboul et al., 1999]), their extension or development of new schema formalisms for property graphs, and the study of efficient algorithms for property graph schema typing are among important directions to undertake in future studies.

Query specification and graph exploration for property graphs. The techniques illustrated in Chapter 5 on query definability and interactive query specification do not fully accommodate the special features of the property graph model. Special attention must be paid to the fact that the results of queries in *RPGQ* are graphs rather than pairs of nodes and connecting paths. Therefore, query specification becomes much harder as the interacting user has to provide examples of input/output pairs that can be as complex as a standalone graph (instead of a single node at a time). Moreover, the graph summarization techniques known so far are limited to labeled graphs and their consideration for property graphs is an interesting open issue. Building property graph summaries and synopses for query specification that can be guided by the underlying queries has not been pursued until present.

Comprehensive comparative study of graph representations.   As laid out in Chapter 6, there is a cornucopia of property graph representations proposed in the research literature and implemented and practically used in actual systems. In other words, the problem of representing a property graph in memory or storage does not lack proposed solutions. However, research works dealing with graph representation usually argue for the advantages of one specific representation in one often very narrow usage scenario. On the side of practical systems, the design decisions—and the rationale involved in them—that lead to a particular representation being implement is typically completely unknown to the public. Graph database systems face large variations in data and workload characteristics. To build systems that prevail in all these scenarios, we require a holistic and deep understanding of the trade-offs involved in property graph representations. Such an understanding is still missing. Comprehensive comparative studies of various property graph representations over a representative range of use cases can help form such understanding.

Efficient evaluation of rich fragments of navigational graph queries.   As mentioned in Chapter 7, currently there are no evaluation approaches which are able to optimize across rich fragments of navigational graph queries such as *UCRPQ*s. Current graph databases fall back to α-RA in order to evaluate complex *UCRPQ*s. This significantly reduces the number of optimization techniques which can be utilized to speed up the query evaluation. A comprehensive study is needed to identify whether the rich body of work on query planning and optimization outside of α-RA can be efficiently used in the context of *UCRPQ*s.

An extensive study of advanced graph query optimization techniques.   As discussed in Chapters 7 and 8, there are numerous different advanced graph query optimization techniques. These techniques come from different domains and research areas. For example, DFS-based refinement techniques are typically not used in the BFS setting. The connection between sideways information passing strategies and worst-case optimal joins is also unexplored. Many optimization strategies have been proposed over time, but the link between different optimization classes is missing. A comprehensive study is needed to establish this link and which will pave the way to new powerful methods for graph query optimization.

Bibliography

Daniel J. Abadi, Adam Marcus, Samuel Madden, and Katherine J. Hollenbach. Scalable semantic web data management using vertical partitioning. In *VLDB*, pages 411–422, ACM,
2007. 99

Christopher R. Aberger, Susan Tu, Kunle Olukotun, and Christopher Ré. EmptyHeaded:
A relational engine for graph processing. In *SIGMOD*, pages 431–446, 2016. DOI:
10.1145/2882903.2915213 100

Serge Abiteboul, Richard Hull, and Victor Vianu. *Foundations of Databases*. Addison-Wesley,
1995. 44, 54

Serge Abiteboul, Peter Buneman, and Dan Suciu. *Data on the Web: From Relations to Semistructured Data and XML*. Morgan Kaufmann, 1999. 35, 141

Rakesh Agrawal. Alpha: An extension of relational algebra to express a class of recursive
queries. *IEEE Transactions on Software Engineering*, 14(7), pages 879–885, July 1988. DOI:
10.1109/32.42731 117

Rakesh Agrawal, Alexander Borgida, and H. V. Jagadish. Efficient management of transitive
relationships in large data and knowledge bases. In *SIGMOD*, pages 253–262, ACM, 1989.
DOI: 10.1145/67544.66950 100

Erik Agterdenbos, George H. L. Fletcher, Chee-Yong Chan, and Stijn Vansummeren. Empirical evaluation of guarded structural indexing. In *EDBT*, pages 714–715, 2016. OpenProcee
dings.org DOI: 10.5441/002/edbt.2016.101. 99

Alfred V. Aho, John E. Hopcroft, and Jeffrey D. Ullman. *Data Structures and Algorithms*.
Addison-Wesley, 1983. 65

Sandra Álvarez-García, Nieves R. Brisaboa, Susana Ladra, and Oscar Pedreira. A compact representation of graph databases. In *MLG*, pages 18–25, ACM, 2010. DOI:
10.1145/1830252.1830255 100

Renzo Angles and Claudio Gutiérrez. Survey of graph database models. *ACM Computing
Surveys*, 40(1), pages 1:1–1:39, 2008. DOI: 10.1145/1322432.1322433 2, 13

Renzo Angles and Claudio Gutierrez. Subqueries in SPARQL. In *AMW*, vol. 749, page 12,
2011. CEUR-WS.org 34

Renzo Angles, Marcelo Arenas, Pablo Barceló, Aidan Hogan, Juan L. Reutter, and Domagoj Vrgoc. Foundations of modern query languages for graph databases. *ACM Computing Surveys*, 50(5), 2017. DOI: 10.1145/3104031 2, 35, 141

Renzo Angles, Marcelo Arenas, Pablo Barceló, Peter A. Boncz, George H. L. Fletcher, Claudio Gutierrez, Tobias Lindaaker, Marcus Paradies, Stefan Plantikow, Juan Sequeda, Oskar van Rest, and Hannes Voigt. G-CORE: A core for future graph query languages. In *SIGMOD*, ACM, 2018a. DOI: 10.1145/3183713.3190654 3, 14, 33, 35, 141

Renzo Angles, Juan Reutter, and Hannes Voigt. Graph query languages. In *Encyclopedia of Big Data Technologies*, Springer, 2018b. DOI: 10.1007/978-3-319-63962-8_75-1 35

Timos Antonopoulos, Frank Neven, and Frédéric Servais. Definability problems for graph query languages. In *ICDT*, pages 141–152, ACM, 2013. DOI: 10.1145/2448496.2448514 59, 61, 71

Alberto Apostolico and Guido Drovandi. Graph compression by BFS. *Algorithms*, 2(3), pages 1031–1044, 2009. DOI: 10.3390/a2031031 100

Marcelo Arenas and Gonzalo I. Diaz. The exact complexity of the first-order logic definability problem. *ACM Transactions on Database Systems*, 41(2), pages 13:1–13:14, 2016. DOI: 10.1145/2886095 58, 59

Marcelo Arenas, Pablo Barceló, Leonid Libkin, and Filip Murlak. *Relational and XML Data Exchange*. Morgan & Claypool Publishers, 2010. DOI: 10.2200/S00297ED1V01Y201008DTM008. 53

Marcelo Arenas, Pablo Barceló, and Leonid Libkin. Graph path navigation. In *Encyclopedia of Big Data Technologies*, Springer, 2018. DOI: 10.1007/978-3-319-63962-8_214-1 35

Abdallah Arioua and Angela Bonifati. User-guided repairing of inconsistent knowledge bases. In *EDBT*, pages 133–144, 2018. OpenProceedings.org DOI: 10.5441/002/edbt.2018.13. 55

William Ward Armstrong. Dependency structures of data base relationships. In *IFIP Congress*, pages 580–583, 1974. 55

Albert Atserias, Martin Grohe, and Dániel Marx. Size bounds and query plans for relational joins. *SIAM Journal on Computing*, 42(4), pages 1737–1767, 2013. DOI: 10.1137/110859440. 139

Sören Auer, Christian Bizer, Georgi Kobilarov, Jens Lehmann, Richard Cyganiak, and Zachary G. Ives. DBpedia: A nucleus for a Web of open data. In *ISWC*, vol. 4825, pages 722–735, Springer, 2007. DOI: 10.1007/978-3-540-76298-0_52 13, 57

Guillaume Bagan, Angela Bonifati, Radu Ciucanu, George H. L. Fletcher, Aurélien Lemay, and Nicky Advokaat.   gMark: Schema-driven generation of graphs and queries. *IEEE Transactions on Knowledge and Data Engineering*, 29(4), pages 856–869, April 2017. DOI: 10.1109/TKDE.2016.2633993. 117, 141

Pablo Barceló and Pablo Muñoz. Graph logics with rational relations: The role of word combinatorics. *ACM Transactions on Computational Logic*, 18(2), pages 10:1–10:41, 2017. DOI: 10.1145/3070822 35

Pablo Barceló, Leonid Libkin, Anthony Widjaja Lin, and Peter T. Wood. Expressive languages for path queries over graph-structured data. *ACM Transactions on Database Systems*, 37(4), pages 31:1–31:46, December 2012a. DOI: 10.1145/2389241.2389250 35

Pablo Barceló, Jorge Pérez, and Juan L. Reutter. Relative expressiveness of nested regular expressions. In *AMW*, pages 180–195, 2012b. CEUR-WS.org 35

Pablo Barceló, Jorge Pérez, and Juan L. Reutter. Schema mappings and data exchange for graph databases. In *ICDT*, pages 189–200, ACM, 2013. DOI: 10.1145/2448496.2448520 54, 55

Pablo Barceló, Gaelle Fontaine, and Anthony Widjaja Lin. Expressive path queries on graph with data. *Logical Methods in Computer Science*, 11(4), pages 1–39, October 2015. DOI: 10.2168/lmcs-11(4:1)2015 35

Hannah Bast, Daniel Delling, Andrew V. Goldberg, Matthias Müller-Hannemann, Thomas Pajor, Peter Sanders, Dorothea Wagner, and Renato F. Werneck. Route planning in transportation networks. In *Algorithm Engineering—Selected Results and Surveys*, vol. 9220, pages 19–80, Springer, 2016. DOI: 10.1007/978-3-319-49487-6_2 100

Kent Beck, Mike Beedle, Arie van Bennekum, Alistair Cockburn, Ward Cunningham, Martin Fowler, James Grenning, Jim Highsmith, Andrew Hunt, Ron Jeffries, Jon Kern, Brian Marick, Robert C. Martin, Steve Mellor, Ken Schwaber, Jeff Sutherland, and Dave Thomas. Manifesto for agile software development, 2001. http://agilemanifesto.org/ 13

Catriel Beeri, Ronald Fagin, and John H. Howard. A complete axiomatization for functional and multivalued dependencies in database relations. In *SIGMOD*, pages 47–61, ACM, 1977. DOI: 10.1145/509404.509414. 55

Tim Berners-Lee, James Hendler, and Ora Lassila. The semantic web. *Scientific American*, 284(5), pages 34–43, May 2001. DOI: 10.1038/scientificamerican0501-34 13

Philip A. Bernstein and Dah-Ming W. Chiu. Using semi-joins to solve relational queries. *Journal of the ACM*, 28(1), pages 25–40, January 1981. DOI: 10.1145/322234.322238 139

Fei Bi, Lijun Chang, Xuemin Lin, Lu Qin, and Wenjie Zhang. Efficient subgraph matching by postponing Cartesian products. In *SIGMOD*, pages 1199–1214, ACM, 2016. DOI: 10.1145/2882903.2915236 117

Meghyn Bienvenu, Diego Calvanese, Magdalena Ortiz, and Mantas Simkus. Nested regular path queries in description logics. In *KR*, pages 218–227, AAAI, 2014. 35

Christian Bizer, Jens Lehmann, Georgi Kobilarov, Sören Auer, Christian Becker, Richard Cyganiak, and Sebastian Hellmann. DBpedia—A crystallization point for the Web of data. *Journal of Web Semantics*, 7(3), pages 154–165, 2009. DOI: 10.1016/j.websem.2009.07.002. 57

Daniel K. Blandford, Guy E. Blelloch, and Ian A. Kash. An experimental analysis of a compact graph representation. In *ALENEX*, pages 49–61, SIAM, 2004. 100

Blazegraph. The bigdata RDF dDatabase, May 2013. https://www.blazegraph.com/white papers/bigdata_architecture_whitepaper.pdf 13

Paolo Boldi and Sebastiano Vigna. The WebGraph framework I: Compression techniques. In *WWW*, pages 595–602, ACM, 2004. DOI: 10.1145/988672.988752 100

Paolo Boldi, Marco Rosa, Massimo Santini, and Sebastiano Vigna. Layered label propagation: A MultiResolution coordinate-free ordering for compressing social networks. In *WWW*, pages 587–596, ACM, 2011. DOI: 10.1145/1963405.1963488 100

Kurt D. Bollacker, Colin Evans, Praveen Paritosh, Tim Sturge, and Jamie Taylor. Freebase: A collaboratively created graph database for structuring human knowledge. In *SIGMOD*, pages 1247–1250, 2008. DOI: 10.1145/1376616.1376746 57

Iovka Boneva, Angela Bonifati, and Radu Ciucanu. Graph data exchange with target constraints. In *GraphQ*, pages 171–176, 2015. CEUR-WS.org 54, 55

Angela Bonifati and Ioana Ileana. Graph data integration and exchange. In *Encyclopedia of Big Data Technologies*, Springer, 2018. DOI: 10.1007/978-3-319-63962-8_209-1 54

Angela Bonifati, Radu Ciucanu, Aurélien Lemay, and Slawek Staworko. A paradigm for learning queries on big data. In *Data4U*, pages 7–12, ACM, 2014a. DOI: 10.1145/2658840.2658842 71

Angela Bonifati, Radu Ciucanu, and Slawek Staworko. Interactive inference of join queries. In *EDBT*, pages 451–462, 2014b. OpenProceedings.org DOI: 10.5441/002/edbt.2014.41. 65

Angela Bonifati, Radu Ciucanu, and Aurélien Lemay. Learning path queries on graph databases. In *EDBT*, pages 109–120, 2015. OpenProceedings.org DOI: 10.5441/002/edbt.2015.11. 57, 59, 61, 62, 64, 65

Angela Bonifati, Radu Ciucanu, and Slawek Staworko. Learning join queries from user examples. *ACM Transactions on Database Systems*, 40(4), pages 24:1–24:38, 2016a. DOI: 10.1145/2818637 65

Angela Bonifati, Werner Nutt, Riccardo Torlone, and Jan Van den Bussche. Mapping-equivalence and oid-equivalence of single-function object-creating conjunctive queries. *The VLDB Journal—The International Journal on Very Large Data Bases*, 25(3), pages 381–397, June 2016b. DOI: 10.1007/s00778-016-0421-x 24

Angela Bonifati, Wim Martens, and Thomas Timm. An analytical study of large SPARQL query logs. *Proc. of the VLDB Endowment*, 11(2), pages 149–161, October 2017. DOI: 10.14778/3149193.3149196 52

Angela Bonifati, Stefania Dumbrava, and Emilio Jesus Gallego Arias. Certified graph view maintenance with regular datalog. *Theory and Practice of Logic Programming. Proc. of the 34th International Conference on Logic Programming*, 18(3–4), pages 372–389, Oxford, UK, July 2018. DOI: 10.1017/S1471068418000224. 34

Mihaela A. Bornea, Julian Dolby, Anastasios Kementsietsidis, Kavitha Srinivas, Patrick Dantressangle, Octavian Udrea, and Bishwaranjan Bhattacharjee. Building an efficient RDF store over a relational database. In *SIGMOD*, pages 121–132, ACM, 2013. DOI: 10.1145/2463676.2463718 100

Christof Bornhövd, Robert Kubis, Wolfgang Lehner, Hannes Voigt, and Horst Werner. Flexible information management, exploration and analysis in SAP HANA. In *DATA*, pages 15–28, SciTePress, 2012. DOI: 10.5220/0004011500150028. 14

Pierre Bourhis, Markus Krötzsch, and Sebastian Rudolph. Query containment for highly expressive datalog fragments. *The Computing Research Repository*, June 2014a. 21

Pierre Bourhis, Markus Krötzsch, and Sebastian Rudolph. How to best nest regular path queries. In *DLOG*, vol. 1193, pages 404–415, 2014b. 21, 35

Mario Briggs, Farzana Anwar, Rajendran Appavu, Ganesh Choudhary, and Priya Ranjan Sahoo. Resource description framework application development in DB2 10 for Linux, UNIX, and Windows, Part 2, Optimize your RDF data stores in DB2 and provide fine-grained access control, October 2012a. https://www.ibm.com/developerworks/data/tutorials/dm-1210rdfdb210/index.html 117

Mario Briggs, Priya Ranjan Sahoo, Gayathri Raghavendra, Rajendran Appavu, and Farzana Anwar. Resource description framework application development in DB2 10 for Linux, UNIX, and Windows, Part 1: RDF store creation and maintenance, May 2012b. https://www.ibm.com/developerworks/data/tutorials/dm-1205rdfdb210/index.html 117

Nieves R. Brisaboa, Susana Ladra, and Gonzalo Navarro. k^2-trees for compact web graph representation. In *SPIRE*, pages 18–30, 2009. DOI: 10.1007/978-3-642-03784-9_3. 100

Diego Calvanese, Giuseppe De Giacomo, Maurizio Lenzerini, and Moshe Y. Vardi. View-based query processing for regular path queries with inverse. In *PODS*, pages 58–66, ACM, 2000. DOI: 10.1145/335168.335207 54, 55

Diego Calvanese, Giuseppe De Giacomo, Maurizio Lenzerini, and Moshe Y. Vardi. Rewriting of regular expressions and regular path queries. *Journal of Computer and System Sciences*, 64(3), pages 443–465, May 2002. DOI: 10.1006/jcss.2001.1805 54, 55

Diego Calvanese, Giuseppe De Giacomo, Maurizio Lenzerini, and Moshe Y. Vardi. On simplification of schema mappings. *Journal of Computer and System Sciences*, 79(6), pages 816–834, 2013. DOI: 10.1016/j.jcss.2013.01.005 54, 55

Šejla Čebirić, François Goasdoué, and Ioana Manolescu. Query-oriented summarization of RDF graphs. *PVLDB*, 8(12), pages 2012–2015, 2015. DOI: 10.14778/2824032.2824124 100

Kristina Chodorow and Michael Dirolf. *MongoDB—The Definitive Guide: Powerful and Scalable Data Storage*. O'Reilly, 2010. 13

Eugene Inseok Chong, Souripriya Das, George Eadon, and Jagannathan Srinivasan. An efficient SQL-based RDF querying scheme. In *VLDB*, pages 1216–1227, ACM, 2005. 99, 117

Eric Chu, Jennifer L. Beckmann, and Jeffrey F. Naughton. The case for a wide-table approach to manage sparse relational data sets. In *SIGMOD*, pages 821–832, ACM, 2007. DOI: 10.1145/1247480.1247571 99

Radu Ciucanu. Cross-model queries and schemas: Complexity and learning. (Requêtes et schémas hétérogènes: Complexité et apprentissage). Ph.D. thesis, Lille University of Science and Technology, France, 2015. 71

Francisco Claude and Gonzalo Navarro. Extended compact web graph representations. In *Algorithms and Applications, Essays Dedicated to Esko Ukkonen on the Occasion of his 60th Birthday*, pages 77–91, Springer, 2010a. DOI: 10.1007/978-3-642-12476-1_5 100

Francisco Claude and Gonzalo Navarro. Fast and compact web graph representations. *ACM Transactions on the Web*, 4(4), pages 16:1–16:31, 2010b. DOI: 10.1145/1841909.1841913 100

Edith Cohen, Eran Halperin, Haim Kaplan, and Uri Zwick. Reachability and distance queries via 2-hop labels. *SIAM Journal on Computing*, 32(5), pages 1338–1355, August 2003. DOI: 10.1137/s0097539702403098 100

Douglas Comer. The ubiquitous B-tree. *ACM Computing Surveys*, 11(2), pages 121–137, 1979. DOI: 10.1145/356770.356776 76

Mariano P. Consens and Alberto O. Mendelzon. GraphLog: A visual formalism for real life recursion. In *PODS*, pages 404–416, ACM, 1990. DOI: 10.1145/298514.298591 35

Mariano P. Consens, Alberto O. Mendelzon, Dimitra Vista, and Peter T. Wood. Constant propagation vs. join reordering in datalog. In *RIDS*, pages 245–259, Springer, 1995. DOI: 10.1007/3-540-60365-4_131 117

Thomas H. Cormen, Charles E. Leiserson, Ronald Rivest, and Clifford Stein. *Introduction to Algorithms*, 3rd ed. MIT Press, Cambridge, MA, 2009. 100

Graham Cormode, Minos N. Garofalakis, Peter J. Haas, and Chris Jermaine. Synopses for massive data: Samples, histograms, wavelets, sketches. *Foundations and Trends in Databases*, 4(1–3), pages 1–294, 2012. DOI: 10.1561/1900000004 139

Douglas Crockford. The application/JSON media type for JavaScript object notation (JSON), RFC 4627, July 2006. `http://tools.ietf.org/html/rfc4627` DOI: 10.17487/rfc4627 13

Isabel F. Cruz, Alberto O. Mendelzon, and Peter T. Wood. A graphical query language supporting recursion. In *SIGMOD*, pages 323–330, ACM, 1987. DOI: 10.1145/38714.38749 35

Isabel F. Cruz, Alberto O. Mendelzon, and Peter T. Wood. G+: Recursive queries without recursion. In *Proc. of 2nd International Conference on Expert Database Systems*, pages 645–666, Benjamin Cummings, Vienna, VA, April 25–27, 1988. 35

Shaul Dar and Raghu Ramakrishnan. A performance study of transitive closure algorithms. In *SIGMOD*, pages 454–465, ACM, 1994. DOI: 10.1145/191843.191928 138

Saumen C. Dey, Víctor Cuevas-Vicenttín, Sven Köhler, Eric Gribkoff, Michael Wang, and Bertram Ludäscher. On implementing provenance-aware regular path queries with relational query engines. In *GraphQ*, pages 214–223, ACM, 2013. DOI: 10.1145/2457317.2457353 117

Orri Erling and Ivan Mikhailov. RDF support in the virtuoso DBMS. In *CSSW*, vol. 113, pages 59–68, GI, 2007. 99, 117

Orri Erling, Alex Averbuch, Josep-Lluis Larriba-Pey, Hassan Chafi, Andrey Gubichev, Arnau Prat-Pérez, Minh-Duc Pham, and Peter A. Boncz. The LDBC social network benchmark: Interactive workload. In *SIGMOD*, pages 619–630, 2015. DOI: 10.1145/2723372.2742786 117

Ronald Fagin and Moshe Y. Vardi. The theory of data dependencies—An overview. In *Proc. of the 11th Colloquium Automata, Languages and Programming*, pages 1–22, Springer, Antwerp, Belgium, July 16–20, 1984. DOI: 10.1007/3-540-13345-3_1 54

Wenfei Fan and Ping Lu. Dependencies for graphs. In *PODS*, pages 403–416, ACM, 2017. DOI: 10.1145/3034786.3056114 45, 50, 55

Wenfei Fan, Floris Geerts, Xibei Jia, and Anastasios Kementsietsidis. Conditional functional dependencies for capturing data inconsistencies. *ACM Transactions on Database Systems*, 33(2), pages 6:1–6:48, June 2008. DOI: 10.1145/1366102.1366103 55

Wenfei Fan, Jianzhong Li, Shuai Ma, Hongzhi Wang, and Yinghui Wu. Graph homomorphism revisited for graph matching. *Proc. of the VLDB Endowment*, 3(1), pages 1161–1172, 2010. DOI: 10.14778/1920841.1920986 67

Wenfei Fan, Jianzhong Li, Xin Wang, and Yinghui Wu. Query preserving graph compression. In *SIGMOD*, pages 157–168, ACM, 2012. DOI: 10.1145/2213836.2213855 72, 100

Wenfei Fan, Zhe Fan, Chao Tian, and Xin Luna Dong. Keys for graphs. *Proc. of the VLDB Endowment*, 8(12), pages 1590–1601, August 2015. DOI: 10.14778/2824032.2824056 49, 55

Wenfei Fan, Yinghui Wu, and Jingbo Xu. Functional dependencies for graphs. In *SIGMOD*, pages 1843–1857, ACM, 2016. DOI: 10.1145/2882903.2915232 38, 55

Raphael A. Finkel and Jon Louis Bentley. Quad trees: A data structure for retrieval on composite keys. *Acta Informatica*, 4, pages 1–9, March 1974. DOI: 10.1007/bf00288933 88

George H. L. Fletcher, Dirk Van Gucht, Yuqing Wu, Marc Gyssens, Sofia Brenes, and Jan Paredaens. A methodology for coupling fragments of XPath with structural indexes for XML documents. *Information Systems*, 34(7), pages 657–670, November 2009. DOI: 10.1016/j.is.2008.09.003 100

George H. L. Fletcher, Marc Gyssens, Dirk Leinders, Jan Van den Bussche, Dirk Van Gucht, and Stijn Vansummeren. Similarity and bisimilarity notions appropriate for characterizing indistinguishability in fragments of the calculus of relations. *Journal of Logic and Computation*, 25(3), pages 549–580, June 2015a. DOI: 10.1093/logcom/exu018 72, 98

George H. L. Fletcher, Marc Gyssens, Dirk Leinders, Dimitri Surinx, Jan Van den Bussche, Dirk Van Gucht, Stijn Vansummeren, and Yuqing Wu. Relative expressive power of navigational querying on graphs. *Information Sciences*, 298, pages 390–406, March 2015b. DOI: 10.1016/j.ins.2014.11.031 35

George H. L. Fletcher, Marc Gyssens, Jan Paredaens, Dirk Van Gucht, and Yuqing Wu. Structural characterizations of the navigational expressiveness of relation algebras on a tree. *Journal of Computer and System Sciences*, 82(2), pages 229–259, March 2016. DOI: 10.1016/j.jcss.2015.10.002 100

Flink. Introducing Gelly: Graph processing with Apache flink, August 2015. http://flink.apache.org/news/2015/08/24/introducing-flink-gelly.html 14

Nadime Francis and Leonid Libkin. Schema mappings for data graphs. In *PODS*, pages 389–401, ACM, 2017. DOI: 10.1145/3034786.3056113 54

Nadime Francis, Luc Segoufin, and Cristina Sirangelo. Datalog rewritings of regular path queries using views. *Logical Methods in Computer Science*, 11(4), December 2015. DOI: 10.2168/lmcs-11(4:14)2015 54, 55

Nadime Francis, Alastair Green, Paolo Guagliardo, Leonid Libkin, Tobias Lindaaker, Victor Marsault, Stefan Plantikow, Mats Rydberg, Petra Selmer, and Andrés Taylor. Cypher: An evolving query language for property graphs. In *SIGMOD*, ACM, 2018. DOI: 10.1145/3183713.3190657 2, 34, 141

Michael J. Franklin, Alon Y. Halevy, and David Maier. From databases to dataspaces: A new abstraction for information management. *SIGMOD Record*, 34(4), pages 27–33, 2005. DOI: 10.1145/1107499.1107502 13

Brian Gallagher. Matching structure and semantics: A survey on graph-based pattern matching. In *AAAIFS*, 2006. 117

Parke Godfrey, Nikolay Yakovets, Zahid Abul-Basher, and Mark H. Chignell. WIREFRAME: Two-phase, cost-based optimization for conjunctive regular path queries. In *AMW*, 2017. CEUR-WS.org 139

E. Mark Gold. Language identification in the limit. *Information and Control*, 10(5), pages 447–474, May 1967. DOI: 10.1016/s0019-9958(67)91165-5 61

E. Mark Gold. Complexity of automaton identification from given data. *Information and Control*, 37(3), pages 302–320, 1978. DOI: 10.1016/s0019-9958(78)90562-4 61, 62

Joseph E. Gonzalez, Reynold S. Xin, Ankur Dave, Daniel Crankshaw, Michael J. Franklin, and Ion Stoica. GraphX: Graph processing in a distributed dataflow framework. In *OSDI*, pages 599–613, 2014. 14

Szymon Grabowski and Wojciech Bieniecki. Merging adjacency lists for efficient web graph compression. In *ICMMI*, pages 385–392, Springer, 2011. DOI: 10.1007/978-3-642-23169-8_42 100

Todd J. Green, Shan Shan Huang, Boon Thau Loo, and Wenchao Zhou. Datalog and recursive query processing. *Foundations and Trends in Databases*, 5(2), pages 105–195, 2013. DOI: 10.1561/1900000017 22, 23

Andrey Gubichev and Thomas Neumann. Exploiting the query structure for efficient join ordering in SPARQL queries. In *EDBT*, pages 439–450, 2014. OpenProceedings.org DOI: 10.5441/002/edbt.2014.40. 139

Fred G. Gustavson. Two fast algorithms for sparse matrices: Multiplication and permuted transposition. *Transactions on Mathematical Software*, 4(3), pages 250–269, 1978. DOI: 10.1145/355791.355796 100

Claudio Gutierrez, Jan Hidders, and Peter Wood. Graph data models. In *Encyclopedia of Big Data Technologies*, Springer, 2018. DOI: 10.1007/978-3-319-63962-8_81-1. 13, 14

Wook-Shin Han, Jinsoo Lee, and Jeong-Hoon Lee. $Turbo_{iso}$: Towards ultraFast and robust subgraph isomorphism search in large graph databases. In *SIGMOD*, pages 337–348, ACM, 2013. DOI: 10.1145/2463676.2465300 117

Olaf Hartig. Foundations of RDF⋆ and SPARQL⋆ (an alternative approach to statement-level metadata in RDF). In *AMW*, 2017. CEUR-WS.org 13, 35

Matthias Hauck, Marcus Paradies, Holger Fröning, Wolfgang Lehner, and Hannes Rauhe. Highspeed graph processing exploiting main-memory column stores. In *Euro-Par*, pages 503–514, 2015. DOI: 10.1007/978-3-319-27308-2_41 99

Tom Heath and Christian Bizer. *Linked Data: Evolving the Web into a Global Data Space*. Morgan & Claypool Publishers, February 2011. DOI: 10.2200/s00334ed1v01y201102wbe001 13

Safiollah Heidari, Yogesh Simmhan, Rodrigo N. Calheiros, and Rajkumar Buyya. Scalable graph processing frameworks: A taxonomy and open challenges. *ACM Computing Surveys*, 51(3), pages 60:1–60:53, 2018. DOI: 10.1145/3199523 2

Jelle Hellings, George H. L. Fletcher, and Herman J. Haverkort. Efficient external-memory bisimulation on dags. In *SIGMOD*, pages 553–564, ACM, 2012. DOI: 10.1145/2213836.2213899 99

Jelle Hellings, Bart Kuijpers, Jan Van den Bussche, and Xiaowang Zhang. Walk logic as a framework for path query languages on graph databases. In *ICDT*, pages 117–128, ACM, 2013. DOI: 10.1145/2448496.2448512 35

Jelle Hellings, Marc Gyssens, Jan Paredaens, and Yuqing Wu. Implication and axiomatization of functional and constant constraints. *Annals of Mathematics and Artificial Intelligence*, 76(3–4), pages 251–279, April 2016. DOI: 10.1007/s10472-015-9473-7 55

Monika Rauch Henzinger, Thomas A. Henzinger, and Peter W. Kopke. Computing simulations on finite and infinite graphs. In *FOCS*, pages 453–462, IEEE, 1995. DOI: 10.1109/sfcs.1995.492576 67

Kai Herrmann, Hannes Voigt, and Wolfgang Lehner. Online horizontal partitioning of heterogeneous data. *IT—Information Technology*, 56(1), pages 4–12, 2014a. DOI: 10.1515/itit-2014-1015 99

Kai Herrmann, Hannes Voigt, and Wolfgang Lehner. Cinderella—Adaptive online partitioning of irregularly structured data. In *SMDB*, pages 284–291, IEEE, 2014b. DOI: 10.1109/icdew.2014.6818342 99

Tony Hey, Stewart Tansley, and Kristin M. Tolle. *The Fourth Paradigm: Data-Intensive Scientific Discovery*. Microsoft Research, 2009. 14

Jan Hidders. *A graph-based update language for object-oriented data models*. Ph.D. thesis, Eindhoven University of Technology, December 2001. 35

Yannis E. Ioannidis. On the computation of the transitive closure of relational operators. In *VLDB*, pages 403–411, Morgan Kaufmann, 1986. 138

Yannis E. Ioannidis. Query optimization. *ACM Computing Surveys*, 28(1), pages 121–123, March 1996. DOI: 10.1145/234313.234367 116

Zachary G. Ives and Nicholas E. Taylor. Sideways information passing for push-style query processing. In *ICDE*, pages 774–783, IEEE, 2008. DOI: 10.1109/icde.2008.4497486 139

Håkan Jakobsson. Mixed-approach algorithms for transitive closure. In *PODS*, pages 199–205, ACM, 1991. DOI: 10.1145/113413.113431 139

Håkan Jakobsson. On tree-based techniques for query evaluation. In *PODS*, pages 380–392, ACM, 1992. DOI: 10.1145/137097.137914 139

Nandish Jayaram, Arijit Khan, Chengkai Li, Xifeng Yan, and Ramez Elmasri. Querying knowledge graphs by example entity tuples. *IEEE Transactions on Knowledge and Data Engineering*, 27(10), pages 2797–2811, October 2015. DOI: 10.1109/TKDE.2015.2426696. 67, 71

Martin Junghanns, André Petermann, Niklas Teichmann, Kevin Gómez, and Erhard Rahm. Analyzing extended property graphs with Apache flink. In *NDA*, pages 3:1–3:8, ACM, 2016. DOI: 10.1145/2980523.2980527 14, 35

Vasiliki Kalavri, Vladimir Vlassov, and Seif Haridi. High-level programming abstractions for distributed graph processing. *IEEE Transactions on Knowledge and Data Engineering*, 30(2), pages 305–324, February 2018. DOI: 10.1109/tkde.2017.2762294 2

154   BIBLIOGRAPHY

Mehdi Kargar and Aijun An. Finding top-k, r-cliques for keyword search from graphs in polynomial delay. *Knowledge and Information Systems*, 43(2), pages 249–280, May 2015. DOI: 10.1007/s10115-014-0736-0 66

Gjergji Kasneci, Maya Ramanath, Mauro Sozio, Fabian M. Suchanek, and Gerhard Weikum. STAR: Steiner-tree approximation in relationship graphs. In *ICDE*, pages 868–879, IEEE, 2009. DOI: 10.1109/icde.2009.64 66

Hyeonji Kim, Juneyoung Lee, Sourav S. Bhowmick, Wook-Shin Han, JeongHoon Lee, Seongyun Ko, and Moath H. A. Jarrah. Dualsim: Parallel subgraph enumeration in a massive graph on a single machine. In *Proc. of the International Conference on Management of Data*, pages 1231–1245, 2016. DOI: 10.1145/2882903.2915209 117

Jinha Kim, Hyungyu Shin, Wook-Shin Han, Sungpack Hong, and Hassan Chafi. Taming subgraph isomorphism for RDF query processing. *Proc. of the VLDB Endowment*, 8(11), pages 1238–1249, July 2015. DOI: 10.14778/2809974.2809985 117

Gordon L. Kindlmann and Carlos Eduardo Scheidegger. An algebraic process for visualization design. *IEEE Transactions on Visualization and Computer Graphics*, 20(12), pages 2181–2190, December 2014. DOI: 10.1109/tvcg.2014.2346325 65

Krys Kochut and Maciej Janik. SPARQLeR: Extended SPARQL for semantic association discovery. In *ESWC*, pages 145–159, Springer, 2007. DOI: 10.1007/978-3-540-72667-8_12 117

André Koschmieder and Ulf Leser. Regular path queries on large graphs. In *SSDBM*, pages 177–194, Springer, 2012. DOI: 10.1007/978-3-642-31235-9_12 117

Danai Koutra and Christos Faloutsos. *Individual and Collective Graph Mining: Principles, Algorithms, and Applications.* Morgan & Claypool Publishers, October 2017. DOI: 10.2200/s00796ed1v01y201708dmk014 2, 65

Dexter Kozen. Lower bounds for natural proof systems. In *FOCS*, pages 254–266, IEEE, 1977. DOI: 10.1109/sfcs.1977.16 61

Longbin Lai, Lu Qin, Xuemin Lin, Ying Zhang, and Lijun Chang. Scalable distributed subgraph enumeration. *Proc. of the VLDB Endowment*, 10(3), pages 217–228, November 2016. DOI: 10.14778/3021924.3021937 139

Grégoire Laurence, Aurélien Lemay, Joachim Niehren, Slawek Staworko, and Marc Tommasi. Learning sequential tree-to-word transducers. In *LATA*, pages 490–502, Springer, 2014. DOI: 10.1007/978-3-319-04921-2_40 61

Jinsoo Lee, Wook-Shin Han, Romans Kasperovics, and Jeong-Hoon Lee. An in-depth comparison of subgraph isomorphism algorithms in graph databases. *Proc. of the VLDB Endowment*, 6(2), pages 133–144, December 2012. DOI: 10.14778/2535568.2448946 117

Michael Levandowsky and David Winter. Distance between sets. *Nature*, 234, pages 34–35, November 1971. DOI: 10.1038/234034a0 82

Leonid Libkin. *Elements of Finite Model Theory*. Springer, 2004. DOI: 10.1007/978-3-662-07003-1 98

Leonid Libkin, Wim Martens, and Domagoj Vrgoc. Querying graphs with data. *Journal of the ACM*, 63(2), pages 14, May 2016. DOI: 10.1145/2850413 35

Yike Liu, Abhilash Dighe, Tara Safavi, and Danai Koutra. Graph summarization methods and applications: A survey. *The Computing Research Repository*, January 2018. DOI: 10.1145/3186727 65, 68, 69, 71

Katja Losemann and Wim Martens. The complexity of evaluating path expressions in SPARQL. In *PODS*, pages 101–112, ACM, 2012. DOI: 10.1145/2213556.2213573 117

Cheng Luo, Zhewei Jiang, Wen-Chi Hou, Feng Yu, and Qiang Zhu. A sampling approach for XML query selectivity estimation. In *EDBT*, pages 335–344, ACM, 2009. DOI: 10.1145/1516360.1516400 139

Yongming Luo, Yannick de Lange, George H. L. Fletcher, Paul De Bra, Jan Hidders, and Yuqing Wu. Bisimulation reduction of big graphs on mapreduce. In *BNCOD*, pages 189–203, Springer, 2013a. DOI: 10.1007/978-3-642-39467-6_18 99

Yongming Luo, George H. L. Fletcher, Jan Hidders, Paul De Bra, and Yuqing Wu. Regularities and dynamics in bisimulation reductions of big graphs. In *GRADES*, pages 13–18, ACM, 2013b. DOI: 10.1145/2484425.2484438 99

Yongming Luo, George H. L. Fletcher, Jan Hidders, Yuqing Wu, and Paul De Bra. External memory k-bisimulation reduction of big graphs. In *CIKM*, pages 919–928, ACM, 2013c. DOI: 10.1145/2505515.2505752 99

Norbert Martínez-Bazan, Victor Muntés-Mulero, Sergio Gómez-Villamor, Jordi Nin, Mario-A. Sánchez-Martínez, and Josep-Lluis Larriba-Pey. DEX: High-performance exploration on large graphs for information retrieva. In *CIKM*, pages 573–582, ACM, 2007. DOI: 10.1145/1321440.1321521 14

Norbert Martínez-Bazan, Sergio Gómez-Villamor, and Francesc Escale-Claveras. DEX: A high-performance graph database management system. In *GDM*, pages 124–127, IEEE, 2011. DOI: 10.1109/icdew.2011.5767616 14

Brian McBride. Jena: Implementing the RDF model and syntax specification. In *SemWeb*, 2001. 99

Robert Ryan McCune, Tim Weninger, and Greg Madey. Thinking like a vertex: A survey of vertex-centric frameworks for large-scale distributed graph processing. *ACM Computing Surveys*, 48(2), pages 25:1–25:39, November 2015. DOI: 10.1145/2818185 2

Alberto O. Mendelzon and Peter T. Wood. Finding regular simple paths in graph databases. *SIAM Journal on Computing*, 24(6), pages 1235–1258, 1995. DOI: 10.1137/s009753979122370x 117

Tova Milo and Dan Suciu. Index structures for path expressions. In *ICDT*, pages 277–295, Springer, 1999. DOI: 10.1007/3-540-49257-7_18 100

Boris Motik, Yavor Nenov, Robert Piro, Ian Horrocks, and Dan Olteanu. Parallel materialisation of datalog programs in centralised, main-memory RDF systems. In *AAAI*, pages 129–137, 2014. 99

Davide Mottin, Francesco Bonchi, and Francesco Gullo. Graph query reformulation with diversity. In *SIGKDD*, pages 825–834, ACM, 2015. DOI: 10.1145/2783258.2783343 71

Davide Mottin, Matteo Lissandrini, Yannis Velegrakis, and Themis Palpanas. Exemplar queries: A new way of searching. *The VLDB Journal—The International Journal on Very Large Data Bases*, 25(6), pages 741–765, December 2016. DOI: 10.1007/s00778-016-0429-2 66, 67, 71

Inderpal Singh Mumick and Hamid Pirahesh. Implementation of magic-sets in a relational database system. In *SIGMOD*, pages 103–114, ACM, 1994. DOI: 10.1145/191843.191860 139

Yavor Nenov, Robert Piro, Boris Motik, Ian Horrocks, Zhe Wu, and Jay Banerjee. RDFox: A highly-scalable RDF store. In *ISWC*, vol. 9367, pages 3–20, Springer, 2015. DOI: 10.1007/978-3-319-25010-6_1 99

Thomas Neumann and Guido Moerkotte. Characteristic sets: Accurate cardinality estimation for RDF queries with multiple joins. In *ICDE*, pages 984–994, IEEE, 2011. DOI: 10.1109/icde.2011.5767868 139

Thomas Neumann and Gerhard Weikum. RDF-3X: A RISC-style engine for RDF. *Proc. of the VLDB Endowment*, 1(1), pages 647–659, 2008. DOI: 10.14778/1453856.1453927 99

Thomas Neumann and Gerhard Weikum. Scalable join processing on very large RDF graphs. In *SIGMOD*, pages 627–640, ACM, 2009. DOI: 10.1145/1559845.1559911 133, 136, 139

Thomas Neumann and Gerhard Weikum. x-RDF-3X: Fast querying, high update rates, and consistency for RDF databases. *Proc. of the VLDB Endowment*, 3(1), pages 256–263, 2010a. DOI: 10.14778/1920841.1920877 99

Thomas Neumann and Gerhard Weikum. The RDF-3X engine for scalable management of RDF data. *The VLDB Journal—The International Journal on Very Large Data Bases*, 19(1), pages 91–113, February 2010b. DOI: 10.1007/s00778-009-0165-y 99

Mark E. J. Newman. *Networks: An Introduction*, 2nd ed. Oxford University Press, 2018. 1

Hung Q. Ngo, Ely Porat, Christopher Ré, and Atri Rudra. Worst-case optimal join algorithms. *Journal of the ACM*, 65(3), pages 16:1–16:40, March 2018. DOI: 10.1145/3180143. 139

Dung T. Nguyen, Molham Aref, Martin Bravenboer, George Kollias, Hung Q. Ngo, Christopher Ré, and Atri Rudra. Join processing for graph patterns: An old dog with new tricks. In *GRADES*, pages 2:1–2:8, 2015. DOI: 10.1145/2764947.2764948 139

Dan Olteanu and Maximilian Schleich. Factorized databases. *SIGMOD Record*, 45(2), pages 5–16, June 2016. DOI: 10.1145/3003665.3003667 139

Marcus Paradies and Hannes Voigt. Big graph data analytics on single machines—an overview. *Datenbank–Spektrum*, 17(2), July 2017. DOI: 10.1007/s13222-017-0255-8 101

Marcus Paradies and Hannes Voigt. Graph representations and storage. In *Encyclopedia of Big Data Technologies*, Springer, 2018. DOI: 10.1007/978-3-319-63962-8_211-1. 101

Marcus Paradies, Wolfgang Lehner, and Christof Bornhövd. GRAPHITE: An extensible graph traversal framework for relational database management systems. In *SSDBM*, pages 29:1–29:12, ACM, 2015. DOI: 10.1145/2791347.2791383 99

Jorge Pérez, Marcelo Arenas, and Claudio Gutiérrez. nSPARQL: A navigational language for RDF. *Journal of Web Semantics*, 8(4), pages 255–270, 2010. DOI: 10.1016/j.websem.2010.01.002. 35, 117

Bryan Perozzi, Leman Akoglu, Patricia Iglesias Sánchez, and Emmanuel Müller. Focused clustering and outlier detection in large attributed graphs. In *SIGKDD*, pages 1346–1355, 2014. DOI: 10.1145/2623330.2623682 69

Minh-Duc Pham, Linnea Passing, Orri Erling, and Peter A. Boncz. Deriving an emergent relational schema from RDF data. In *WWW*, pages 864–874, ACM, 2015. DOI: 10.1145/2736277.2741121 99

François Picalausa. Guarded structural indexes: Theory and application to relational RDF databases. Ph.D. thesis, Université Libre de Bruxelles, 2013. 99

François Picalausa, Yongming Luo, George H. L. Fletcher, Jan Hidders, and Stijn Vansummeren. A structural approach to indexing triples. In *ESWC*, pages 406–421, Springer, 2012. DOI: 10.1007/978-3-642-30284-8_34 72, 98

François Picalausa, George H. L. Fletcher, Jan Hidders, and Stijn Vansummeren. Principles of guarded structural indexing. In *ICDT*, pages 245–256, 2014. `OpenProceedings.org` DOI: 10.5441/002/icdt.2014.26. 98

Neoklis Polyzotis, Minos N. Garofalakis, and Yannis E. Ioannidis. Approximate XML query answers. In *SIGMOD*, pages 263–274, ACM, 2004. DOI: 10.1145/1007568.1007599 139

Alexandra Poulovassilis and Peter T. Wood. Combining approximation and relaxation in semantic web path queries. In *ISWC*, pages 631–646, Springer, 2010. DOI: 10.1007/978-3-642-17746-0_40 71

Miao Qiao, Hao Zhang, and Hong Cheng. Subgraph matching: On compression and computation. *Proc. of the VLDB Endowment*, 11(2), pages 176–188, October 2017. DOI: 10.14778/3149193.3149198 139

Juan L. Reutter, Miguel Romero, and Moshe Y. Vardi. Regular queries on graph databases. *Theory of Computing Systems*, 61(1), pages 31–83, 2017. DOI: 10.1007/s00224-016-9676-2 15, 21, 35

Benjamin Rossman. Homomorphism preservation theorems. *Journal of the ACM*, 55(3), pages 15:1–15:53, July 2008. DOI: 10.1145/1379759.1379763 98

Michael Rudolf, Marcus Paradies, Christof Bornhövd, and Wolfgang Lehner. The graph story of the SAP HANA database. In *BTW*, vol. 214, pages 403–420, GI, 2013. 14, 99

Stuart J. Russell and Peter Norvig. *Artificial Intelligence—A Modern Approach* (3rd international ed.). Pearson Education, 2010. 65

Sherif Sakr, Sameh Elnikety, and Yuxiong He. G-SPARQL: A hybrid engine for querying large attributed graphs. In *Proc. of the 21st ACM International Conference on Information and Knowledge Management*, pages 335–344, ACM, 2012. DOI: 10.1145/2396761.2396806 117

Simone Santini. Regular languages with variables on graphs. *Information and Computation*, 211, pages 1–28, February 2012. DOI: 10.1016/j.ic.2011.10.010 35

Mohamed Sarwat, Sameh Elnikety, Yuxiong He, and Mohamed F. Mokbel. Horton+: A distributed system for processing declarative reachability queries over partitioned graphs. *Proc. of the VLDB Endowment*, 6(14), pages 1918–1929, 2013. DOI: 10.14778/2556549.2556573 117

Praveen Seshadri, Joseph M. Hellerstein, Hamid Pirahesh, T. Y. Cliff Leung, Raghu Ramakrishnan, Divesh Srivastava, Peter J. Stuckey, and S. Sudarshan. Cost-based optimization for magic: Algebra and implementation. In *SIGMOD*, pages 435–446, ACM, 1996. DOI: 10.1145/233269.233360. 139

Stephan Seufert, Avishek Anand, Srikanta J. Bedathur, and Gerhard Weikum. FERRARI: Flexible and efficient reachability range assignment for graph indexing. In *ICDE*, pages 1009–1020, IEEE, 2013. DOI: 10.1109/icde.2013.6544893 100

Julian Shun and Guy E. Blelloch. Ligra: A lightweight graph processing framework for shared memory. In *PPoPP*, pages 135–146, 2013. DOI: 10.1145/2517327.2442530 100

George M. Slota, Sivasankaran Rajamanickam, and Kamesh Madduri. BFS and coloring-based parallel algorithms for strongly connected components and related problems. In *IPDPS*, pages 550–559, IEEE, 2014. DOI: 10.1109/ipdps.2014.64 92

Christian Sommer. Shortest-path queries in static networks. *ACM Computing Surveys*, 46(4), pages 45:1–45:31, April 2014. DOI: 10.1145/2530531 100

Shaoxu Song, Boge Liu, Hong Cheng, Jeffrey Xu Yu, and Lei Chen. Graph repairing under neighborhood constraints. *The VLDB Journal—The International Journal on Very Large Data Bases*, 26(5), pages 611–635, October 2017. DOI: 10.1007/s00778-017-0466-5 52, 53

Giorgio Stefanoni, Boris Motik, and Egor V. Kostylev. Estimating the cardinality of conjunctive queries over RDF data using graph summarisation. In *WWW*, pages 1043–1052, ACM, 2018. DOI: 10.1145/3178876.3186003 135, 139

Konrad Stocker, Donald Kossmann, Reinhard Braumandl, and Alfons Kemper. Integrating semi-join-reducers into state of the art query processors. In *ICDE*, pages 575–584, IEEE, 2001. DOI: 10.1109/icde.2001.914872 139

Larry J. Stockmeyer and Albert R. Meyer. Word problems requiring exponential time: Preliminary report. In *STOC*, pages 1–9, ACM, 1973. DOI: 10.1145/800125.804029 61

Jiao Su, Qing Zhu, Hao Wei, and Jeffrey Xu Yu. Reachability querying: Can it be even faster? *IEEE Transactions on Knowledge and Data Engineering*, 29(3), pages 683–697, 2017. DOI: 10.1109/tkde.2016.2631160 89, 100

Fabian M. Suchanek, Gjergji Kasneci, and Gerhard Weikum. Yago: A core of semantic knowledge unifying WordNet and Wikipedia. In *WWW*, pages 697–706, ACM, 2007. 57

Wen Sun, Achille Fokoue, Kavitha Srinivas, Anastasios Kementsietsidis, Gang Hu, and Guo Tong Xie. SQLGraph: An efficient relational-based property graph store. In *SIGMOD*, pages 1887–1901, ACM, 2015. DOI: 10.1145/2723372.2723732 100

Dimitri Surinx, George H. L. Fletcher, Marc Gyssens, Dirk Leinders, Jan Van den Bussche, Dirk Van Gucht, Stijn Vansummeren, and Yuqing Wu. Relative expressive power of navigational querying on graphs using transitive closure. *Logic Journal of the IGPL*, 23(5), pages 759–788, 2015. DOI: 10.1093/jigpal/jzv028. 35

Robert Endre Tarjan. Depth-first search and linear graph algorithms. *SIAM Journal on Computing*, 1(2), pages 146–160, June 1972. DOI: 10.1137/0201010 92

Alfred Tarski. On the calculus of relations. *Journal of Symbolic Logic*, 6(3), pages 73–89, September 1941. DOI: 10.2307/2268577 35

Alfred Tarski and Steven R. Givant. *A Formalization of Set Theory Without Variables*, vol. 41. American Mathematical Society, 1987. DOI: 10.1090/coll/041 35

The Coq Development Team. The Coq proof assistant, version 8.7.2, February 2018. 34

Frank Tetzel, Hannes Voigt, Marcus Paradies, and Wolfgang Lehner. An analysis of the feasibility of graph compression techniques for indexing regular path qeries. In *GRADES*, ACM, 2017. DOI: 10.1145/3078447.3078458 100

Jeffrey D. Ullman. *Principles of Database and Knowledge-Base Systems*, vol. I and vol. 14. Computer Science Press, 1988. 27

Jeffrey D. Ullman. *Principles of Database and Knowledge-Base Systems*, vol. II. Computer Science Press, 1989. 27

Patrick Valduriez and Haran Boral. Evaluation of recursive queries using join indices. In *Proc. of the 1st International Conference on Expert Database Systems*, pages 271–293, Benjamin Cummings, Charleston, SC, April 1–4, 1986. 138

Wouter van Heeswijk, George H. L. Fletcher, and Mykola Pechenizkiy. On structure preserving sampling and approximate partitioning of graphs. In *SAC*, pages 875–882, ACM, 2016. DOI: 10.1145/2851613.2851650 99

Oskar van Rest, Sungpack Hong, Jinha Kim, Xuming Meng, and Hassan Chafi. PGQL: A property graph query language. In *GRADES*, page 7, ACM, 2016. DOI: 10.1145/2960414.2960421 2, 14, 34

Elena Vasilyeva. Why-query support in graph databases. Ph.D. thesis, Dresden University of Technology, Germany, 2017. 71

Elena Vasilyeva, Maik Thiele, Adrian Mocan, and Wolfgang Lehner. Relaxation of subgraph queries delivering empty results. In *SSDBM*, pages 28:1–28:12, ACM, 2015. DOI: 10.1145/2791347.2791382 71

Elena Vasilyeva, Maik Thiele, Christof Bornhövd, and Wolfgang Lehner. Answering "Why empty?" and "Why so many?" queries in graph databases. *Journal of Computer and System Sciences*, 82(1), pages 3–22, February 2016. DOI: 10.1016/j.jcss.2015.06.007 71

Todd L. Veldhuizen. Triejoin: A simple, worst-case optimal join algorithm. In *ICDT*, pages 96–106, 2014. DOI: 10.5441/002/icdt.2014.13. 139

Hannes Voigt. Declarative multidimensional graph queries. In *Business Intelligence—6th European Summer School, eBISS*, pages 1–37, Tours, France, July 3–8, 2016, Tutorial Lectures, Springer, 2017. DOI: 10.1007/978-3-319-61164-8_1 35

Denny Vrandecic and Markus Krötzsch. Wikidata: A free collaborative knowledgebase. *Communications of the ACM*, 57(10), pages 78–85, 2014. DOI: 10.1145/2629489 13

W3C. Resource description framework (RDF): Model and syntax specification, February 1999. https://www.w3.org/TR/1999/REC-rdf-syntax-19990222/ 13

W3C. Resource description framework (RDF): Concepts and abstract syntax, February 2004. http://www.w3.org/TR/2004/REC-rdf-concepts-20040210/ 13

W3C. Extensible markup language (XML) 1.0, 5th ed., November 2008. http://www.w3.org/TR/2008/REC-xml-20081126/ 13

W3C. SPARQL 1.1 overview, March 2013. http://www.w3.org/TR/2013/REC-sparql11-overview-20130321/ 34

W3C. RDF 1.1 concepts and abstract syntax, February 2014. http://www.w3.org/TR/2014/REC-rdf11-concepts-20140225/ 13

Hao Wei, Jeffrey Xu Yu, Can Lu, and Ruoming Jin. Reachability querying: An independent permutation labeling approach. *Proc. of the VLDB Endowment*, 7(12), pages 1191–1202, August 2014. DOI: 10.14778/2732977.2732992 100

Cathrin Weiss, Panagiotis Karras, and Abraham Bernstein. Hexastore: Sextuple indexing for semantic web data management. *Proc. of the VLDB Endowment*, 1(1), pages 1008–1019, 2008. DOI: 10.14778/1453856.1453965 99

Yaacov Weiss and Sara Cohen. Reverse engineering SPJ-queries from examples. In *PODS*, pages 151–166, ACM, 2017. DOI: 10.1145/3034786.3056112 71

Horst Werner, Christof Bornhövd, Robert Kubis, and Hannes Voigt. MOAW: An agile visual modeling and exploration tool for irregularly structured data. In *BTW*, vol. 180, pages 742–745, GI, 2011. 13

Kevin Wilkinson. Jena property table implementation. In *SSWS*, 2006. 99

Kevin Wilkinson, Craig Sayers, Harumi A. Kuno, and Dave Reynolds. Efficient RDF storage and retrieval in Jena2. In *SWDB*, pages 131–150, 2003. 99

Ross Willard. PP-definability is CO-nexptime-complete. In *The Constraint Satisfaction Problem: Complexity and Approximability*, vol. 09441, Schloss Dagstuhl–Leibniz-Zentrum für Informatik, Dagstuhl, Germany, October 25–30 2009. 59

Peter T. Wood. Query languages for graph databases. *SIGMOD Record*, 41(1), pages 50–60, 2012. DOI: 10.1145/2206869.2206879 35

Yinghui Wu and Arijit Khan. Graph pattern matching. In *Encyclopedia of Big Data Technologies*, Springer, 2018. DOI: 10.1007/978-3-319-63962-8_74-1 35

Nikolay Yakovets, Parke Godfrey, and Jarek Gryz. Evaluation of SPARQL property paths via recursive SQL. In *AMW*, 2013. CEUR-WS.org 117

Nikolay Yakovets, Parke Godfrey, and Jarek Gryz. Query planning for evaluating SPARQL property paths. In *SIGMOD*, pages 1875–1889, ACM, 2016. DOI: 10.1145/2882903.2882944 117, 139

Da Yan, Yingyi Bu, Yuanyuan Tian, and Amol Deshpande. Big graph analytics platforms. *Foundations and Trends in Databases*, 7(1–2), pages 1–195, January 2017. DOI: 10.1561/1900000056 2

Mohan Yang and Carlo Zaniolo. Main memory evaluation of recursive queries on multicore machines. In *BD*, pages 251–260, IEEE, 2014. DOI: 10.1109/bigdata.2014.7004240 139

Hilmi Yildirim, Vineet Chaoji, and Mohammed J. Zaki. GRAIL: A scalable index for reachability queries in very large graphs. *The VLDB Journal—The International Journal on Very Large Data Bases*, 21(4), pages 509–534, August 2012. DOI: 10.1007/s00778-011-0256-4 100

Jeffrey Xu Yu and Jiefeng Cheng. Graph reachability queries: A survey. In *Managing and Mining Graph Data*, vol. 40, pages 181–215, Springer, 2010. DOI: 10.1007/978-1-4419-6045-0_6 100

Harald Zauner, Benedikt Linse, Tim Furche, and François Bry. A RPL through RDF: Expressive navigation in RDF graphs. In *Web Reasoning and Rule Systems—Proc. of the 4th International Conference, RR*, pages 251–257, Bressanone/Brixen, Italy, September 22–24, Springer, 2010. DOI: 10.1007/978-3-642-15918-3_25 117

J. W. Zhang and Y. C. Tay. GSCALER: Synthetically scaling A given graph. In *EDBT*, pages 53–64, 2016. OpenProceedings.org DOI: 10.5441/002/edbt.2016.08. 117

Ning Zhang, M. Tamer Özsu, Ashraf Aboulnaga, and Ihab F. Ilyas. XSEED: Accurate and fast cardinality estimation for XPath queries. In *ICDE*, pages 61–72, IEEE, 2006. DOI: 10.1109/icde.2006.178 139

Ning Zhang, Yuanyuan Tian, and Jignesh M. Patel. Discovery-driven graph summarization. In *ICDE*, pages 880–891, IEEE, 2010. DOI: 10.1109/icde.2010.5447830 69, 70, 72

Moshé M. Zloof. Query-by-example: The invocation and definition of tables and forms. In *VLDB*, pages 1–24, ACM, 1975. DOI: 10.1145/1282480.1282482 67

Lei Zou, M. Tamer Özsu, Lei Chen, Xuchuan Shen, Ruizhe Huang, and Dongyan Zhao. gStore: A graph-based SPARQL query engine. *The VLDB Journal—The International Journal on Very Large Data Bases*, 23(4), pages 565–590, August 2014. DOI: 10.1007/s00778-013-0337-7 100

Authors' Biographies

ANGELA BONIFATI

Angela Bonifati is a full professor of computer science at Université Claude Bernard Lyon 1 and affiliated with the CNRS Liris research lab. She received her Ph.D. from Politecnico di Milano in 2002 and right after she was a postdoctoral researcher at INRIA Roquencourt. Her current research interests are on the interplay of relational and graph-shaped data paradigms, particularly on schema mapping and data exchange, query processing, and learning for these data models. She was Vice Chair of ICDE 2018 for the information extraction, data cleaning, and curation track and Vice Chair of ICDE 2011 for the semi-structured data track. She is Associate Editor of the *VLDB Journal*, *ACM TODS*, and *Distributed and Parallel Databases*. She is a member-at-large of the ICDT council and serving on the program committees of SIGMOD, PODS, PVLDB, ICDE, and EDBT.

GEORGE FLETCHER

George Fletcher is an associate professor of computer science at Technische Universiteit Eindhoven where he is chair of the Database Group. He defended a Ph.D. at Indiana University Bloomington in 2007. His research interests span query language design and engineering, foundations of databases, and data integration. His current focus is on management of massive graphs such as social networks and linked open data. He was a co-organizer of the EDBT Summer School on Graph Data Management (2015) and is currently a member of the LDBC Graph Query Language Standardization Task Force. His other recent activities include co-organizing an NII Shonan seminar on Graph Database Systems (2018) and serving on the program committees of SIGMOD, VLDB, ISWC, ICDE, EDBT, and IJCAI.

HANNES VOIGT

Hannes Voigt is a software engineer at Neo4j since June 2018, where he is part of the Query Languages, Standards, and Research team. Before that he was a post-doctoral researcher at the Dresden Database Systems Group, Technische Universität Dresden and obtained his Ph.D. from the same university in 2014. As a researcher, he worked on various database topics such as declarative graph query languages, database evolution and versioning, management of schema-flexible data, and self-adapting indexes. He is member of the LDBC Graph Query Language Standardization Task Force. Other recent activities include co-editing the section on graph analytics in the *Encyclopedia of Big Data Technologies*, co-presenting a tutorial on graph query processing at EDBT 2017, and serving on the program committees of VLDB, ICDE, and CIKM.

NIKOLAY YAKOVETS

Nikolay Yakovets is an assistant professor of computer science at Technische Universiteit Eindhoven. He obtained his Ph.D. from Lassonde School of Engineering at York University in 2017. He worked on various database topics at IBM CAS Canada and Empress Software Canada. His current focus is on design and implementation of core database technologies, management of massive graph data, and efficient processing of queries on graphs. His recent activities include co-presenting a tutorial on graph query processing at EDBT 2017, co-organizing the 2017 edition of the Dutch-Belgian Database Day, and serving on a program committee of ICDE.

Printed in the United States
by Baker & Taylor Publisher Services